PRAISE
THE PRINCESS PROBLEM

"Hains has given us a very insightful look at our princess culture. And she doesn't stop there. Her ideas and suggestions on how parents can help their children navigate the overwhelming princess marketing, media, and negative stereotypes are refreshingly perceptive. She points out the problem and offers realistic solutions. Parents—this is a must read!"

—Brenda Chapman, writer/director,
Disney/Pixar's *Brave*

"Blending fact, analysis, and compelling research with expert interviews and eye-opening narratives from actual moms, Rebecca Hains paints a troubling picture of princess culture and media messaging. But like a true fairy godmother, she swoops in to mentor parents on how to rescue girls from the diabolical clutches of the self-serving marketing machine by offering real-world solutions and teachable techniques to counter its effects."

—Jen Jones, cofounder and managing editor,
WomenYouShouldKnow.net

"Media and marketers bombard girls at ever-younger ages with 'fun' products that promote pernicious stereotypes. So what's a parent to do? Enter Rebecca Hains, a wise, optimistic guide through the princess industrial complex. *The Princess Problem* is an indispensable tool kit, full of concrete, practical advice. I only wish it had been around when my daughter was in preschool!"

—Peggy Orenstein, author of
Cinderella Ate My Daughter

"*The Princess Problem* offers sound, sensible, and parent-tested advice for helping children thrive in today's consumer culture. Hains...lays out a family-centered strategy for raising media-smart kids."

—Jo B. Paoletti, author of *Pink and Blue: Telling the Boys from the Girls in America*

"With warmth, humor, and in-depth research, *The Princess Problem* thoughtfully explores the production of princess culture, its impact on children, and why we should all care about it. As an expert in media literacy for children, Hains provides concrete and effective (and often fun) strategies and activities to help parents raise girls and boys who are confident, critical, and compassionate."

—Chyng Sun, PhD, clinical professor of media studies, McGhee Division, School of Continuing and Professional Studies, New York University, and producer of documentary film *Mickey Mouse Monopoly: Disney, Childhood & Corporate Power*

THE PRINCESS PROBLEM

Guiding Our Girls through the Princess-Obsessed Years

REBECCA C. HAINS, PhD

Published by Sourcebooks, Inc.
P.O. Box 4410, Naperville, Illinois 60567-4410
(630) 961-3900
Fax: (630) 961-2168
www.sourcebooks.com

Library of Congress Cataloging-in-Publication Data

Hains, Rebecca C.
  The princess problem : guiding our girls through the princess-obsessed years / Rebecca C. Hains, PhD.
       pages cm
  Includes bibliographical references.
  (trade : alk. paper) 1. Girls—Psychology. 2. Princesses. 3. Mass media and girls. 4. Identity (Psychology) 5. Parenting. I. Title.
  HQ777.H235 2014
  305.23082—dc23
                              2014009884

Printed and bound in the United States of America.
VP 10 9 8 7 6 5 4 3 2 1

To Theo and Alex
Forever and ever and always

Contents

PART ONE

The Pleasures and Problems of
Princess Culture—and a Solution

Introduction

I work at my computer in jeans and a sweater, wearing glasses and no makeup, as usual. My three-year-old son playfully sticks hair clips into my long, dark brown hair, willy-nilly. The look, I'm sure, is haphazard.

He stops to admire his work and says, "Mommy, you're pretty."

I smile and hug him tightly. "Thank you, Theo!"

Pressing closer to me, he says, "I love you, Mommy. You're my princess."

I look *nothing* like a princess. But at preschool, Theo has seen that girls love dressing up as princesses. The girls in his class play often with princess toys, draw princess pictures, and love being called "princess."

How could he avoid it? It's a cultural norm.

★ ★ ★

Three weeks later, I am impeccably dressed in a gorgeous silvery-blue gown with gold trim. Its skirt is full and flattering, thanks to the crinoline I wear beneath it. My upswept blond wig perfectly covers my dark hair. My eyeglasses are in their case. Now I wear contacts, and my eyelashes are long and curled. Having spent more than an hour dressing and applying makeup, I look stunning.

A woman ushers me into her living room. Guests snack on party food, chat, and play. Suddenly, a small voice cries, "It's Cinderella! It's Cinderella!" The children flock to me. Using my best manners, I smile and reach out to each child, greeting them by taking their hands in mine. I hope none of them get food on my silver evening gloves.

From among the twelve children, ages two to eleven, I locate the four-year-old birthday girl; she wears a Disney-brand Cinderella

THE AUTHOR AS CINDERELLA

dress and party hat. Giving her a hug, I gently smile and say, "I am so pleased that I could attend your party." I inflect my words like a proper princess.

The birthday girl smiles shyly but does not speak. She is too awestruck.

I take her hand and lead her to the front of the room. Her elderly relatives beam at me with palpable affection. "Oh, Cinderella!" they call. "Hi!" I pause to smile and curtsy at them, and their eyes sparkle, perhaps with nostalgia. "Isn't she beautiful," one says.

During the party, I mingle with the children, read them fairy tales, paint their faces, and make them balloon animals. I enjoy the attention and relish the children's delight.

I tell the children that I have enough time to make each of them a second balloon animal, and the birthday girl asks me to make her a sword. Suddenly, everybody wants one. I whisper conspiratorially to a group of girls that they look very strong. "I really want you to fight those boys," I say. "I'm certain you could beat them in a sword fight." They grin wickedly. One says, "Yeah, I think we could!" and off they run.

The eleven-year-old girl hovers as I work. "You know," she offers, "I think Cinderella does a lot more things now than she did when I was a little kid. I don't remember Cinderella doing so many things."

I smile and reply, "Well, of course! It's important for all of us to continue to grow and learn new things. Even me." She nods, then asks if I can show her how to make a balloon animal. I help her practice a few simple twists.

When I catch a glimpse of a clock, I realize that I am short on time. I have only forty-five minutes left in which to excuse myself, transform into Sleeping Beauty, drive to another party, and park a few blocks away from the next birthday girl's home. I'm obliged to ensure the children don't see a storybook princess arrive in a run-down car.

As I leave, the birthday girl's parents thank me for my perfor-mance. Her mom comments, "I have never seen a group of kids sit still that long and listen!" The dad shakes my hand and gives me a twenty-five-dollar tip. I am grateful. As I later tell my colleagues at Salem State University where I teach, this money will help fund my field research in a few weeks at Walt Disney World, where I plan to see the Disney brand of princess culture in action. Rushing out into the cold winter air, I hurry on my way, careful not to lose a slipper.

I know why preschool girls love to play princess. Dressing up in cos-tume is a pleasure. What fun to transform into a glamorous beauty, to be adulated, to be treated as royalty! And during the months I spent as a princess performer, I found it to be a fun source of extra income, too.

That wasn't the main reason I worked as a princess performer, though—far from it. As a professor who studies and writes about girls' media culture, I've spent the last three years studying the rise of princess culture from multiple angles. Working at children's birthday parties was a research opportunity, a chance to make a first-person journey into princess culture. By transforming myself into storybook princesses—as Cinderella, Belle, the Little Mermaid, Rapunzel, Aladdin's princess (I was playing generic princesses, not the Disney versions), and Sleeping Beauty—I gained a unique perspective on princess culture in young girls' lives. For a couple of hours every weekend, I was in the eye of the storm.

I also interviewed more than fifty parents about their perspectives on princess culture, listening with care to what they had to say. (Note: In this book, the names of the parents I interviewed—and their children's names—have been changed.) I heard all about the things they like about princess culture, and also about the aspects of princess culture that worry them. On the one hand, many moms have nostalgia for the princesses of their own childhoods, and compared with other popular girls' toys and media, like the edgy Monster High dolls, parents see princesses as innocent and safe.

But at the same time, now that princess culture has become a dominant force in little girls' lives across the United States, moms and dads alike have concerns. They are concerned about the way princess culture stereotypes girls' behaviors and interests. They are concerned about its unhealthy emphasis on romance and the way its focus on physical beauty might affect girls' body images and self-esteem. They also feel concerned about the deficiencies in princess culture's racial diversity and race representation, which just aren't in sync with the realities of modern life in the United States.

Since princess culture is here to stay—and, with it, these problems alongside the fun—I want to offer some solutions: tips that thoughtful parents can easily implement in their everyday lives to raise resilient, media-savvy girls. To this end, I reviewed dozens of scholarly studies to learn more about the issues the parents I interviewed raised. I spoke with experts, too—psychologists, educators, media-literacy experts, and girl empowerment advocates. The best of these studies and conversations are interspersed throughout *The Princess Problem: Guiding Our Girls through the Princess-Obsessed Years*.

In the process, I developed a better understanding of the ways in which little girls across the nation become enamored with princess toys, princess movies, and princess play clothes. Disney Princess is the number-one brand for licensed entertainment merchandise in the United States and Canada, selling $1.52 billion in merchandise in 2012 and besting runners-up Star Wars ($1.46 billion) and Hello Kitty ($1.08 billion) for the top spot. No wonder, then, that Disney continues to expand its Princess line and diversify other elements of its portfolio with princesses, as well. Minnie Mouse is available in "princess" varieties, and late in 2012, Disney Junior released *Sofia the First*, a television cartoon for girls ages two to seven about a little girl who suddenly becomes royalty when her mother marries a king. Since then, *Sofia*—which is considered separate from the Disney Princess line—has been a marketing bonanza for Disney Junior.

Although countless little girls are buying into the princess identity, not all of their parents are on board. While many loving parents enjoy spoiling their "little princesses" every year, another crop of new parents is stunned by how pervasive princess marketing is. In some cases, they are also stunned by the extremity of their daughters' princess obsessions—realizing too late that once "princess" is introduced to their toddlers, life can quickly become all princess, all the time.

Even parents whose little girls aren't fully obsessed with princesses are often ambivalent about princess culture—that aspect of children's popular culture that makes "princess" a central part of girls' identities and lives and, in so doing, promotes old-fashioned ideas of what the ideal girl should be like, what she should do, and even whom she should love. They are concerned about what their daughters are learning from princess culture: the lessons they're taking in about consumerism, about the beauty ideal, about gender stereotypes (including people's roles within romantic relationships), and about racial stereotypes.

Experts agree that parents are right to be concerned. What young girls learn from the media about princesses also teaches them lessons about what it means to be a girl. Those lessons can, in turn, influence how they think about *themselves* as they grow up. What little girls learn from princess culture can shape their own identities and self-images—whether or not they embrace the idea that they, too, are princesses.

Faced with problems of this nature, many parents wonder: what is the solution? Short of improving princess culture itself—a feat that would require collective action for longer than our own children's childhoods will last—how do we raise little girls who feel empowered to break free of the princess stereotypes and ideals surrounding them?

The Solution: Parents as Pop Culture Coaches

I have an answer, and it's the central idea of this book. Every parent can guide their girls through the media world around them with what I've dubbed "pop culture coaching." To become their daughters' pop culture coaches, parents begin by reflecting on their own values—giving conscious thought to what they believe about various issues relevant to girls. Then, with these values in mind, parents coach their children to become media-literate individuals.

Media-literate people are able to think critically about all media—the contexts of their production and the messages they convey. As critical viewers, media-literate people are good at questioning what they see on-screen and can build resilience to the media's negative aspects. Therefore, this is an important task for twenty-first-century parents. We must coach our children, guiding them to become critical viewers of media culture in general and of princess culture in particular.

The goal is not to persuade girls that princesses are bad or to "de-princess" them. Rather, it is to help girls reason through the problems with princesses and see that there are many other ways to be a girl—to help unfetter their imaginations and help them dream a multiplicity of dreams.

To this end, *The Princess Problem* offers parents clear instructions on handling four key areas of concern: the insidious marketing, the restrictive beauty ideal embodied by princesses, the gender stereotypes, and the racial stereotypes. Each chapter in Part Two of *The Princess Problem* begins by unpacking one of these four issues to help parents gain a comprehensive, informed view of the problem in question. Then, each chapter offers parents general strategies and specific recommendations they can implement with their kids.

Note that I've used a multifaceted approach in creating these recommendations. After all, I know how fun it can be to play princess. I don't deny the appeal of this pleasure. (After one of my first Saturday mornings spent performing at children's birthday parties, I came home and told my husband, "This is such a great job for me!") So while I support girls in their princess interests, I also hold toy makers and marketers accountable for the problems in their films, products, and marketing tactics.

Using the pop culture coaching approach discussed in *The Princess Problem*, parents can help their children understand their family's individual values and perspectives, while still being respectful of girls' interests and princess pleasures. Teaching our children media-literacy skills *now*, in their preschool and early elementary years, is important. It equips them to question, resist, and negotiate the marketing strategies and the ideals presented by Disney and other producers. In today's media-saturated world, the earlier children learn these skills, the better. They'll use them their entire lives.

Note that while *The Princess Problem* is about young girls' princess culture and often highlights the Disney Princess brand because it dominates the marketplace, the pop culture coaching principles in this book are applicable to other media products and properties, as well—princesses and beyond. These principles can also be used to help boys. In fact, some of the examples I offer will be based upon my own exchanges with my young son as we negotiate the positives and negatives of popular culture together. (See my website, RebeccaHains.com, for a parent-child discussion guide for each of the Disney Princess films, as well as discussion guides for pop culture coaching that go beyond princess culture.)

Today's world is so media-saturated that becoming a savvy consumer of television, films, and other media texts can be empowering for anyone. With marketers expending more time and money on courting children to purchase their products than ever before, becoming media literate is especially important for our children. That's why I've written this book—and why I hope you'll find it useful.

CHAPTER ONE
The Problems with Princess Culture

✶

Today's parents are smart and thoughtful, and we are terrific at finding the information we need to do right by our kids. Thanks to the Internet, a world of information is at our fingertips. We can find the answers to just about any parenting challenge we face, whether big or small: Childhood illnesses. Toy safety. Car seat installation. Birthday party themes. The age-appropriateness of specific movies. Avoiding BPA. Creative ideas for *The Elf on the Shelf*. Healthy recipes.

But one parenting challenge has been flummoxing even the most resourceful parents: how to deal with the way pretty, pink princess culture has taken over girlhood. In the past decade, princess toys have become *the* most popular item for girls. As we've said, Disney Princess is the number-one licensed entertainment line in the United States and Canada, and there are countless additional princess toys beyond that brand. This means that princess culture is an unavoidable part of modern girlhood. Princess is *everywhere*.

Unfortunately, with princess culture's exceptional rise, preschool boys and girls have come to experience very different childhoods. Boys' toys feature superheroes, trains, cars, building sets, and a range of colors. Girls' toys, swathed in an endless sea of pink and purple, are dominated by princesses. In consequence, boys grow up in an active, rough-and-tumble, building-oriented world, while girls grow up in a passive, frilly, image- and appearance-oriented world. Girls get the short end of the stick. They are separate and unequal.

Making matters worse, the stories told about princesses in the media—which are so beloved by little girls—are incredibly limiting. Scholars and critics have carefully analyzed the stories told about princesses, and a laundry list of concerns has emerged:

They're too skinny.

They're too buxom.

They're too weak.

They're too helpless.

They're too often white.

In other words, princess movies by studios, including but not limited to Disney, teach girls that they should be pretty and passive; and for the most part, the characters they depict lack racial and cultural diversity. This is unacceptable to modern parents, who are working to raise strong, empowered girls of many diverse backgrounds.

In this cultural context, the wildfire success of anything critical of princesses is really telling. Hordes of parents want more than just princesses for their daughters.

On the social-media front, a humorous approach reigns. Nearly every month, a new image or video making fun of princess culture goes viral. *Saturday Night Live*'s skit "The Real Housewives of Disney" hilariously satirized what the princesses' lives would be like after their "happily ever afters." (Hint: not so great.)

The Second City Network, a sketch comedy troupe from Chicago and Toronto whose alumni include Stephen Colbert and Tina Fey, released a series of YouTube videos called *Advice from a Cartoon Princess*, full of "wonderful" life lessons for young girls presented by comedians dressed in princess attire—like the Little Mermaid offering retrograde tips including, "Don't ever talk to a man until he kisses you on the lips first. Then, as a woman, you're allowed," and "Never be comfortable in the body that you're given."

And thanks to Pinterest and Facebook, cartoon images go viral constantly—like cartoonist Bill Walko's "What If Wonder Woman Was a Disney Princess," in which Wonder Woman—wearing a princess-style gown and carrying a blood-stained sword—tells a perplexed fairy godmother, prince, and two woodland creatures: "Oh dear, I'm afraid I have already slain the dragon, defeated the evil queen, and saved the kingdom. But it is truly splendid you all offered to help!"

Alongside the humor, more serious critiques of princess culture have gone viral, as well. For example, social media went ablaze with the release of *Fallen Princesses*, a series of somber photographs depicting fairy-tale characters in starkly realistic modern-day scenarios. (Photo gallery available at fallenprincesses.com.) Artist Dina Goldstein was inspired to create the series when her three-year-old daughter became a princess devotee.

Goldstein has explained on her website that after her daughter became interested in the Disney Princesses, "I began to imagine Disney's perfect princesses juxtaposed with real issues that were affecting women around me, such as illness, addiction, and self-image issues." According to her website, the series "was born out of deep personal pain, when [Goldstein] raged against the 'happily ever after' motif" that dominates girlhood.

The resulting images are jarring and compelling and often sad. For example, one photo finds Snow White and her prince in a suburban living room with four young children. Two of them are in Snow White's arms while one pulls at her skirt, and a fourth child plays on the floor in the background. The prince is watching television with his feet up, and Snow White looks unamused. In another photo, an unconscious, middle-aged Belle is undergoing plastic surgery. One surgeon slices her skin open for an eye-lift, while another injects her lips with a needle full of collagen. Other portraits are equally grim: Ariel is trapped in an aquarium, Jasmine is in a Middle Eastern war zone, and a hairless Rapunzel is undergoing chemotherapy.

Once *Fallen Princesses* went viral online, it was covered by media outlets worldwide, including MSN, the *New York Daily News*, Yahoo! News, the *New Zealand Herald*, the *Huffington Post*, and the *Daily Telegraph*. Along the way, Jack David Zipes, PhD—a retired professor of German history at the University of Minnesota and renowned fairy-tale expert—argued about the series' tremendous appeal.

He noted that *Fallen Princesses* "comment critically on the Disney world and raise many questions about the lives women are expected to lead and the actual lives that they lead. [Goldstein's] photos are not optimistic. Rather, they are subtle, comic, and grotesque images that undo classical fairy-tale narratives and expose some of the negative results that are rarely discussed in public." This is key to understanding why the photos became a sensation. They speak to the impossibility of princess culture's promises to women and girls, which we rarely discuss. Romance is flawed. Beauty is short-lived. Life is difficult.

Fantasy, meet reality.

Consider, too, the immense popularity of articles critiquing princess culture in the *New York Times* and the *Christian Science Monitor;* the existence of well-read blogs like *Princess Free Zone* and *Disney*

Princess Recovery, dedicated to pushing back against princess culture's takeover of modern girlhood; and the bestseller status of Peggy Orenstein's book *Cinderella Ate My Daughter: Dispatches from the Front Lines of the New Girlie-Girl Culture*, whose success I'll describe later. All have captured readers' interest, sparking a ton of conversation.

For the past few years, I've been a strong voice in that conversation myself. I've written about princess culture on my own blog and the *Christian Science Monitor*'s blog, *Modern Parenthood*, chatting with countless parents about the issues by email and on social media. I've talked about princess culture in live interviews on Huffington Post Live, CBC Radio, and *Fox & Friends*. I've discussed it with journalists from the *Boston Globe*, the *Atlanta Journal-Constitution*, and *Cosmopolitan* magazine. I've even been interviewed about princess culture for two documentary films—*Girl Attitude: The Making of Girls* and *Mickey Mouse Monopoly: Disney, Childhood & Corporate Power* (second edition)—which are slated for release in 2015 and 2016, respectively.

And I'm here to tell you there's nothing inherently wrong with princesses, pink and purple, sparkles, or frills. Princesses are pretty, and sparkles and frills are fun! Girls have been playing princesses for generations. But there *is* something wrong when that's the main type of girlhood marketed to girls. Princesses should be one of a vast range of options for little girls. Compared with the choices boys have, preschool girls' play choices have become exceedingly limited. As a result, parents are concerned about what girls are learning from princess culture—and as a media studies professor who specializes in the study of girls and media culture, I know they're right to worry.

Even Disney has, in a roundabout way, admitted that princesses are not generally the healthiest option for little girls. When Disney Junior announced the impending release of its new television cartoon

Sofia the First, the channel explained that the title character would be a little girl, rather than a teenager like those in the Walt Disney Studios princess films—and Disney execs promised that *Sofia the First* would be "age-appropriate" for preschoolers. The cartoon would feature not just "plenty of pretty dresses and sparkly shoes," but also lessons relevant to little ones, such as "the importance of getting along with siblings and how to be a kind and generous person."

The announcement caused savvy critics of girls' princess culture to raise a collective eyebrow. For example, Orenstein was incredulous. She accused Disney of trying to have it both ways: claiming that their princess-themed feature films are harmless fun for young girls while also claiming that *Sofia* would address some of the problems found in princess-themed feature films. What a contradiction.

Unfortunately, solutions to the problems of princess culture have been hard to come by. So, in this book, I explore the major areas of concern with princess culture and then offer parents solutions to each of those problems:

1. The endless gender-segregated marketing.
2. The emphasis on appearance.
3. The regressive gender stereotypes.
4. The limited amount of race representation.

Let's take a quick look at each one before turning to the solutions.

The Problem with Princess Marketing

Princesses are so heavily marketed that they're inescapable. They're featured on everything from furniture to clothing to food items, to such an extent that if marketers want to suggest that a product is "for girls," all they have to do is slap a princess on it, color it pink, and call it a day.

Unfortunately, this excessive princess marketing is contributing to a broader problem—the division of boys and girls into separate and unequal spheres. In Chapter 3, I'll go into more detail about why that has been a successful strategy for marketers (hint: it exploits a normal developmental phase), and why it's such a problem for our kids.

But meanwhile, consider what my family and I witnessed at our local Stride Rite, the popular children's shoe store. Stride Rite was selling sneakers for preschool boys featuring characters such as Spider-Man and Lightning McQueen from Disney's *Cars*, and sneakers for preschool girls featuring characters such as Cinderella, Sleeping Beauty, and Hello Kitty.

Signs in the store and promotional copy on the Stride Rite website encouraged boys to be active, energetic, and powerful—with "light-up powers" that are "good for your little adventurer's feet," "no matter what kind of web he spins." The *Cars* shoes promised to help boys be "as fast as the legendary Lightning McQueen."

Meanwhile, Stride Rite exhorted girls to be princesses who "sparkle" and "shine" with "the cutest sneakers on the block." Cinderella and Sleeping Beauty sneakers promised to "transport your little princess to a world of fantasy." There was not a word about girls using their sneakers to play actively or adventurously like the boys; it was all about appearance and princess dreams.

To parents who are working hard to raise active, empowered girls, this kind of marketing is incredibly frustrating. By implying that boys prefer physical play and girls prefer looking good, Stride Rite's marketing strategies—like other companies', for they are definitely not alone—were reinforcing the sex role biases that keep boys active and girls passive.

As author Colette Dowling has argued, these biases are at the root of what she calls the Frailty Myth. Boys learn "to use their bodies in skilled ways, and this gives them a good sense of their physical capacities and limits," while girls "hold themselves back from full, complete movement. Although it's usually something girls are unaware of, they actually learn to hamper their movements, developing a 'body timidity that increases with age.'"

Absorbing this lesson has lifelong consequences for little girls, as Dowling explains in *The Frailty Myth: Redefining the Physical Potential of Women and Girls*. Some little girls defy marketers' expectations, playing sports or collecting bugs in their princess dresses—but they are the exceptions to the rule. Ultimately, girls are dropping out of sports at two times the rate of boys. Studies show that this is in part because girls feel worried about how they look while exercising, when their focus should be on how well their bodies are working—not whether they look good. Combined with eschewing activities that might mess up their hair and makeup, all of these factors lead girls and women to have less healthy lifestyles than they might otherwise.

I've witnessed more extreme examples of this at Walt Disney World in Florida. Little girls wear beautiful Disney Princess dresses all around Disney's parks, and Disney employees—all of whom Disney calls "cast members," including janitors and the kids who run the soft drink machines—provide positive reinforcement for this through adulatory comments: "Hello, little Cinderella!" "Why, Ariel, don't you look lovely today!"

Some little girls wear Disney Princess dress-up shoes, purchased from the Disney Store or chains like Target, around the theme park.

The dress-up shoes are not sneakers, but sparkly plastic high heels featuring a plastic emblem emblazoned with the face of the princess whose dress they are supposed to match.

I've worn high heels frequently enough to say with confidence that these little plastic shoes cannot *possibly* be comfortable. They're meant for in-home dress-up play, not walking around in public. And so, unable to run around the parks playfully like their peers, the girls who wear their Disney-brand dress-up shoes to the Magic Kingdom can only walk a little at a time before returning to their strollers.

Just like the marketing strategies that divide the girls from the boys, the shoes restrict them.

The Problems with the Beauty Ideal, Gender Stereotypes, and Race

When it comes to the problems with princess culture, gender-segregated marketing is only the tip of the iceberg. In Chapters 4 through 6 of this book, I discuss three other problems that are quite pervasive. Chapter 4 is dedicated to the problems with princess culture's emphasis on appearance. I dub it "The Pretty Princess Mandate." Chapter 5 is about the problems with the gender stereotypes that pervade princess culture—specifically, with what princess culture suggests are appropriate behaviors for girls. And in Chapter 6, I detail the problems with race representation, exploring why there aren't enough princesses of color and what that means for real girls. These three problems have been a source of concern for many years, especially in relation to Walt Disney Studios' princesses—with critics pointing them out even before Disney Princess became a brand.

Let's take a look at how these criticisms emerged, what their basic points are, and when they went mainstream.

As early as 1975, scholar Kay Stone—a folklorist and professor at the University of Winnipeg—was concerned about how passive and pretty modern-day fairy-tale heroines were. She conducted a study in which she compared the contents of the original Grimm collection of fairy tales to the modern fairy-tale collections being sold to children in North America.

Here's what she found: In the original Grimm collection, only 20 percent of the stories featured passive heroines—while in contemporary children's fairy-tale collections, passive heroines appeared in as many as 75 percent of the stories. That's a remarkable difference! She said there are many old folktales about aggressive heroines—spirited girls who go out into the world and do remarkable things. They're not always *nice* stories, Professor Stone noted, but they're interesting. Modern anthologies have ignored these heroines' stories in favor of their weak and wimpy sisters.

Stone then turned her eye to Walt Disney Studios' animated films. Contradicting the popular belief that Disney's films just reflect the contents of old-fashioned fairy tales, she made a startling discovery. The films took folktale heroines and depicted them as more regressive than they originally were. According to Stone, Disney made its princesses "not only passive and pretty, but also unusually patient, obedient, industrious, and quiet"—in her view, significantly worse examples for modern children than their folktale predecessors were.

Since then, many other studies have agreed that the fairy tales selected for the silver screen are too focused on beauty and stereotypically feminine behavior. Scholars have also criticized the fact that modern princess films were always about romance (usually involving an unhealthy "love at first sight" and an outdated type of couple who are not equal partners in the relationship), and they also argued that these films don't handle race representation very well.

Then, in 2001, around the time that the Disney Princess line was launched, filmmaker Chyng Sun, PhD—an associate professor of media studies at New York University—created a film called *Mickey Mouse Monopoly: Disney, Childhood & Corporate Power*. The film, which is distributed by the Media Education Foundation (MEF), brings together many of these criticisms.

Because the MEF is a nonprofit organization that produces and distributes documentary films for use in classrooms, *Mickey Mouse Monopoly*'s main buyers have been professors and university libraries. The MEF's mission is to inspire students to think critically about American mass media. Now, *Mickey Mouse Monopoly* is held in nearly six hundred libraries in the United States, many of which are university libraries. Hundreds of copies have also been sold to academic departments and individual professors at universities. Professors screen these copies for their students semester after semester, year after year.

Although *Mickey Mouse Monopoly* was about more than Disney's princesses, the film foreshadowed the Disney Princess criticisms that would soon go mainstream. For example, the film argued that in the ever-popular *Snow White and the Seven Dwarfs* (1937), Snow White seemed fulfilled by cooking and cleaning—which perhaps made sense in its social context then, but is hopelessly outdated today. It pointed out that in *The Little Mermaid*, Ariel gives up her voice and alters her body to pursue a man she doesn't even know.

It noted that in *Beauty and the Beast*, Belle falls in love with a beast-man, even though experts note that his emotional abuse of Belle and others in his household resembles real-life domestic violence—perpetuating the misguided fantasy that a good girl can change a bad boy. In *Aladdin*, the film notes, Jasmine behaves as a seductress to manipulate the film's villain, suggesting that women's greatest power is their sexuality—a horrible message for kids to absorb.

Meanwhile, *Pocahontas* trivializes the accomplishments of the real Pocahontas, reducing her actual history and political significance to a fictitious love story, and *Mulan* (also considered part of the Disney Princess line although Mulan is not actually a princess) fabricates from whole cloth the concept that the Chinese engaged in matchmaking—characterizing social norms in Mulan's time as more oppressive than they were. This has racist undertones, for it makes Western culture seem more enlightened in the process.

In addition to these problems, in story after story, every Disney princess character (until Merida in *Brave*—we'll get to her later) always needed a male character to rescue her, no matter how independent she might otherwise have seemed.

Classroom Conversations about Disney Princess Problems

At Salem State University in Salem, Massachusetts, where I am an associate professor, my undergraduate communications majors' reactions to *Mickey Mouse Monopoly* are typical. Having grown up on Disney films, they are stunned by the problems the documentary reveals. "I never thought about it that way before," they say. Some immediately agree with the film's perspectives, while others struggle to process the idea that Disney—a locus of childhood nostalgia—is imperfect.

Some students even feel angry or defensive. For their whole lives, they have regarded Disney as a wholesome company, and they resent the film's arguments. The criticisms can feel personal, as though the critics are attacking their own childhoods and their parents' choices for them. Others simply dismiss the film. "Those professors in the movie are reading too much into things," they tell me. "It's *Disney*. It's just entertainment."

These reactions vary significantly, but they all have something in common: They reveal that the typical undergraduate has never once thought critically about the Disney franchise or the problems with Disney's princesses. They have not approached the films from a media-literate perspective, so they can't see them for what they are. As the Chinese proverb states, if you want to know what water is like, don't ask the fish.

Every once in a while, though, a student tells the class about grappling with these issues as a small child, with the help of his or her parents—the kind of help that I advocate for in this book.

For example, one of my students was raised by her father and his wife. Because of Disney's portrayals of evil stepmothers, her family had many conversations when she was young about what was wrong with these films' portrayals of family structures and older women. This, she said, helped her become a more critical viewer of the films.

Another student explained that as the daughter of a Chinese American man and a Caucasian woman, she was riveted by Mulan when the film came out, delighted to finally see a character who looked like her. She watched the video obsessively, enjoying Mulan's victories against the monstrous-looking, gray-skinned Huns and their leader, Shan Yu—a frighteningly enormous man with beady yellow eyes and fangs.

Then, one day, my student's father explained something to her: "You are not Mulan. You know how she fights against the Huns? That's us. Our people were the Huns." In this way, as a small child, she came to recognize that despite its fantastic heroine, *Mulan* is imperfect. Disney's grotesque depiction of the Huns is a thread of ugly racism running through the film.

Out of the Classroom, into the Home

Since *Mickey Mouse Monopoly*'s release, concerns about Disney Princesses have leaped out of the classroom and gone mainstream. They are no longer confined to scholarly journals and educational films. And as the Disney Princess brand evolved into a megabrand worth $4 billion, parents' reactions to the brand's critics have been as diverse as my students'. They range from stunned acceptance to dismissiveness to defensiveness.

In 2006, for those parents who felt ambivalent or anxious about their daughters' princess adoration, and even for some who had never really considered it before, Orenstein's *New York Times Magazine* article "What's Wrong with Cinderella?" proved a cultural touch-stone. Writing about her own young daughter, Orenstein lamented, "I worry about what playing Little Mermaid is teaching her. I've spent much of my career writing about experiences that undermine girls' well-being, warning parents that a preoccupation with body and beauty (encouraged by films, TV, magazines and, yes, toys) is perilous to their daughters' mental and physical health. Am I now supposed to shrug and forget all that? If trafficking in stereotypes doesn't matter at three, when does it matter? At six? Eight? Thirteen?"

The response to Orenstein's article was incredible. It was one of the *Times*' "Most E-Mailed" articles for several days. Orenstein later expanded her argument into a bestselling book, *Cinderella Ate My Daughter*, prompting an even broader conversation. For example, the *Christian Science Monitor* covered the issue in an article called "Little Girls or Little Women? The Disney Princess Effect," connecting the popularity of the Disney Princesses with popular culture's increasing sexualization of young girls and a range of related problems.

This article was so successful that it prompted the *Monitor* to launch a new blog called *Modern Parenthood* in 2012, to which I have been a frequent guest contributor. The blog often features pieces about princess culture, because it has proven to be an ongoing challenge in the lives of families with preschool-aged girls.

Making Progress in Films but Not Products

Walt Disney Studios executives are savvy, and it's clear that they have been attuned to these conversations. And when powerful stars add their voices to the mix—as Meryl Streep did in an awards ceremony speech in 2014, calling Walt Disney himself a "gender bigot" who had "racist proclivities"—how can Disney executives ignore their critics?

I'm happy to say that every new princess film in recent years has made strides in addressing these problems. In *The Princess and the Frog*, Tiana is African American, adding more much-needed racial diversity to the princess line. In *Tangled*, Rapunzel is not helpless. She wields a frying pan as a weapon, and she takes the lead in orchestrating her own escape from her tower.

In *Brave* (produced by Pixar Animation Studios, a Disney subsidiary), Merida is both strong and independent. She's a skilled archer who has no interest in romance, and she is the first Disney Princess who is not married at the end of her film. In *Frozen*, the bond between sisters is shown to be more important than the pursuit of romance. This is clearly progress.

It's also good business—and it's terrific when business interests and girls' best interests sync up in this way. As author Gerard Jones explains in the book *Killing Monsters: Why Children Need Fantasy, Super Heroes, and Make-Believe Violence*, "As girlhood changes, girls' fantasies are changing. As their fantasies change, the entertainment industry scrambles to create stories that will speak to them. Its motives may be nothing more than profit, but in trying to find stories and images that will sell, it discovers girls' most powerful yearnings. Right now, girls are yearning for more power, while trying to weave it, in many different ways, into a new kind of female self. We can help them with that if we let them follow their fantasies and play their games, while we also go on teaching them that they can be anything they want to be."

It's a pity, then, that numerous licensed products from Disney's Consumer Products Division based on these films betray their better messages, as we'll discuss in more detail later—watering the modern princesses down in ways that make them seem weaker than their on-screen counterparts. Also, in the marketplace, the princesses who are often pushed the most are still classic princesses, like Cinderella and Sleeping Beauty, who were passive and valued for their appearances. They grace more Disney Princess products than, say, Mulan, who was active and valued for the things she accomplished, rather than what she did.

The leading ladies from Disney's historic princess films have real staying power—and unfortunately, for all the reasons Stone outlined back in 1975, their stories are the most problematic. Little girls born in the 2010 decade are growing up immersed in decades-old stories with outdated messages about women's roles in society and culture, about who can be a princess. And many experts agree that this is dangerous for our girls.

In short, princess culture is no longer child's play. No more wide-eyed innocence: princess is *controversial*.

But fortunately for parents, there's a way to address these problems with our children. We can use a technique called pop culture coaching, as discussed in the next chapter, to talk with our children about what they see in stores and on-screen. In so doing, we can raise them to be media literate, with the skills to assess and evaluate the stories the media tell them.

And of equal importance, when we practice pop culture coaching with our children, we establish healthy patterns of interpersonal communication with them. That means that as our children grow up and get beyond the princess years, they will feel comfortable coming to us with whatever new problems they may face—a healthy goal for every parent-child relationship.

CHAPTER TWO
Raising Media-Literate Children

For young children, viewing media critically is a challenge. But in today's media-saturated world, learning how to do so is essential. Media are so influential in our society that we need to understand how they work and be capable of analyzing the messages they convey. These media-literacy skills don't come naturally; they take guidance and practice. Fortunately, parents can put critical viewing in children's reach with pop culture coaching.

Pop culture coaching is a flexible, child-centered, proactive approach to raising media-savvy kids. When we act as our children's pop culture coaches, we give them support and feedback about their media interests—princess-related and otherwise. We show them what it means to think critically about media content, and we guide them to become critical thinkers themselves.

It's never too early to start pop culture coaching. We can talk with our preschoolers about the media in age-appropriate ways, giving them tools to foster their media literacy. Over time, our conversations can become more complex, growing with our children.

As pop culture coaches, we can help our kids to:

Understand how the media work.
Think critically about media content.
Create their own media—empowering them not just to consume, but also to create.

As our children grow up, the fact that they have been empowered by their critical-thinking abilities will benefit them in other areas of life, too—from the lessons taught at school to the things their peers say and do. So, pop culture coaching offers valuable short-term and long-term payoffs.

In this chapter, we'll consider effective pop culture coaching practices in a broad context. Pop culture coaching relates to all media—television, movies, video games, Internet, magazines, handheld devices such as LeapPads and iPads, and books—so it includes but is not limited to princess culture. Therefore, I discuss the principles of pop culture coaching in detail here and then apply them to girls' interests in pop culture princesses in the rest of this book.

Pop Culture Coaching: An Overview

To practice pop culture coaching, we must do a little preparation. We begin by *reflecting on our family's values*. What is important to us as a family, especially when it comes to our children's media use and the content they see? What values do we want our children to share with us? For some families, the answers will be clear and straightforward; others will require some reflection.

Once our values are clarified, we can use them to parent pro-actively. This means that instead of primarily reacting to problems that arise, we anticipate potential problems. How could the media contradict our values and negatively affect our children? What can we do to prevent or mitigate these negative effects?

For one thing, we can practice *media management*—making sure our children's media consumption is part of a balanced day of activities and establishing a healthy media diet for them to follow. For another, we can *talk about media* with our children, teaching them to think about the media we see, hear, and read, and fostering critical-viewing habits. As our children grow older, we can also coach them to develop higher-level skills—understanding how the media work and thinking critically about media messages.

Finally, we can help children of all ages *create their own simple media*. There are many benefits to being not just a media consumer, but also a creator. It gives children a sense of empowerment to know that they can use their voice to communicate their visions and ideas with others. It also takes their critical-thinking skills to a higher level, because understanding that media are created by other people helps children to question the goals and motives that underpin the media we all consume.

The ultimate goal is for our children to become their own coaches. We want them to understand how media work so that their experiences are rich and engaging, rather than passive; and we want them to internalize the skills and resilience necessary to navigate any problems that they may encounter in popular culture for years to come.

Putting Pop Culture Coaching in Action, Step by Step
Step 1: Identify Your Family's Values

What are your family's most important values? By values, I mean the personal beliefs that guide your family's behaviors and decisions. Values are general concepts, like obedience, rather than specific instructions, like "Don't talk back to your mother—do what she says."

Although we all have values that guide us, many people don't give their values much conscious thought. But conscious or not, they are there.

Families' values might include concepts like honesty, generosity, education, creativity, religious devotion, open communication, creativity, independence, frugality, and so on. Some values will have higher priority than others. (For example, in this book, I prioritize critical thinking as an important value.)

Think it through: What do you value? What drives the decisions you make for your family as a whole and your children as individuals? What values do you wish to instill in your children through your guidance and by your example?

It's also important to think about your *media* values. What's important to your family regarding media use? Questions you might ask yourself include:

What is your stance on television? Movies? Video games? The Internet? For example, is your position that these media are a source of fun times for your family, or that they are potential sources of problems—or maybe some of each?

Do you think it is important to limit the amount of time children spend with media?

Do you value content that is noncommercial? Educational? Prosocial—teaching lessons about positive behaviors?

Clearly identified values—both in general and in relation to the media—are useful for pop culture coaching because they help you decide what to coach your children *about*, and they help you be *consistent* in what you focus on. For example, if one of your most important values is open-mindedness, you might regularly coach your children to identify the stereotypes in the media that lead to closed-minded thinking and help them see how limiting stereotypes are. Or if you value self-esteem, you might coach your children to understand that the body types that are idealized in the media are unhealthy.

Beth Mayer is a nationally known eating-disorder expert who serves as president of the Multiservice Eating Disorders Association. In her therapy practice, Mayer has helped hundreds of parents to identify their values so that their values can serve as a reference point in their parenting. But she notes that it's not always easy. "What do you really value in your world?" Mayer asks. "It's a big question for people. What do I value? What's important to me? A lot of people don't know the answer."

In therapy, Mayer guides her clients through this process by asking questions about different values. "For example, I might ask, 'How do you want to raise your child? What kind of world do you want them to be in? How safe do you want them to feel?' Some parents say, 'I want them to live in the real world, so if there's a red alert in this country, I'm going to let them know.' If you think back to 9/11, some parents shielded their kids and some people let their kids listen to everything. That's a good example of a decision to make, in advance, of what you want for your children as they grow up. Do you want them to deal with reality, or do you want to shield them a little bit?"

Sometimes, when a family's values haven't been articulated, individual parents don't realize that they have conflicting values. This can lead to inconsistencies in their parenting and cause tension in the family. Mayer explains that when two parents aren't on the same page, or when the parents are inconsistent, kids received mixed messages. "Children learn very quickly: 'If I want some cookies, I'll go to Daddy, because Mommy never lets me have any,'" she explains.

Once you've articulated your family's values, you can use those values for pop culture coaching by *parenting proactively*. When you parent proactively, you anticipate that your children might become exposed to values that conflict with your family's, and you respond to this anticipated conflict in advance. In other words, proactive parents don't just wait for a conflict to arise—they do something about it ahead of time. The two main strategies are 1) to *protect* our children from encountering things we object to, and 2) to *prepare* them, teaching them strategies to handle the messages they receive that conflict with our values.

As you'll see in the pages that follow, Step 2 of pop culture coaching involves *media management*—establishing a media diet that is healthy and balanced with other activities. This falls under *protecting*. Step 3 emphasizes *preparation*, or coaching children to think critically about media messages and learn how to resist them. And Step 4 empowers children to create their own media as a way of understanding that all media are created by people—which further encourages critical thinking about the goals of and motivations behind media messages.

STEP 1 TIPS

Spend some time thinking about your values. Jot them down on paper. If you need a sounding board, talk them over with a trusted friend or family member.

If you have a spouse or partner, compare notes. Have a conversation. What are your points of agreement? Disagreement? Which values can you prioritize as a couple to help you be more consistent as you raise your children?

Consider writing a family values statement that encompasses media values. If your children are old enough, involve them in this process, too.

Share your values with your children in age-appropriate ways. Studies show that children are more likely to internalize their parents' values if they know exactly what those values are. Spell out your values for them.

Step 2: Establish a Healthy Media Diet

Children need a healthy media diet—one that balances their screen time with other activities and considers the quality of the content they consume.

Monitor screen time. The American Academy of Pediatrics (AAP) recommends that children over the age of two use media for no more than two hours per day. Too much media consumption is harmful to children. The AAP argues that time spent watching television, movies, and playing video games can displace other healthy and important activities that children should be engaged in—like physically active play, homework, and sleep.

According to the AAP policy on media and children, potential types of harm from too much screen time include attention problems, disordered eating and sleeping, and even obesity. So, it's important to make sure that children's screen time is balanced out with a range of other activities and interests.

Keeping the AAP's recommendation in mind, consider how much time you would like your children to spend with the media each day. Add up the time they currently spend watching television and DVDs, playing video games, and so on. (If your children attend day care, don't forget to check how much time they spend with media there, too. One study found that children in home-based day cares watch a daily average of 2.4 hours of television at day care, versus 0.4 hour a day in a child-care center.)

Do you think your children's average daily screen time is reasonable? Is this time well-balanced with other activities, like reading, toys, crafts, and outdoor play?

If your answer to either of these questions is no, it's time to cut back.

Take stock of *where* your children spend time with the media, as well. Do you let your child play with apps on your iPhone while you're driving or shopping, or watch videos on a Kindle or iPad while you're on the go? That can add up very quickly and is worth reconsidering.

Also, the AAP suggests having screen-free zones at home. For example, they suggest eliminating entertainment media from children's bedrooms—a great idea, as bedroom televisions can interfere with sleep time. The AAP also suggests turning off the television set during dinner, a great way to encourage family conversation. Several parents I spoke with mentioned that there is no TV in their family room or the kids' bedrooms. The only TV is in the master bedroom, which helps them to limit the children's access.

Finally, remember that advertising is also a cause for concern. In most households, kids' increased screen time exposes them to more ads. (The exception to this is families that use a DVR or an account such as Netflix for their children's media access.) Ads permeate the media, including the Internet and video games, and they can be very appealing. But it is only at about eight years old that children typically understand the persuasive intent of advertisements. Until that age, our children are typically vulnerable to the commercials on-screen—yet another reason why some experts advocate for minimizing children's screen time.

Organizations that advocate for this do so because the interests of media creators—to gain high ratings and big profits—are generally at odds with our children's best interests. Minimizing their exposure is a way of protecting them from the negative effects of big media's profiteering.

Content matters. Beyond minimizing screen time, parents face the critically important task of establishing a healthy media diet for their children—one full of high-quality programming. The devil, however, is in the details. It's easier to watch the clock or set a timer and say, "No more than two hours of screen time a day," than to monitor kids' media choices. Nevertheless, it's worth the effort.

The AAP recognizes this fact. Their policy statement on media and children notes, "To help kids make wise media choices, parents should monitor their media diet. Parents can make use of established ratings systems for shows, movies, and games to avoid inappropriate content, such as violence, explicit sexual content, or glorified tobacco and alcohol use." If content isn't monitored, children can easily see acts of violence, sexual content, and scenes in which bad behavior is glorified or rewarded.

Some argue that the media are just for entertainment, and that we needn't worry about content. Readers of my blog posts on the *Christian Science Monitor* and elsewhere occasionally snipe: "Why do you have to take things so *seriously*?"

My response is this: Most of young children's screen time tends to be spent on television. As adults, we know that the world shown on the television screen is largely a fantasy. But to children ages five and under, what's on television is real. Many preschoolers and kindergartners believe that the screen is actually a window into another part of the world—and for them, seeing is believing.

Sometimes, this involves a sense of magic and wonder that is very sweet. In their innocence, children believe in many things that are not real, from Santa Claus to the Tooth Fairy, and the blurred boundaries between the fantasy world and the real world can be darling. At age four, my son still believes in fairies. Last summer, when we planted a fairy garden in our backyard, he loved checking it in the morning for signs that the fairies had visited the previous night.

But unfortunately, children's television viewing can also cause some problems, as our children—lacking incredulity—can easily learn lessons we don't want them to learn. After all, people learn how to behave by observing and imitating others, and the media serve up countless people and situations to witness. When children see characters rewarded or punished for their actions and attitudes, they learn about cultural norms and rules that might apply to them, and they often believe and behave accordingly.

For example, when children see superheroes rewarded for fighting the bad guys, they might learn that fighting solves problems. But resorting to blows to resolve conflicts contradicts many families' values. Or, when our children see princesses loved and admired for their beauty, they might learn that prettiness is the most important quality in a girl—contradicting the values of families who believe the entire child is important, that what's inside counts.

Even shows that are rated appropriately for children may contain content that does not align with our values, and which may have undesirable effects on our children. For example, popular children's shows like *Mighty Morphin Power Rangers* and its many variants feature extended scenes of fantasy violence, in which conflicts are resolved by fighting. When researchers conducted an experiment on how *Mighty Morphin Power Rangers* influenced children's behavior, they found that children who watched the show committed many more aggressive acts than children who did not—seven times as many, in fact.

This is not surprising to some researchers who study children's media and health. Although there are disagreements on this point, a 2010 report in the journal *Pediatrics* argued, "The relationship between media violence and real-life aggression is nearly as strong as the impact of cigarette smoking on lung cancer: not everyone who smokes will get lung cancer, and not everyone who views media violence will become aggressive themselves. However, the connection is significant."

Other programs considered age-appropriate for children also have negative effects on them. For example, researchers studying the effect of fast-paced shows on preschool children conducted an experiment with *SpongeBob SquarePants*. The results: Because of *SpongeBob*'s fast pacing (its scenes change every eleven seconds, on average), children who viewed it had a harder time concentrating on tasks than children who watched a slower-paced show. The children also did poorly on tests measuring executive function skills such as self-regulation and delayed gratification—meaning they had trouble behaving well.

Therefore, in addition to adding up and evaluating your children's screen time, it's important to take stock of *what* they're watching. Do a media census. What TV shows are your children watching and how often? Which DVDs? Video games? Websites? Apps? Of those, what percentage would you consider "high-quality"? How much of it is the kind of educational and prosocial programming you find on PBS? How many of the video games and websites actively foster your children's learning? How much of it do you feel is mindless, or the visual equivalent of junk food?

(Remember that deciding what programs constitute junk food will depend on your family's values. As Faith Rogow, PhD, founding president of the National Association for Media Literacy Education, explains, "Because everyone interprets through the lens of their own experience, what one child takes away from a program might make it junk food, while another finds it thoroughly nutritious. I know I was initially appalled at a neighbor who let their four-year-old watch *Rescue 911*, until I realized that his dad was a firefighter and the child felt like he was watching his father be a hero.")

Write a prescription. Once you have a complete picture of the media situation in your children's lives, you can act as their media dietician, writing a prescription for a healthier, more balanced media experience. Maybe you'll want to remove free apps like Disney's Palace Pets that are basically glorified toy ads for their new princess-themed pet toys, and stock up on educational apps like Endless Alphabet instead. But there is no one-size-fits-all prescription, because every family's values and priorities are different. Spend some time thinking about your options to find something that will work for your family.

Also, while it's important to include enough "good stuff" in your kids' media diet, media-literacy experts argue that children need access to a range of media. They shouldn't necessarily be limited to "good stuff" exclusively. Cyndy Scheibe, PhD, is an associate professor of psychology at Ithaca College and a nationally recognized media-literacy expert. She explains: "Just as teaching kids to read is not about keeping them away from certain kinds of books, raising critical viewers is not about keeping kids from seeing certain media content. We do make choices about the books we expose kids to, and we try to expose them to a wide range of high-quality books. In the same way, it's important for parents and caregivers to help kids make choices about how they spend their time."

As I will explain in Step 3, when children have access to a range of media, you will have many more opportunities for productive conversations with them about your values in relation to the content they are viewing on-screen.

That said, with young children especially, media choices shouldn't be wide open. It's okay to say "no" to media that deeply conflict with your values. Rogow explains: "With young children, you're still gatekeeping and establishing core values. Parents should realize that kids' default thinking is, 'My parents keep me safe, so if this were really bad for me, they wouldn't allow it in our house.' So what's in the house has your tacit seal of approval; the media you allow is a reflection of your values. When our children get older, we allow them to make choices because we want them to become good decision makers. But when you're dealing with little ones, keep out stuff that really counters core family values, because otherwise they're getting mixed messages."

Note that age matters, too. The smaller the children, the simpler the solution can be. As our children grow older, their lives become more complex—and a simple media diet that suits a toddler will not be appropriate for a school-aged child. *I want to emphasize the importance of establishing a media diet as soon as possible, before your children reach their teenage years.* Studies show that children acquire television-viewing patterns in early childhood, and the types of programs they watch—and the time they spend watching—tend to be consistent in the long term. Because of this, setting healthy patterns as early as possible is key. So whether your child is two or twelve, there's no time like the present to start them on a healthier media diet.

Here are some ideas to get you started:

For children ages two to three, consider making a simple list of the TV shows, networks, apps, or DVDs they are allowed to choose from, and note the maximum time they should spend with those on a given day.

A reasonable media diet for a two-year-old child might say, "No more than one hour of screen time per day; TV shows must be age-appropriate programs from PBS only." It could even be more specific than that, listing exactly which shows your child will watch and which apps she may use, based on your preferences and perhaps those of your child, as well. For example: "Every day, Maggie may watch one episode of *Sesame Street* and one episode of *The Wonder Pets*. She may then spend five to ten minutes playing with the Kids Doodle drawing app on the iPad." You can curate a list of apps and shows from networks like PBS, Baby First, Nick Junior, and Disney Junior that make sense for your child.

For example, Lynn established a media diet for her two-year-old son that is similar to this. His diet focuses on particular times of day that he can watch television. "When my son is with me all day, he only watches TV in the early morning and after dinner," she says. And for content, she emphasizes the networks she approves of: "I only let him watch PBS shows and the Baby First network."

For children ages four to five, consider building in some choices. At this age, having some control over situations is important to children, so it is developmentally appropriate to give them a little bit of power over what they watch when they seem ready for it.

A reasonable media diet for children in this age range might say,

"No more than two hours of screen time per day, or three TV shows and some video game or app time. Two of the shows must be age-appropriate shows from PBS. The third show may be chosen freely from any age-appropriate programs." You could also add caveats such as, "No more than one movie every other day," or "Movies are not part of the daily schedule. They will only be watched on family movie nights."

Family movie night works well for Katha's family of three. "We have family movie night on Sundays, with who chooses on a rotation schedule," she explains. "All films must be appropriate for our four-year-old." Beyond that, her daughter's media diet consists of only one hour of television a day, with exceptions made on vacations and during illnesses. "We have Netflix, not cable—so we all have to be thoughtful about TV time," Katha notes. "We never just have it on for background noise."

. . . .

THEO'S MEDIA DIET

My son, Theo, is now four years old. Over the past year, he figured out how to use the remote control to access all the programs available on our Netflix account. This gave him easy access to educational shows like *LeapFrog* and *Blue's Clues*, but it also gave him easy access to junk food programs like *Power Rangers*.

I knew that the AAP stressed the importance of high-quality content, yet slowly but surely, my son was making his way through the *Power Rangers* canon: *Mighty Morphin Power Rangers. Power Rangers Samurai. Power Rangers Time Force. Power Rangers Turbo. Power Rangers Ninja Storm. Power Rangers Zeo.* Oy.

Then I had a new baby. Tending to a fussy nursling and a four-year-old at the same time was such a challenge! I started using the television to occupy Theo while I tried to get the baby to nap. I was so focused on tracking how often the baby had eaten or wet a diaper that I lost track of how much screen time Theo was getting—and of just how much *Power Rangers* he was watching.

When my husband and I realized this, we started actively suggesting to Theo that he watch other programs, too—and when we pressed the point, he would get angry. But we weren't trying to take it away. We knew he really loved the show, and we just wanted him to watch other things, too. Clearly, we needed a new approach. What to do?

While I was wrestling with this question, I attended the 2013 summit of the Campaign for a Commercial-Free Childhood (CCFC) in Boston. I gave a presentation about pretty princess problems, and I also attended as many of the other presentations as I could, baby in my arms.

In one presentation, Michael Rich, MD, director of the Center on Media and Child Health at Harvard University, spoke about the positive and negative effects that media can have on children's health. He reminded the audience of the importance of content choices. He discussed the results of the *Power Rangers* study (in which children who had viewed the show were more aggressive than their nonviewing peers), and then brought up the decades of research on *Sesame Street*, which documents the myriad positive effects of the show's curriculum on its young viewers.

The conference had lit a fire under me. I came away determined to establish a media diet for my son, test it out, and see how it went.

I explained what I had in mind to my husband, and together, we collaborated on a media diet that went beyond establishing screen time limits. It also prescribed the type of content our son was allowed to watch. Here's what it said:

THEO'S TV RULES

We need to have a healthy media diet! So, we have a few rules:

1. <u>If</u> Theo is to watch TV, he must begin with an episode of *Sesame Street*.

2. After *Sesame Street*, he may watch <u>one</u> show of his choosing.

3. <u>If</u> he wishes to watch any further TV, his next program must be one of the following:
    - *Mister Rogers' Neighborhood*
    - *Sesame Street*
    - *Blue's Clues*
    - *Dragon Tales*
    - *LeapFrog*
    - *Super Why!*

4. He may then watch <u>one</u> additional show of his choice <u>or</u> play on his LeapPad.

As you can see, although this media diet limits time and prescribes good stuff, it also gives him a lot of latitude to make his own decisions. At his age (four), I don't mind that he'll use some of the freedom afforded in this diet to watch *Power Rangers*. The way I see it, if I want him to be a critical thinker who can analyze and evaluate what he sees on-screen, he needs access to a range of media. I just want to make sure he sees a lot of healthy stuff, as well.

After getting our list down on paper, we let Theo know that we had created a healthy media diet. We explained that we created it because we love him and want him to be healthy, and then we made a big deal out of showing him this document and taping it to the side of the TV set where everyone can see it.

At first, he protested. He didn't want a media diet! But we were firm and made it clear that these were the new rules.

We were also consistent about implementation. When Theo asked for shows that would deviate from the plan, we would say, "Let's look at the list together!" Then we'd read the relevant sections back to him and gently discuss his options.

Within a week, he had adjusted to the new schedule. He grew to love *Sesame Street* very much, even though he had gotten to the point of being so into *Power Rangers* that he claimed he didn't like Big Bird anymore. Now, when he gets home from preschool, he's likely to announce, "I haven't watched *Sesame Street* yet!" and sit down with a happy smile on his face.

In short order, he also began asking for less and less television. He would often watch only two or three shows and then be done with television for the day, clocking in at less than the two hours recommended by the AAP. We're happy with that!

. . . .

Children ages six, seven, and eight can have even more latitude to self-monitor what they watch, with more autonomy the older they get. However, the parents still need to be the ultimate authority, as there is a wide range of content targeting this age group, some of which is bound to conflict with an individual family's values.

A media diet for children in this age group might read: "We trust you to choose content that is age-appropriate and in line with the family's values. However, Mom and Dad have veto power. If we object to what's on-screen, you will change the channel or turn the device off." The parents might also wish to make a list of specific channels, shows, apps, or video games that are off-limits (for example, no MTV or no using their older cousins' copy of *Grand Theft Auto*).

Have open conversations about what you consider "healthy" and why to foster understanding and encourage children's cooperation. Also, explain to your children what the terms "appropriate" and "inappropriate" mean, and chat with them about why certain shows are or are not age-appropriate.

Angela, mom to a six-year-old girl, notes, "I think limiting my child's viewing to specific shows, channels, and movies is still good at this age, as most TV shows are still not appropriate for a six-year-old." Angela and her husband don't allow TV until her daughter's homework is done, and they maintain control over what she watches by using their DVR to record almost everything she sees.

"By having the shows on DVR, we know exactly what she's watching and avoid commercials, while simultaneously allowing her some freedom of choice. She can select the show on her own, knowing which ones are for her. But she always has to ask permission to turn on the TV," Angela adds, "and arguing when it's time to turn it off can result in lost TV privileges."

Shara and her husband also set restrictions on what their eight-year-old daughter is allowed to view. They let her watch no more than an hour and a half of television a day. "She gets about a half hour in the morning while she is getting ready for school—and maybe an hour at night," Shara says. "We watch a lot of sports with her—baseball and basketball. When she watches by herself, we really try to know what she is watching and have restricted the Disney Channel because of the more teen-oriented shows. She knows to ask if she can watch specific shows. She also uses the on-demand function a lot—which takes her directly to the cartoons she likes without the ads, which I really love."

Interestingly, during the school year, a healthy media diet for children ages six and up often includes *less* screen time than they had prior to beginning elementary school. This is because as children become increasingly involved in extracurricular activities and face a heavier homework load, demands on their time increase, reducing the time available for media in the first place.

Katherine is the mom of two boys, ages seven and thirteen, and she explains: "During the school year, the boys are limited during the week to almost no screen time because homework and reading must be done first, and dinner and the bedtime routine often fill the rest of the awake time." On the weekend, however, they are allowed two hours per day per the AAP's maximum recommendation—but, Katherine says, "I always have veto power on whatever show they are watching, and if they argue, they lose their privileges."

Amy, who is the mother of a seven-year-old girl and a ten-year-old boy, agrees. During the school week, there is no time for screen time. "Our kids get no screen time during the school year Monday through Thursday, really," she explains. "There is no extra time beyond activities, outside time, homework, dinner, showers, reading, and bedtime. But Friday afternoon is kind of a free-for-all and often involves two-plus hours, and we have a family movie night once a month or so. On Saturday and Sunday during the school year, most of the time the max is two hours total screen time each day."

But summertime is different. Many parents of school-aged children have two sets of rules: one for the school year and one for the summer. Both Katherine and Amy's children are allowed a maximum of two hours per day when school is out, just like on the weekends. In both families, however, the children have to *earn* these screen-time hours by engaging in other activities that balance out the media diet.

Katherine's boys must read books to earn their screen time, because reading is an important value to their family. "During the summer," she explains, "every day the boys have to prove to me that they have read at least a hundred pages in a book that has age- and reading-level-appropriate paragraphs and literary value before I let them turn on the TV or do any screen-based activity. They have to tell me what they've read in some detail to prove it, or else I send them back to reread the same hundred pages. Then I try to limit their screen time to two hours per day."

Meanwhile, Amy's family prioritizes physical activity as an important value, so her children earn screen time by engaging in physical activities. "In the summer we allow some screen time most days, but try to keep it in check. They 'earn' screen time—a minute for every minute they are active outside. Screen time is a privilege, not a right, and I don't hesitate to take it away if it becomes a problem."

Apparently this strategy has been around for some time. One thirtysomething mom recalls with a grin: "When I was growing up, my sitter made us run laps to earn TV time. One lap around the double-lot-sized front yard for each minute of TV time," she says. "If it was nice out and we wanted to veg, she'd say, 'It's a beautiful day for growing children,' and send us outside."

WHAT ABOUT YOUNGER SIBLINGS?

For children under the age of two, the AAP recommends no screen time at all. Media use is not considered developmentally appropriate for such young children. For one thing, experts say that babies who *seem* interested in media may actually not be. Their attention to what's on-screen may be due to a basic human reflex known as the orienting response. When an unfamiliar sight or sound occurs, the orienting response makes babies focus on it, in case it is a threat. But what's on-screen is always changing—always novel and new—so babies' "interest" in the screen may not be what it seems. They may actually be unable to look away.

Moreover, babies thrive on human interaction, and a screen can never replace that need. As Rich has argued, "A growing infant brain needs human interaction, face to face. Babies should be acting on their physical environment and engaged in open-ended, imaginative free play—not engaged with a screen."

Rogow points out, however, that screen time and free play don't have to be mutually exclusive. "If we're concerned about the influence of media," she asks, "shouldn't we start helping them become literate from birth, rather than waiting until after a child's second birthday? Screens are present in families' lives, and whether we like it or not, children are internalizing messages about them (and from them) from birth. Saying 'no TV' doesn't give anyone any helpful strategies to think about how to help babies become media literate from day one." If a baby is going to be in front of a screen with an older sibling, then it is important to interact with the baby as much as possible—

talking to the baby about what's on-screen and engaging with her actively.

Scheibe agrees. "I personally don't go along with the strict AAP recommendation of no screen time at all before the age of two. It's much more about the quality of what they see and the balance of lots of different activities. I'd avoid watching adult media content that might sound scary around little kids—but when young children watch small quantities of good quality, educational, prosocial TV, that gives parents a chance to make dinner or change their clothes, or to de-stress and be better parents."

The takeaway: With siblings under the age of two, be very conscious of what media they are around. Keep media consumption to a minimum and balanced out by other activities, and make it as age-appropriate as possible. Don't let older kids watch scary-sounding content around younger siblings. Emphasize that what's best for the family is what's good for the baby, so gentle programming is a must. And as much as possible, engage with the baby about what's happening on-screen, rather than expecting him or her to watch passively. All interaction is a good thing.

STEP 2 TIPS

Be warm. Studies show that children are more likely to accept their parents' values when those values are communicated with warmth and good humor. So, when explaining that you are setting limits on media use, try to be firm and warm, rather than harsh. Make it clear that the media limits reflect your family's values and a desire for the children to be as healthy as possible—and are not meant as a punishment or a threat to their autonomy. Research suggests that with young children especially, when parents use a warm approach, the children's desire to identify with their parents increases. The children want to be more like their parents, so they become more willing to follow their rules.

Be consistent. Don't make occasional exceptions to the limits you set, or you'll be in for a hard time. In her therapy practice, Mayer has seen many families struggling because the parents have enforced their rules inconsistently. "When parents are inconsistent, children often learn, 'The more I scream, the more I'll get,'" Mayer explains. "That sets up a really negative dynamic in the family system because the kids know that if they push their parents hard enough, they may crack. For this reason, I promote parents taking their stand and being consistent."

Good news: Parenting with warmth and consistency will pay off in the long run. Studies indicate that 96 percent of teenagers lie to their parents, often about really big issues. But which teens lie the least? Those whose parents consistently enforce rules while being the warmest and having the most conversations with their children. They explain why rules exist but are supportive of their children's autonomy and freedom.

Be authoritative. The key to being successful with the media diet is to be firm but warm and consistent when implementing it—to be authoritative, rather than authoritarian. Studies show that authoritative parenting is most effective at producing socially competent, responsible children—children who follow their parents' wishes "without sacrificing curiosity, originality, and spontaneity."

Being authoritative means setting firm controls on children's behavior, but not being overly harsh or punitive. Making it clear that it's about the child's *health*, and that it's not a punishment of some kind, is important.

It's okay to change the media diet. Being consistent doesn't mean being inflexible; authoritative parents are open to their children's input. You can reconsider the rules if your child's suggestions seem reasonable. For example, after a few months following his media diet, Theo wondered if we could add a few more shows to his "healthy shows" list. When we asked what he had in mind, he made some suggestions that didn't fit (*Voltron Force*) and some that did (*Super Why!* and *Word Girl*). We had some great conversations surrounding that. We explained that healthy shows were shows that would teach him things, so no, *Voltron Force* couldn't join the list—but yes, *Super Why!* and *Word Girl* could.

It's okay to ban toxic media. If something is toxic to your child or your family—truly harming your child or your relationship—don't be afraid to ban it from your home. How do you identify what's toxic? Rogow notes it's easier to think about this in terms of the extremes we might see with older kids. "Suppose your fourteen-year-old comes home and wants to listen to white supremacist rock-and-roll," she says. "You have a right to say, as a parent, 'You are a member of a family. That's a community. You have a responsibility as a member of this community not to hurt other people in the community, and we deem this to be so upsetting that it's hurtful. You can't have this here.'"

With little kids, it's more about the effects that certain media have on the child. "Really pay attention to kids' immediate reaction to media," she suggests. "After they've watched a certain show or played a certain video game, what's their mood like? What's their behavior like? If you see a pattern where every time they watch that show, they wind up in a fight with their sibling within five minutes, that's a signal that your child is not ready for it.

"It might be a developmental issue—it's not meant for their age and they're not ready for it yet—or it just might be the personality of the kid. They might be likely to act out in certain ways because of what they see. Or it might be the media itself, that it's really designed to wind kids up, and it did. And if you don't want that, or if the kid can't handle that, then maybe that's not a good match for that child."

BOOKS ABOUT BALANCING SCREEN TIME WITH OTHER INTERESTS

Want help broaching the idea of limiting your children's screen time? Look for age-appropriate books on the topic that you and your children can read together. For example, here are some books on the topic that are appropriate for preschoolers:

Aunt Chip and the Great Triple Creek Dam Affair by Patricia Polacco. What happens when people no longer read? A cautionary tale: don't let TV take over your life!

The Berenstain Bears and Too Much TV by Stan and Jan Berenstain. The bears go without TV for a week and find all kinds of other things to do, instead.

Box-Head Boy by Christine Winn. Denny learns about the consequences of watching too much television.

Mama Rex and T Turn Off the TV by Rachel Vail. No power means no TV! Mama proves to T that there are other fun things to do besides watch television all day.

Mouse TV by Matt Novak. A mouse family squabbles over what to watch. No one can agree. But when the television breaks, they learn to enjoy all kinds of other activities together.

Step 3: Watch and Talk about On-Screen Content with Your Kids

Besides limiting screen time, watching television and movies with your kids—a.k.a. "co-viewing"—may be the most common media-related advice parents encounter (in part because it's one of the AAP's recommendations). But if we want to encourage our children's critical thinking, co-viewing is not enough. We also need to *talk about* what's happening on-screen, during the screening, and afterwards.

Studies show that many times, when parents don't like what they and their children see on-screen, they're inclined to ignore it—to just let it go. Unfortunately, however, children can take parents' silence regarding negative material as a form of endorsement—the opposite of what co-viewing would hope to achieve. Because of this, "parents should be aware that the popular advice to 'watch television with your children' may produce undesirable effects if parents do not contradict the negative messages that are co-viewed," warns Amy Nathanson, PhD, an associate professor of communication at Ohio State University.

If you want to cultivate critical-viewing skills in your children, the simple advice to watch television together may actually be counterproductive. The consequence is the same as allowing popular culture you dislike inside your house. Kids will interpret it as having your tacit approval.

This means that limiting screen time and watching or using media alongside one's children are most effective when parents actively talk with their children about content. Be present to see and hear your children's reactions, and talk with them about what you are seeing. Think of your reactions as a demonstration of critical thinking. When you talk back to the screen or share your concerns with your children, you are modeling the kind of behavior you hope your children will adopt. Respond to anything the children say, too. Pick up on any cues they give you.

Try to make these conversations routine in your family. Don't think of it as one big talk. Think of it as an ongoing conversation.

Respect your children's media tastes. As previously mentioned in Step 2, it is okay for children to have access to a range of media—sometimes even content that you dislike. Children are entitled to have interests that differ from their parents. Respecting their individuality is important.

As Rogow explains, "We often don't share kids' tastes. If adults used their own taste to choose shows, very few kids would ever see *Barney and Friends*. It's important to actually distinguish taste issues from values issues. There's a difference between not liking a show or a game and actually deciding that the show conveys troubling values. We do require agreement on following established family rules; what we don't require agreement on is what we *like*."

Furthermore, she argues that unless a specific program or video game is actually toxic or dangerous to your child or to the family, there's no need to ban specific media. Likewise, it's fine to ban apps that can actually be dangerous to your kids—like Snapchat, which allows users to send photos to each other that will self-destruct in ten seconds.

Snapchat gives kids a false sense of security and encourages them to send one another inappropriate photos. It is also used for "sexting."

So even though Snapchat and similar apps may be popular among preteens and teens, it's okay to make them completely off limits to a child who nevertheless wants them. (Also keep an eye out for apps like Poof, which lets kids hide apps they don't want their parents to see. You definitely don't want those on the family iPad or your child's smartphone!)

Otherwise, letting children see the content you disagree with can be highly productive, because it provides you with opportunities for conversations. Rogow explains: "In the long run, kids will benefit from watching media you do not like, if you talk it through with them. When you react to what's on-screen and explain why you don't like what you're seeing, you're giving your children *language*. Young kids don't yet have the vocabulary to think through the negative aspects of media the way that adults do, and they need words if they're going to think critically about it. The more that you can talk through the content you object to with them, the better."

Respect your children's opinions about media content. Your child may not always agree with your value judgments about certain television programs, media, or video games. For example, you may comment that a certain behavior is inappropriate, and your child may defend it, saying that it's funny. Remember that as pop culture coaches, our goal is not to change our children's minds or to coax a specific answer out of them. Instead, it's to *foster their critical thinking*. As Rogow notes, this can be tricky to remember. As parents, we get used to focusing on helping our children answer questions correctly—but in pop culture coaching, there is not always one right answer. For that reason, try to remember that your pop culture conversations are a way to:

- Let your children know where you stand, without requiring their agreement (except in the case of rules—established family rules must be followed).
- Encourage your children to be critical viewers, rather than passive consumers.
- Establish healthy patterns of communication between yourself and your child, so that chatting about what's on-screen becomes the norm in your household.

So, be sure to respect your children's interests and their right to form their own opinions. If they feel comfortable being honest when they disagree with you, the lines of communication will stay open—a pattern that's important to establish before the teenage years.

Discussing Media with Children: Conversation Ideas

Talking with your children about media can feel awkward or forced if you're not used to it. To begin, try making simple declarative statements to share your reactions to what's on-screen. For example:

- "I like this part because [reason]."
- "I don't think he should be lying about that."
- "I don't agree with her decision."
- "No one is listening to her! They should listen to their friend."
- "Wow, he's being greedy! People shouldn't be greedy like that."

Ask questions to solicit your child's opinion during a screening. Yes or no questions are okay, but open-ended questions are even better:

- "Do you think it's a good idea for her to do that?"
- "Why do you think he is keeping that secret?"
- "Uh-oh. What did her mom say to her earlier? Can you remember what she's supposed to be doing?"

If your child seems annoyed by questions during a program or movie (which is more likely the older your child gets), save your major questions or comments for later. Jot them down if you need to. And feel free to silently give the screen the evil eye when something happens that you disapprove of. Kids pay more attention to our reactions than we realize.

Then, at dinner or when you're driving somewhere together in the car, you can introduce the topic. Just make sure to give enough of a reminder of the content so that your child will remember what you're talking about. You might combine declarative statements with open-ended questions as you do so:

- "I noticed that in the Miley Cyrus video we watched today, the girls wore a lot less clothing than the guys did. That kind of bothered me. What did you think of that?"
- "In the movie we were watching earlier, the popular girls were really mean to that girl they didn't like. What would you do in that situation?"

To help your children identify whether the values in a media text are appropriate or inappropriate for them, consider this suggestion from Rogow: Look closely at video games with your child and explain that what the *game* values is what you can earn points for. For example, if you win when you spell words correctly, that game values reading and spelling. If you get points for shooting bad guys, that game values shooting. "Ask your child, 'Does that fit our values? Does it fit the values you want to have?'" By modeling this kind of thinking for your children, they can begin to ask these questions about media independently, even when you are not around.

A final important tip: If your child says something about what's on-screen or reacts in some way, be sure to respond. You might express agreement ("Yes, that's true!") or support ("Good point"), or follow up for more info ("Why did you cringe?" or "What do you mean by that?"). What's key is to let your child know that when you're watching or using media together, you're *listening* and you *care*.

Lynn keeps her media conversations with her two-year-old son simple. She points out various things to him, getting him used to the idea that media is something parents and children can talk about. For example, Lynn says, "I try to read him a book within a half hour of him watching TV, and I'll point out anything similar from the show. I think *Super Why!* is his favorite show right now, and I love it because it promotes reading."

With her four-year-old daughter, Katha's current focus is on the insults and violence found in children's television. "Usually when someone uses a not so-nice-word (G-rated words but not the kind of words we use)," Katha says, "or if a bad guy or even a good guy does something violent, usually someone getting bopped on the head, we talk about how what so-and-so just did isn't very nice."

Dina has a ten-year-old son and a six-year-old daughter. She co-views their cartoons with them ("There are so many that are really fresh!" she complains), and she likes to ask questions that will get them thinking about what they see on-screen. "Just the other day,

I asked them what made the fish in *Finding Nemo* look like boys or girls," Dina says. "They stared and stared, and then they agreed. They thought it was the eyelashes."

Her repeated conversations with her children about media have also helped them self-regulate in certain areas—like video games. "We have had tons of talks because I don't allow killing games in our house," Dina says. "My son sometimes tries to validate certain games because they aren't people, or the blood doesn't look real. He will always come ask me—but then he realizes if he is asking, it is probably because he knows it is too violent."

Angela, whose daughter only watches television programs that have been saved to DVR, also talks constantly with her daughter about what's on-screen. "Sometimes I will pause a show just so we can talk about what happened," she explains. "I try to keep the conversations simple, since she's only six, and I'm not always sure if she gets it or is just parroting emphatically back to me. But at least we're talking about it, and maybe it will sink in later."

Angela and her daughter have had conversations about the contents of video games, as well. "I had to explain why there were certain video games I didn't feel were appropriate for her to play, even though they are included in a game-filled website the kids all access in the after-school program at their elementary school. The video games in the 'Games for Girls' section were all about fashion and makeup, with the girls and women looking like Bratz dolls. I told her to stick to the cartoony zombie bunnies, jumping pandas, and wannabe Mario."

Tara's daughters are ages eight and twelve, and she wants them to know that the way the media present women's bodies is unrealistic. "When I look through a magazine, I ask, 'So, do you think this is airbrushed?' 'Do you think this girl really looks like this in real life?'" These kinds of questions and conversations have made an impact. Tara says, "My daughters picked up on this very quickly."

And indeed, such conversations can pay off in the long term, as well. Sonya, a nineteen-year-old college student, feels that learning critical-thinking skills in early childhood benefitted her tremendously. "I was raised on Disney movies, and my parents gave me the tools to critically analyze the movies very early on," she says. "This allowed me to watch the movies obsessively—I watched *The Little Mermaid* at least once a day, every day, between the ages of two and five—and recognize the flaws in them.

"I remember being annoyed with all the pink in my Pocahontas-themed sixth birthday party, and I remember sitting in my kitchen plotting ways around my peers' typical 'Oh my gosh, what do you want your wedding to be like?' conversations. I knew that the best part about Belle's character was that she was true to her bookish self, despite the majority's disapproval, and that the prince was secondary to Ariel pursuing her dreams above ground."

TALKING ABOUT BAD BEHAVIORS

In my family, with a four-year-old child, we wind up talking about characters' behaviors a lot. Lots of kids' programs focus on bad behaviors. Academic studies show that even prosocial children's media, like the kind found on PBS that are meant to teach lessons about good behavior, spend way too much time modeling bad behavior. The result: Little kids often don't pick up on the resolution or good behavior that such programs mean to encourage. The exciting and interesting bad behaviors get all the attention.

Because I'm aware of this problem, when my son, Theo,

and I are watching movies or television programs together, I'm quick to point out on-screen behaviors that I don't like—in a gentle way, of course. I might say, "Thomas should tell Sir Topham Hatt the truth!" or "Gee, I don't like the way the witch is talking to Rapunzel right now—that's cruel," or "Uh-oh, Spike is being really greedy! That's not nice."

In the interest of positive reinforcement, I'll point out good behaviors, too. "That was really kind of Kanta to let the girls take his umbrella," or "It was so clever how Word Girl figured that out," or "Rarity is so generous with her friends."

Sometimes, I'll phrase my commentary as questions: "Do you think that's a good idea?" or "What do you think of that?"

What's great is that the older he gets, the more often he'll turn to me and offer the kinds of commentary that I model for him. For example, when we watched *Beauty and the Beast* together for the first time, he said, "The Beast shouldn't yell like that. It's naughty." Then, later, when Belle appeared in her gold dress for the ballroom scene: "Hey, where did her blue dress go that I like?" (Blue is his favorite color.) Whatever his comments are, I like to hear them—and I make sure to give him an answer so he knows I'm listening.

Sometimes, it's helpful to have longer conversations when the TV is off. By paying attention to Theo's interests and his reactions while we're viewing things together, I can gauge what he might like to talk about later.

For example, Theo has been interested in the concept of "thieves" since he was about two and a half years old. One day, our family was enjoying a picnic on a park bench in Salem, Massachusetts, when a seagull stole Theo's sandwich through the slats in the bench. He was really upset about losing his sandwich this way, so we encouraged him to shoo the nearby seagulls away by shouting, "Go away, thieves!" He seemed empowered by his ability to fight back.

Now, anytime we are at the beach or another location where seagulls approach, he is vigilant about shooing them away, saying, "You can't have our food, thieves!" He's even noticed seagulls creeping up on other families and seems to have made it his personal mission to try to scare encroaching seagulls away. He doesn't like thieves.

About a year ago, he had an experience with a real thief when my iPhone was stolen while we were running errands in the mall. We were able to recover it, thanks to Find My iPhone and the help of our local police. But in the midst of all the excitement, Theo was amazed to learn that people could be thieves, too—not just seagulls.

Oh.

Yes, we said. Some people are thieves!

Then came the inevitable, perplexed question: "Why?"

Well, because sometimes, people make bad decisions.

So, between the seagulls and the iPhone theft, thieves have been an occasionally recurring topic of conversation. (Key questions he's asked have included: "Do thieves live in houses?" and "Do thieves have teeth?")

Soon after becoming enamored with the Disney films *Tangled* and *Aladdin*, Theo realized that Flynn and Aladdin are thieves. Thieves! Uh-oh. He had a hard time making sense of this, since both are really likable characters, and he feels very keenly that stealing is wrong.

So we've talked a lot about *why* Flynn and Aladdin are thieves, and the differences between the two characters. Flynn seems to steal because he's greedy and thinks it's fun. In his verse of the "I've Got a Dream" song, he sings that his only dream is to be "surrounded by enormous piles of money." In contrast, Aladdin is a boy without parents who steals food because otherwise, he won't eat. And he's not greedy, either. In an early scene in the film, he gives his stolen bread to littler kids who are also hungry, showing that he is a kind person.

As a result of these conversations, when we're watching *Tangled*, Theo will sometimes offer his own running commentary. He'll say things to me like, "Flynn shouldn't be a thief! That's too naughty," or "Poor Aladdin! He is a thief because he doesn't have any mommy or daddy or food. He doesn't want to be a thief."

In my opinion, being able to identify differences between on-screen characters and their motivations is a terrific outcome of pop culture coaching. It's the result of talking and thinking critically about how people are represented, and why characters are shown doing the things they do. I'm glad that my child has a basic understanding that depictions of bad behaviors don't make those bad behaviors okay, even when the characters engaged in them are fun and exciting.

Moreover, these conversations are laying important groundwork for the future, making it clear that we discuss and think critically about media content in our family. Considering the content he'll likely see later in childhood and in adolescence, it's crucial to establish parent-child communication and critical-thinking practices as the norm now.

STEP 3 TIPS

Chat while you're co-viewing. Sometimes, it will be obvious. Something will directly reinforce or contradict one of your values, and you'll want to mention or address it. Other times, possible discussion topics may seem less obvious. One strategy: Consider which people are represented, and how. Are the bad guys people of color? Do men vastly outnumber women? As you're viewing, you might ask yourself: "Who is harmed, who benefits, and who is left out?"

Are you concerned with the underrepresentation of women in media? If so, you can also make a game of deciding whether different movies pass the Bechdel test. It's simple—to pass the test, a movie must meet the following criteria:

1. It has to have at least two [named] women in it
2. Who talk to each other
3. About something besides a man

Sadly, far fewer movies pass this test than you'd think—offering lots of opportunities for discussion with children about why men are featured more often than women in films, and why they're so often depicted doing a more interesting range of things (for example, not always focused on romance).

Step 4: Teach Children about Media Creation

As our children's pop culture coaches, we need to help them understand authorship—that media are created by people. And if other people created the media we see on our screens, that means we can create our own media, too. This concept is easiest for older children to grasp. Very young children can have a hard time understanding that what's on-screen is created by other people, and not just a window into some other location in the world.

Media-literacy experts assert that if we give children the tools to create their own media, they will better understand how mass media are created. They will know that other people have made decisions about what stories to tell, what shots to show on-screen, and what words the characters will say. This kind of knowledge is truly a form of literacy. It's at odds, though, with the way marketers position kids as consumers—people who spend and buy, not create.

Teach your child that all media are created by people, and that he or she can be a creator, too. Here are some ideas on how to do so, grouped roughly by the age appropriateness of the activity.

Ages Three to Five (as suggested by Faith Rogow):

- Next time you do something special as a family, help your child to take photos to document the trip. Then print the photos and ask your child to help you put them back together in order. This will teach the child about *sequencing*—a great skill for creating media.

- At the end of a family outing, take a photo of something fun that represents the experience, and send it to a family member (like a grandparent) or a family friend. Then ask that family member to have a conversation with the child about it: "Madison, can you tell me about the photo you sent me? What's in it? Why did you take that photo?" This helps children understand *choices*— that in creating media, people choose what to depict.

- When watching television programs and movies, pause the action and ask your child to imagine what you would see if you could look up above the action, or to either side. What is outside the frame of the screen? (You can do the same with illustrated books.) This helps children understand *framing*—that not everything could be pictured, so someone selected only a portion to share with the audience.

- Ask your child to draw a picture of her bedroom. Then ask questions about what's in the picture. How do you know it's *her* bedroom and not somebody else's? What clues are there to whose room it is? For example, is her favorite stuffed animal included in the drawing? "This kind of questioning will get children thinking about the *props* used in the media," Rogow notes.

Ages Five and Six

- Once your child has experience talking about his or her own photos, you can start to talk about the photos shown on toy boxes. "Why do you think the people who made this toy chose that photo?" Rogow explains, "By the age of six, children can give pretty good answers to this kind of question."

- Give your child an inexpensive camera or camcorder. Teach him or her to document his world. Ask him or her to direct your actions. How should you pose for a photo? What should you say or do on video?

- If your child enjoys telling stories and drawing, have him or her tell you a story and write it down. Then, ask your child to draw pictures to illustrate it. Now you have a homemade book.

- After your child has told you a story, ask your child about *why* he or she told you a story in a certain way. This will encourage deeper thinking about the choices media creators make.

- Take the homemade book one step further: help your child

take a photo of each image. Upload the images together to your computer. Put them together in a software package you're comfortable with—it doesn't matter if it's PowerPoint or iMovie. Now your child's story is on-screen.

- If you're good with video editing or want an excuse to learn, you can help your child make videos featuring his or her toys. You could take inspiration from a favorite program. For example, a lot of families have created video remakes of the "Accidents Happen" song from *Thomas and Friends*. Or you can help your child use dolls or stuffed animals to act out a story that you videotape. Technology is so ubiquitous nowadays, and so affordable, that there's lots of potential for making cute, creative stuff.

Ages Six through Eight

- If your child is passionate about a cause or an issue, help him or her create a video to express his or her position.
- Watch YouTube videos together before creating your own video. Find videos made by other kids or families, and try to figure out *how* they were made. Did they use one camera or two? A continuous shot or several edits? Is there a soundtrack—any music underneath? What else do you notice about how it was produced? You can even use the comments to ask questions about how they did anything impressive.
- Teach your children about *storyboards*. A storyboard is a sequence of sketches or drawings that outline the actions or plot planned for a video. If you do a web search for "storyboard template," you will find printable storyboard pages. For each storyboard, a drawing of a scene goes in the box on top (stick figures are

okay!), and a caption describing the action or dialogue goes in the space below. Work together to imagine a commercial or short story that would make an interesting video, and use storyboards to visualize it. You can use characters your children already know and love, or make up new ones.

. . . .

TEACHING MY DAUGHTER ABOUT MEDIA CREATION

CHRISTA TERRY, COFOUNDER OF MOM MEET MOM (MOMMEETMOM.COM)

When it comes to books and other print media, we're lucky because I'm a writer. My four-year-old daughter, Paloma, knows I wrote a book and that most of my work involves writing, so by extension she has always known that everything we read was created by someone like me. That has led to us creating more than a few picture books and illustrated poems together—which I hope is helping her understand that you don't simply have to *consume* media.

To that end, my husband, Tedd, and I do whatever we can to encourage her creative endeavors, and we make sure she sees us being creative. Tedd is a music lover who composes his own pieces, and he and Paloma have recorded songs together. Thanks to his extensive knowledge of musicians, she knows who composed or performed the music she likes and can even identify some genres.

Paloma was three when she received her first camera—one of our old point-and-shoots—and since then she has taken hundreds of photographs of people, our home and neighborhood, toys, and nature. It's really amazing to watch her efforts to frame her chosen subject, direct the action when she's photographing or filming people, check the focus, and then review her shots.

It was only recently, though, that we realized we'd forgotten a very important piece of the puzzle: TV and movies. They were easy to overlook because she doesn't have a lot of that kind of screen time and we're pretty strict about controlling what she does see. She does, however, go to day care where our provider lets the kids watch an hour or so a day so she can get a sanity break, and because there are kids of different ages, Paloma occasionally sees movies and shows we might as a family deem too scary or mature.

I only realized our mistake when she came home after watching *Labyrinth*, and bedtime was becoming an ordeal because she was worrying the Goblin King was going to come for her. The usual questions—like "Is the Goblin King real?" and "Are movies real?"—weren't working to calm her down. That's when it dawned on me that we'd never really talked about actors.

"Do you know that movies are just a story and that someone writes the stories you see in movies just like stories in books?" I asked, and she nodded. "And did you know that all of the people in movies are actors? That means pretending to be characters is their job. Even if you see a monster in a movie, it's someone in a costume. In *Labyrinth*, the Goblin King is really an actor named David Bowie, and pretending to be the Goblin King was his work."

She sat up in bed, wide-eyed.

"You mean David Bowie whose songs I like?" When I said yes, she said: "Mama, that means David Bowie has *two jobs*! He's in movies and he makes music!"

I loved that reaction because she seemed pretty clear on a couple of points I think are important for kids to internalize to be able to watch thoughtfully. Namely, that TV and movies are pretend, that the people she sees in them are not their characters, and that being a part of them is work. We've also been able to talk about how people in print ads and TV commercials are also working, not just really enjoying products, and create our own shows, thanks to the aforementioned camera. My hope is that helping her appreciate these concepts at four years old will lay the groundwork for both a lifelong healthy skepticism where media is concerned and the understanding that media are products of people.

STEP 4 TIPS

Read books about media creation with your child. Age-appropriate books can help you and your child learn about the media production process. For example, for preschoolers, check out *How a Book Is Made* by Aliki, which is all about the publishing process. It shows how a book progresses from an author's idea to a published work. Also consider reading *The Bionic Bunny Show* by Marc Brown, which offers a behind-the-scenes look at a show-within-a-show featured on the program *Arthur*. It describes how an ordinary bunny seems to have superpowers on-screen, even though it's all make-believe. Both books are good prompts for discussing how media are created.

Children learn best by making things. Learning how to make their own books, videos, and storyboards will help children develop creative skills and problem-solving skills, as well.

Talk with your children about media creators' intentions.

As they gain experience creating their own media, children will understand that the creators of the mainstream media they enjoy made many decisions along the way. Help them reflect on why characters might be shown doing certain things, or why advertisements use certain language, and so on.

Make Pop Culture Coaching Work for You!

By following the four steps featured in this chapter, you can become an excellent pop culture coach for your children. As a parent whose values are clear, you can guide your children to consume media in healthy ways and empower them to think critically about what they encounter on-screen.

Now, let's apply pop culture coaching principles to princess culture. How can we help our daughters think critically about princess culture—about all the marketing, the beauty ideal, the gender stereotypes, and the racial stereotypes? That's what Part Two of this book is all about.

RECAP: POP CULTURE COACHING IN FOUR STEPS

1. Identify your family's values.
2. Establish a healthy media diet for your children.
3. Watch and talk about media content with your children.
4. Teach your children about media creation.

PART TWO

Guiding Our Girls: Pop Culture Coaching in Action

★ CHAPTER THREE
The Problem with Princess Marketing

★

"Oh, for the past four years, everything has been princesses. Every book, every movie, every backpack. All princesses, all the time."
"Sounds fun!"
"…It's a nightmare."

—*Parks and Recreation*

Princesses: what a marketing phenomenon! Every children's product category—whether toys, games, books, clothing, home decor, or even food—teems with sparkly pink princesses.

This unavoidable toy-industry trend began with *The Little Mermaid* in 1987, according to toy industry expert Jim Silver. "*The Little Mermaid* was a surprise hit for Disney," Silver explains, "and in terms of toys, the brand became a very popular line." Afterwards, the most successful Disney toys followed a similar pattern. They were from films like *Beauty and the Beast* and *Aladdin*, which had princesses in them—not *Hercules* or *The Hunchback of Notre Dame*.

"So," Silver explains, "from 1987 through about 1994, princess-related items were extremely popular with young girls," one movie at a time.

Then, about a decade ago, Disney executives had an incredible new marketing idea. "They thought, 'Hey! We have all these prin-cesses, but each one has such a small market share,'" recalls Silver, who is editor in chief of *Time to Play* magazine. "I mean, kids still watched *Aladdin*; they still watched Belle; they still watched *Cinderella*, and *Sleeping Beauty*; but each was so small by itself that they didn't have a large effect on the marketplace. So they created the Disney Princess collection. And when the Disney Princesses were put together, the whole was greater than the sum of its parts."

How much greater? Nearly twice as large. While Disney Princess films have earned more than $2.6 billion at the box office worldwide, the Disney Princess brand boasts more than $4 billion in global retail sales. In the United States, Disney Princess is actu-ally the number-one licensed toy brand among all girls, and it's also the number-one toy brand for dolls and role play among two- to five-year-old girls.

Naturally, when the Disney Princess brand took off, other brands wanted to cash in. Competitors from Barbie to Dora the Explorer vied for a slice of Disney's pie, as did brands like Candyland and Mega Bloks. Today, countless popular toys come in carefully planned princess form. Take the new version of the *My Little Pony* television cartoon. When the show was in development, Hasbro vetoed plans to make a queen the ruler of ponydom. The reason? Execs knew that pink *princess* pony toys would sell better than toys based on a *queen*. The show's creator, Lauren Faust (also known for her work on *The Powerpuff Girls* and *Foster's Home for Imaginary Friends*), was outranked. Her queen character was nixed, so she devised Princess Celestia to rule Equestria, instead.

Another recent offering is Barbie's *The Princess and the Popstar*. A line of dolls supported by a direct-to-video release, the Princess and the Popstar brand craftily grafts together two major interests of little girls: pop music and princesses. While Disney has always had its own princesses and pop stars (think of young Britney Spears and of *Hannah Montana*), Barbie is gambling on gaining some of Disney's market share by combining both in a single line. From a marketing standpoint, it's genius.

Here's the premise: Princess Tori is tired of her boring royal duties and wishes she could have the fun, exciting life of a pop star. Meanwhile, pop star Kiera is tired of her busy tour schedule and wishes she was a pampered princess. So when Tori and Kiera meet and realize how similar they are in appearance (well, yeah—they're both *Barbie dolls*), they channel *The Parent Trap* and *Hannah Montana* and secretly trade places, briefly living a double life. Hijinks ensue—and thus a new line of nearly one hundred heavily marketed pop star and princess products was born.

And because marketers want to extend the shelf life of princesses as long as possible, 2013 saw the introduction of two new princess toy lines—Ever After High and Fairy Tale High. Mattel launched Ever After High as a spin-off of its successful Monster High franchise, which is extremely popular among young girls. Ever After High imagines the children of famous fairy-tale characters (such as Snow White, Sleeping Beauty, the Mad Hatter, Cinderella, and Little Red Riding Hood) in a high school setting. The Ever After High dolls are dressed in a sort of modernized Victorian style, with princess-type gowns that are cut short.

Meanwhile, new contender S-K Victory's Fairy Tale High dolls imagine the fairy-tale characters themselves (Rapunzel, Alice, Belle, Little Mermaid, Sleeping Beauty, Cinderella, Snow White, and Tinker Bell) as contemporary high school students. They are provocatively dressed in skimpy modern attire, with ultrashort skirts and exposed midriffs.

Both lines are accompanied by other media—webisodes, books, and so on—but their raison d'être is clearly to sell more princess products. Each company is angling to reel in kindergarten girls who have been immersed in princess culture since birth, and who—thanks to successful, edgy lines like Monster High—may soon find Disney Princesses "babyish." And the girls are buying these princess products hook, line, and sinker.

Princess Marketing and GoldieBlox

To compete in the girls' princess-oriented marketplace, even brands that are not really about princesses find that they must create princess offerings. La Dee Da and Glimma Girlz dolls both include princesses in their fashion-doll lineups, making a grab for a portion of the Disney and Mattel dolls' market shares.

Meanwhile, toy brand Melissa and Doug, which has a great reputation for producing many high-quality, gender-neutral toys, has several princess offerings, too. These range from a Princess Paint with Water kit to a Jumbo Princess and Fairy Coloring Pad to several Princess Magnetic Dress-Up Wooden Doll and Stand items. They even make a Deluxe Wooden Folding Princess Castle—with lots of pink, of course—and gendered crayon sets: a truck crayon set for the boys, and a princess crayon set for the girls. (Parents have noticed the limitations of these sets, observing that the princess set contains "no primary colors. Even 'princesses' need green for coloring leaves or a proper brown!")

But perhaps the most interesting example of using princesses to compete is GoldieBlox, which in 2013 was a hot new toy for girls.

GoldieBlox is meant to inspire girls to become engineers. The toy's "hook" is that it combines construction toys with books to appeal to girls' interest in stories. The books feature stories about Goldie, a girl who loves engineering, which culminate in building instructions that teach girls how to use their GoldieBlox toys to create the same devices as Goldie does.

GoldieBlox was created by Debbie Sterling, a seasoned marketer with a strong engineering background. Sterling launched her brand with a successful crowd-funding campaign on Kickstarter.com, where she raised $285,881 with this inspiring pitch:

> My name is Debbie and I'm a Stanford engineer. When I was a little girl, I thought the word "engineering" was nerdy and intimidating and just for boys. I've since learned I was so wrong. Engineers build all the important things we use every day…things that make our lives better. The scary truth is that only 11 percent of engineers are women, and girls start losing interest in science as young as age eight! This is our chance to change that statistic.
>
> I'm creating GoldieBlox to inspire girls the way LEGOs and Erector sets have inspired boys, for over a hundred years, to develop an early interest and skill set in engineering. It's time to motivate our girls to help build our future.

The initial GoldieBlox offering was called "GoldieBlox and the Spinning Machine," in which Goldie builds a spinning machine to help her dog, Nacho, chase his tail. It was an immense success, selling out before Christmas 2013.

According to the GoldieBlox Kickstarter page, the second GoldieBlox set was to be called "GoldieBlox Goes to the Parade."

But when the set debuted in late 2013, the toy and story—now called "GoldieBlox and the Parade Float"—were not about your typical parade. Instead, it was about a *princess* parade. The toy's original promotional copy read as follows:

> In this much-anticipated sequel, Goldie's friends Ruby and Katinka compete in a princess pageant with the hopes of riding in the town parade. When Katinka loses the crown, Goldie and Ruby team up to build her a parade float as well as other fun rolling, spinning, and whirling designs.

Here is the basic plot of the book that comes with the set: Ruby (who happens to be an African American girl—a definite plus in terms of representation) has been preparing for "the biggest event of the school year"—the "Miss Princess Pageant." Goldie assures her she's going to win, but their friend Katinka, a pink dolphin, exhibits mean girl behavior and is determined to win the crown. (She butts into the competition, saying rudely, "Step aside, girls. You're making me yawn. Judges watch *me* as I twirl my baton.")

When Ruby wins the Princess Pageant, Katinka bursts into tears. The girls are kind and want to make her feel better, despite her mean behavior. So, what do they do? As a reader, I was hoping they'd engage in some other activity together and assure her that princesses and pageantry aren't very important. But that's not what happens. Instead, Ruby and Goldie build a float that Katinka can ride on, too. It ends with the whole town cheering "for Katinka and Ruby, the Miss Princess Engineer."

Perplexingly, the GoldieBlox ad that was created to promote the brand at the time of the Parade Float toys release came across as being strongly antiprincess. With a song parodying the Beastie Boys' song "Girls" (which, as an aside, got GoldieBlox into hot water with the band—they did not consent to their song's use, and therefore the ad can no longer be found online), the advertisement argued against the idea that girls get pink princess stuff while boys get *everything else*. The fierce little girls in the ad sang about wanting a change. They said they can use their brains and engineer, because they are more than just princesses.

Upon the ad's release, it went viral, gaining 3.5 million views on YouTube in only three days alone. So when I learned that the ad was marketing the Princess Float toy (which was only featured in the ad itself for a few seconds), I was shocked. I had no idea that such an antiprincess-sounding ad was shilling a princess-themed toy! Many of my colleagues from the Brave Girls Alliance felt the same way and wrote about it on their blogs.

The way we saw it, GoldieBlox was trying to have it both ways. On the one hand, the brand was claiming to be antiprincess, depicting girls who declared they were *not* princesses and who wanted to learn interesting new things, and offering the GoldieBlox toy as a solution to parents who were experiencing princess fatigue. On the other hand, GoldieBlox was nevertheless offering girls a "princess parade" toy to play with.

Why did this happen?

As I explained in interviews on CBC Radio's *The Current* and in the *National Journal*, as well as in an article I published in the *Christian Science Monitor* online, independent brands like GoldieBlox walk an awfully fine line in the marketplace. When they try to provide girls with something different, something STEM-oriented to foster an interest in science, technology, engineering, or math, they wind up swimming in a sea of princess products. They are competing with everything from the girly-girl LEGO Friends line (which also drew heavy criticism upon its release) to Barbies and Disney Princesses. So, to get picked up by major retailers and better appeal to girls shopping in toy stores, GoldieBlox apparently has to take a product meant to be nonconformist—as indicated by the ad campaign—and conform to the dominance of princess culture.

If that doesn't prove that "princess" is the dominant marketing force in girl culture, I don't know what does.

BREAKING INTO THE TOY INDUSTRY

It's difficult for independent brands to break into the toy industry, says Kaye Toal, GoldieBlox's community manager. "In most cases," she argues, "independent toymakers with good ideas are bought by major toy companies and flattened into the stereotyped nonsense that populates the pink aisle today."

In an effort to make sure girls have as many choices as possible, Toal says that Sterling and the rest of the GoldieBlox team are committed to staying independent. And so they are offering a princess-themed toy to girls, despite the prevalence of the stereotype. "We don't have a problem with princesses being *one of many* options," Toal explains. "There are many, many girls who love princesses and ballet and pink, just as there are many, many girls who would rather roll in mud. And there are girls that love both.

"We're not interested in putting them in boxes," Toal adds. "We're interested in giving them choices that encourage their innate creativity and inventiveness, and characters that they can love and look up to."

For this reason, none of GoldieBlox's forthcoming toys involve princesses, Toal says. Instead, the new kits will appeal to girls who like carnivals, tree houses, lighting things up, flying, climbing, and other diverse interests. But perhaps the princess-themed Parade Float toy will act as a "hook" for girls who might otherwise not be interested in a building toy.

Disney Princesses in the Marketplace

Although toy aisles are full of princesses, when we think of popular princess characters, Disney Princesses usually come to mind first. They really are *everywhere*. Their faces don't just adorn children's toys; Disney Princesses sell everything from grapes (sold in clear plastic bags festooned with the princesses' faces) to prom gowns. Retail stores like Walmart and Target—and the average grocery store, too—contain dizzying numbers of Disney Princess products. "You can't really go into any store without being assaulted by all the princess stuff," laments Cindy, mother to three-year-old princess-obsessed Ava.

My friend Shayla Thiel-Stern, a professor at University of Minnesota, is mom to two-and-a-half-year-old Adelaide—a role that's made her all too aware of the endless princess product push. One day, as Shayla pushed Adelaide in the grocery cart, Addie reverently gasped, "Look, Mama! That's for *girls*!" Shayla looked to see what had enthralled Addie so much and saw…a can of SpaghettiOs, placed carefully at the eye level of a child being pushed in a grocery cart. Addie could tell these special SpaghettiOs were for girls, and therefore she wanted some—very, very much.

"We have never bought SpaghettiOs or canned pasta before," Shayla recalls, "so she didn't know what they were or that it might be something that she'd like to eat. She just recognized the princesses."

Even more remarkable was that Adelaide had never been allowed to watch any Disney Princess films and didn't own any Disney Princess items! "She would not have had much of a clue about who Belle or Cinderella were," Shayla recalls. "I'd intentionally kept them out of her life. It's so amazing that she felt the product was 'for girls'—in really kind of an aspirational way."

Later that summer, walking through the mall, Addie was captivated by a Snow White display at the Disney Store. Shayla snapped a picture of her entranced daughter and sent it to me with this note: "We walked by and she gasped, 'Mama! It's a *girls'* store!'" Shayla added, "It's insane how good they are at marketing to her age group."

Want to know of an even more surprising Disney Princess product than SpaghettiOs? House paints—Disney Princess interior paints by Behr, to be exact. The line is dominated by shades of pink, purple, and pale blue, with saccharine names like "Pretty in Pink," "Fairest of Them All," "Snow White Song," "Kissed Awake," and "Blushing Belle." Their brochure depicts a princess-themed bathroom (giving a whole new meaning to "the princess and the pea") and a lavish Sleeping Beauty bedroom. Disney Princess paints, pieces from the Disney Princess Furniture Collection, Disney Princess bedding, and many other Disney Princess products adorn the bedroom in the brochure. Make no mistake: the room is 100 percent princess.

Why *paints*? What's going on here?

Lifestyle Branding

In class, my undergraduates and I screen the Media Education Foundation documentary *No Logo*, based on Naomi Klein's book by the same name. In the video, Klein explains why consumers and critics wind up protesting certain brands: the insidiousness of brand marketing. Brands no longer seek popularity. Instead, Klein says, they "want to be everywhere and be everything." In so doing, a brand becomes a *megabrand*.

Because of this outlook, Klein says megabrands (and megabrand wannabes) regularly ask questions like, "If it's a line of clothing, can it be a house paint?"

The answer, of course, is yes. Megabrand Ralph Lauren makes clothes…and home goods…and, yes, house paints. Even though Ralph Lauren paint looks just like other paints that cost much less, the Ralph Lauren brand has prestige, making it appealing to brand-conscious consumers.

In this way, megabrands—by being everywhere and everything—become something bigger. They transform into *lifestyle brands*.

Lifestyle brands permeate every aspect of a consumer's lifestyle, intertwining the brand identity with the consumer's personal identity. Virgin is the quintessential lifestyle brand. Its subsidiaries include everything from music to travel to wine. A consumer with a strong preference for a megabrand's products and services may think, "This is my brand," or "This brand is part of me."

Disney Princess as Lifestyle Brand

Like Disney as a whole, Disney Princess has been following the megabrand playbook for years. The result is that, in the past decade, Disney Princess has become a lifestyle brand, completely intertwined with little girls' identities. Disney Princess isn't just about the movies and the toys. It's about food, clothing, home goods. As I've said, a Disney Princess product exists for just about every aspect of life.

Although Disney Princess is primarily for girls ages two to eight, with its strongest devotees ages two to five, they are not its only target. With "cradle-to-grave" marketing, Disney marketers extend engagement with the brand well beyond these years. The goal is for children to grow into loyal, lifelong customers.

This has played out very well for Disney: when children too young to ask for Disney products are swathed in them from birth, it's often because of their parents' understandable nostalgia and fondness for Disney. Parents who loved Disney when they were children are likely to be tempted by Disney-branded diapers, onesies, teething rings, bassinets, car seats, strollers, mobiles, crib bedding, pacifiers, sippy cups, and baby toys.

Then, as children begin developing brand preferences, nostalgic parents who enjoy the fun, wholesome aspects of Disney are happy to fulfill their children's requests, buying them Disney videos, toys, books, apparel, video games, apps, and room furniture and decor. I saw so many examples of this during my stint as a birthday party princess. Excited kids would give me tours of their playrooms, showing off their cherished dolls, dresses, costume jewelry, and other toys. "Look, look!" they would shout, placing assorted trinkets in front of my nose. From what I could see, the Disney Princess products were *way* too many to count.

But for a lifestyle brand like Disney Princess, purchases on behalf of children are not enough. It's even better for business if adults want to buy Princess products for *themselves*. So, the cradle-to-grave strategy culminates in high-end goods for adult women, including Disney Princess–inspired shoes by Christian Louboutin, Marc Jacobs, and—for those of us who aren't full-fledged fashionistas—mainstream retailer DSW.

There are also Disney Princess running shoes from New Balance (the better to run Walt Disney World's annual Disney Princess Half-Marathon in, I suppose) and Disney Princess lingerie from Belle Maison, a popular retailer in Japan whose princess-themed designs went viral on social media. Better still are high-end goods targeted to moments in life when people make expensive purchases, such as weddings. That's why we see Disney Princess-inspired prom gowns and wedding dresses by designers such as Vera Wang and Alfred Angelo; Disney Princess-inspired wedding rings; and even big-bucks "Fairy-Tale Weddings" in Disney's Magic Kingdom.

So, if Disney wants its princesses to be everything, everywhere, then *of course* your home's walls are in its sights. The paint line is just the tip of the giant pink iceberg. As a special bonus, the Disney Princess paint catalog cross-promotes other products, like Disney Princess bedding and the furniture collection—a nice example of what marketers call "synergy":

When synergy happens, one plus one no longer equals two. It can equal three, four, five, or more. Synergy in marketing is when two marketing initiatives create a response greater than the sum of the combined response the two would have elicited alone.

If this language sounds familiar, it's because it echoes Silver's words—that "when the Disney Princesses were put together, the whole was greater than the sum of its parts." That's synergy, which is basically the Holy Grail of integrated marketing campaigns. Disney Princess is absolutely synergistic: as a collective, it's worth much more than the sum of its parts.

Why It Works: Princesses and Developmental Psychology

In my conversations about the Disney Princess phenomenon with parents, journalists, and so on, I am asked one question over and over: *But* why *is Princess marketing so effective?*

The answer is simple but infuriating: it exploits a developmental stage of childhood.

Most children begin paying close attention to gender in preschool. By this point, they have seen that gender is a major organizing category in our society—that we separate "girls" and "boys," "women" and "men," and tend to characterize them as opposites. But preschoolers are so little, so innocent, that they're unsure what makes boys boys and girls girls.

It's only at about the age of seven that children understand that sex is both biological and stable over time. At that point, they finally realize that people remain male or female despite superficial changes in clothing, accessories, hairstyles, and so on.

Until then, kids search the culture around them for clues about what determines who is a boy and who is a girl. And they see stereotypes. That girls have long hair and boys have short hair. That girls like dolls and boys like trucks. That girls like Disney Princesses and boys like vehicles, superheroes, and Star Wars. That girls wear pink, and boys wear blue.

By pre-K and kindergarten, most children have come to think of stereotypes as hard-and-fast rules that they must follow. Roughly two-thirds of girls ages three to four, and roughly half of boys ages five to six, develop what researchers call "appearance rigidity." They become completely obsessed with wearing stereotypical clothing— which for girls often equals pink, frilly dresses. This is so common, in fact, that researchers use the acronym "PFD" to describe this syndrome. During this developmental stage, boys and girls will typically play only with children of their own sex and reject anything associated with the opposite sex. It's really important to them.

How important is it? So important that, according to the kids' inner logic, they could *change sexes* if they don't follow the "rules" they've picked up on. This idea scares boys and girls alike, because most kids have really positive feelings about their own sex. As a general rule, boys really like being boys, and girls really like being girls. So when young kids treat gender stereotypes as religion, they are joyously telling the world: "This is who I am!"

Girls and boys announce their genders in very different ways, though. Girls embrace all things girlish, as epitomized by the PFD— while boys *reject* all things girlish, avoiding femininity like a deadly disease. And this learned rejection can last for years: When I was at the Magic Kingdom, I overheard a couple of college-aged men laughing at a dad a few feet ahead of us who was carrying his little girl's pink princess backpack. "Oh, man, I'm glad I'm not *that* guy," one of them chortled.

One consequence of this is that boys are now avoiding movies like *Cinderella* and *Snow White*, which were originally marketed as family films, because they are now being marketed as *princess* properties, which means they are *for girls*. Therefore, Disney has had to market its most recent films—*Tangled*, *Brave*, and *Frozen*—in ways that downplay their "princessy" natures. No more girls' names like *Cinderella* and *Sleeping Beauty* in Disney's movie titles. In the Princess brand era, such names cut out too much of the boy audience at the box office.

Overall, these facts about child development explain a lot about Disney's marketing success. In aggressively marketing stereotypically feminine princesses in big, frilly dresses to preschool girls, Disney is hitting a sweet spot. The brand captures girls' attention just as they are using stereotypes to figure out who they are. It's really genius.

Disney has been so successful in this that they've been desperately trying to bottle the same magic for boys. Sure, since acquiring Pixar, *Cars* and *Toy Story* have been lucrative with boy audiences, but those characters are not aspirational like princesses. Boys don't pretend to *be* Lightning McQueen and dream of growing up to be a vehicle. They can't embody these characters the way girls embody princesses.

So Disney tried to build a boy brand on the success of *Pirates of the Caribbean* and *Jake and the Neverland Pirates*. The idea was to make "pirate" the boy version of "princess." Disney's marketing made this clear. For example, a clever billboard in Orlando made the two categories equivalent, stating: "Pirate takeovers. Princess makeovers. Shop World of Disney."

But pirate hasn't caught on in the same way that princess did— at least, not yet. So Disney simply bought up the properties that already boasted devoted boy followings: first Marvel—home of superheroes like Spider-Man, Iron Man, and the Incredible Hulk— and then Star Wars.

That's the logic of capitalism today: if you can't beat 'em, buy 'em.

The Downside to Gender Segmentation

But there's a real downside to all of these marketing schemes that bifurcate children into two completely separate audiences. By treating boys and girls as inherently different from one another, gender segmentation leads to gender *segregation*. Children have always separated themselves into segregated play groups by kindergarten or first grade, but the successful preschool marketing techniques of companies like

Disney are causing gender segregation to happen at increasingly early ages, and with higher levels of rigidity.

Carol Spencer, director of the Hoosier Courts Nursery School at the University of Bloomington, has been working with preschool children since 1978, and she attests to the changes that have resulted from recent marketing strategies. "Marketing has taken a very natural stage of children's gender development and encouraged it to happen earlier and last longer," she explains. "By marketing these stereotypical roles to kids in this age group, they're making this phase even more rigid than it used to be."

According to psychologist and educational consultant Lori Day, author of *Her Next Chapter: How Mother-Daughter Book Clubs Can Help Girls Navigate Malicious Media, Risky Relationships, Girl Gossip, and So Much More*, this stronger and longer gender division is troublesome. It robs boys and girls of a shared childhood that can serve as a foundation for future healthy relationships.

"Now even the littlest girls are playing princesses on one side of the classroom while the boys are playing Spider-Man on the other," Day observes. "This means that when kids eventually have romantic relationships with each other in adolescence, they will have spent less time being friends and playing with each other in nonromantic ways. Having friendships with the opposite sex in childhood makes us better romantic partners later on—better able to understand and relate to one another."

Meanwhile, new research has found that in elementary school, children don't necessarily avoid playing with the opposite sex—but they largely believe that it's not normal to do so. They insist that boys only play with boys, and girls only play with girls. Jennifer Watling Neal, PhD, from Michigan State University explains: "While gender does matter a great deal in the formation of children's friendships, children think it is nearly the only relevant factor."

Holding such an inaccurate belief to be true can have negative consequences later in life beyond the personal sphere. It can impact workplace success, as well. "In adulthood," Neal explains, "we know that people who have accurate perceptions of workplace relationships tend to be perceived as more powerful and have better reputations than their colleagues." In this way, the belief that boys and girls inhabit separate spheres—which is so pervasive and promoted with such vigor by marketers—does a disservice to our children.

A related downside of gender segmentation is that in everyday life, kids who don't conform to gender stereotypes wind up excluded by their peers. As I mentioned earlier, about two-thirds of three- to four-year-old girls go through an appearance-rigid phase. This means that one-third of girls do *not*. What about them?

"Girls need more choices in the marketplace," suggests Jo Paoletti, author of *Pink and Blue: Telling the Boys from the Girls in America*. "Two-thirds of girls are going to pick a princess. But one-third are not. And they need options that aren't marketed as 'boys' toys,' but as either being *for girls* or *for girls and boys*."

The same goes for clothing, Paoletti adds. "Now, once you get out of the newborn sizes, choices that are neutral in any way are hard to find," she explains. "The choice is 'girly' or 'for boys.' Although stores previously offered gender-neutral and unisex clothing choices, today's children cannot choose from a complete range of possible ways of presenting themselves. They're choosing between *looking like a princess* and *looking like a boy*."

Melissa Wardy, author of *Redefining Girly: How Parents Can Fight the Stereotyping and Sexualizing of Girlhood, from Birth to Tween* and mother to Amelia, seven, and Benny, five, couldn't agree more. "I went into parenthood *not* hating princesses and *not* hating pink," she explains, "until I realized that those are the only choices given to my daughter. But she is more interested in watching a volcano explode or a shark attack or dinosaurs.

"When she was three, when most girls are completely enraptured with princesses, she carried around this rubber Tyrannosaurus rex. She made people call her 'Amelia Dinosaur,' or she would not answer them." In other words, Amelia wasn't a girly girl; she was her own person. But Wardy didn't see a place for a girl like Amelia in children's media culture, and that was infuriating.

Michele Yulo had a similar experience with her daughter, Gaby. When Gaby was young, Yulo realized that she refused to use girly things, and she wouldn't wear dresses at all. She preferred boyish clothes and characters, and as a result, she even wore boy underwear for a while. "She liked Spider-Man," Yulo recalls, "but they don't make Spider-Man underwear for girls."

Yulo felt bad. "As a parent, I wanted my girl to feel like a girl. I would say, 'Gaby, there's nothing wrong with being a girl. It's okay to wear dresses sometimes. There's nothing wrong with that.'"

But soon, Yulo began noticing that quite a few other girls were just like Gaby. "We met other girls who also preferred boy stuff," Yulo says. "Then I read a study that Harvard put out that says that one out of every ten kids is gender nonconforming."

Frustrated at the lack of clothing and toys for girls that weren't pink and princessy, and noticing more and more girls in the world who reminded her of Gaby, Yulo became convinced that there was a market for other types of products for girls. So she launched a website and blog called Princess Free Zone to advocate for more choices for girls, where she also sells T-shirts that break out of the princess trope. She also wrote *Super Tool Lula*, a children's book about a little girl who likes to build things—just like Gaby.

Wardy took similar action. Finding the culture lacking, she took matters into her own hands and launched the website and blog Pigtail Pals, where she sells clothing for girls that comes in a full rainbow of colors. "There are lots of ways to be a girl." Then, as her son, Benny, grew older, and she saw that boys' options are almost as limiting as girls, she expanded her business. Now, she offer products for both boys and girls, and has changed the business name to "Pigtail Pals and Ballcap Buddies" to reflect this. Her Facebook page boasts a dynamic, engaged community of 15,000 people—evidence that she's really hit a nerve.

SPOTLIGHT ON APPEARANCE RIGIDITY

Four-year-old Hailee loved bold colors, especially orange. She wore her hair short and gravitated away from pink princess sparkles. She loved to play with toy animals and to draw. When she began preschool, she was friendly with all of her classmates, but her best friends were the boys. She came home from school talking with delight about her new friends Nicholas, Jacob, Michael, and Christopher.

Then, one day, as her best friend Nicholas chatted with his mom about Hailee, he referred to her as a "he." His mom loved Hailee and thought this was a funny mistake. She gently corrected him: "Nicholas, Hailee is a girl."

Nicholas wasn't convinced, so Hailee's mom, Colette, cheerfully confirmed this for Nicholas at school the next day: "Oh, no, no, she's a girl! Hailee is a girl!"

But Colette might not have been so cheerful if she had known what would happen next. Hailee's friends abandoned her, refusing to play with her because she was a girl. "From that moment on," Colette recalls, "the boys would not have anything to do with Hailee. It really hurt her feelings."

Hailee just couldn't understand it. Why had her best friends rejected her in that way?

Prior to that, a classmate had told Hailee that as a girl, she should forget about orange, because girls like pink best. After all, the pretty, pink princess palette dominated her female peers' toys, dolls, games, art, and attire. It was everywhere.

At first, Hailee—who enjoyed choosing comfortable T-shirts and sweatpants from the boys' clothing department—was defiant. "I like all the colors!" she insisted.

But when the boys stopped being her friends, Hailee got the message. "I kind of realized that all the girls liked pink," Hailee would later recall, "and that I was the only girl who had other preferences in colors. So I tried to be like them."

Hailee made a switch. She left behind her identity as a girl who liked all the colors and became a girl obsessed with pink.

"It was a complete reversal," Colette confirms. "Hailee got into a pink phase, big time. She insisted, 'I'm going to only wear dresses.' She understood that she could no longer be ambiguous about what gender she was. It was clearly a conscious decision of, 'Okay, well, I'm not a boy; I'm a girl. And I have to really make sure that I announce that loud and clear.'"

"It was a shock," Colette adds.

But children's culture is so stereotypical and so divisive that it's no surprise the boys excluded Hailee for being a girl. Nor is it surprising that she coped with this rejection by embracing pink with a passion so that she would fit in with the other girls at her school. Young children learn from our culture that boys and girls are supposed to be polar opposites, and they take this lesson to heart. While boys are built up as powerful, active heroes, girls are diminished as powerless and passive—and with such clear demarcations, there is little room for overlap between their worlds.

It's fairly clear that when the boys expelled Hailee from their social circle, they were going through a period of appearance rigidity. They were rejecting anything associated with girls—including Hailee—to protect their identification with masculinity.

Colette's recollections support this interpretation. "I remember having a conversation with one of the boys' mothers, who had bought a package of drinking straws in all different colors," she recalls. "She told me, 'My son won't even drink from pink straws, because he says they're for girls!'" At that point, because pink is the ultimate marker of girl culture today, pink avoidance had become an established pattern. "He was just refusing anything that was pink."

Colette says that eventually, the boys' moms were "pulling their hair out" over how obsessed the boys were with gender.

The moms wanted their sons to be open-minded.

They wanted their sons to keep playing with Hailee.

But the boys wouldn't budge. They were set on rigidly avoiding girls and "girly" things, and there was no changing their minds.

Hailee's pink phase lasted about a year. "For a while, I tried to be like the other kids," she recalled, "but after a while, that just wasn't really me." Fortunately, the end of her pink phase coincided with her peers' appearance-rigidity stage lessening.

Asked if any of the other kids gave her trouble when she went back to loving orange, she replied, "Oh, I was fine! And I was happy," she said, beaming.

Her family was thrilled, too—happy to welcome "Orange Hailee" back into their lives.

Parenting Young Consumers: Resisting Princess Lifestyle Branding

What do princesses everywhere mean for parents? Well, imagine this scenario:

Four-year-old princess-obsessed Madison wants to eat, sleep, and breathe nothing but Disney Princess products, and it's becoming a point of contention in her household. Her parents are tired of all the little battles over what she will wear, watch, and play with.

Madison's mom blames herself for this situation. She loved princesses when she was a little girl, so she's been buying princess products for Madison since her daughter was an infant. She thinks sadly, "I can't believe I did this to my daughter."

But summer is coming, and Madison's parents look forward to spending time outdoors. They think involving their daughter in a little gardening might encourage her to branch out a bit—develop new interests.

It's time to start planting, so they plan a visit to their local garden shop. Building up Madison's enthusiasm, they tell her, "You can choose any seeds you want to plant! We'll help you take care of them and you can see how they grow." She is excited. "Maybe I'll plant some carrots," she says.

But then, imagine that Madison comes across an appealing display of Disney Princess seed packets—a product line that really exists. Gardening-supply brand Burpee has licensed the names and likenesses of Belle, Sleeping Beauty, Jasmine, and Cinderella to adorn their flowers' seed packets, capitalizing on the princesses' popularity.

Upon seeing the display, Madison wants princess flowers and nothing else. Her discouraged parents remind her that she wanted carrots, but Madison insists. "I want a princess garden, Mommy! Daddy, don't say no."

Looking around the corner, her parents see that Burpee does offer Disney-branded vegetables—but they're not princess-themed. The logic must be that princesses are meant to be gazed upon. They are delicate beauties, so they only adorn the packages of flowers, which share these qualities. The veggie seed packs go to Mickey and friends.

Madison's parents never dreamed Disney would co-opt their gardening experience, and they *did* tell her she could choose any packets she wants...so despite her parents' reluctance, the princess flowers win.

For the "privilege" of purchasing seed packages adorned with Disney characters, her parents will spend $1.99 for each, instead of the $1.00 to $1.19 Burpee charges for otherwise identical seed packages with no licensed characters on them—making the outing twice as expensive as it should have been.

Oh, and don't forget the princess-themed plant labels, which cost $2.97 for a package of six—*way* more than the plain ones, which cost $1.99 for a package of twenty. Yikes.

Now, I don't mean to knock Burpee for licensing Disney characters on their products. Gardening isn't necessarily exciting for modern kids. Though some love it, it's a slow-moving hobby compared with other pastimes. Maybe Disney-branded seeds are a great way get kids involved in a healthy, satisfying activity that requires more patience and work than they're used to.

No, my point is this: the Disney Princess marketing machine is *so* huge, so far reaching, that it's hard to avoid and even harder to resist. Parents sometimes blame themselves for their daughters' princess obsessions, but who's really to blame—the parents, or the multibillion-dollar industry that profits by both shaping little girls' dreams and exploiting their developmental stage—their nascent understanding of what it means to be a girl?

The answer is clear. In this kind of context, it's hard to choose freely—and that's something for families to think critically about.

How to...
Help Kids Think Critically about Marketing

No matter who made it, every princess product has one thing in common: the *nag factor*, or the likelihood that kids will beg and whine and wear their parents down until they fold and make the purchase. Marketers have studied how to best encourage children to beg and plead. Unfortunately, when we give in to our children's nagging, we are rewarding their behavior—so the nag factor only intensifies as kids get older.

As our kids' pop culture coaches, we can fight back by teaching our children that marketers are manipulating them, and that when they do so, they are contradicting our family's values. No one likes to be used—not even little kids. Children have a strong sense of fairness, and if they feel that something is unfair, they will try to resist it. So, as parents, we can coach our children to resist marketers' schemes.

PREP WORK: TEACH YOUR CHILDREN SOME
SIMPLE DEFINITIONS

Talk about commercials, advertisements, and marketing with your little ones. Provide definitions: "Commercials try to sell us things we don't need." "Commercials try to trick us into buying things." (One of my proudest pop culture coaching moments was the day my preschooler called out in annoyance, "Momm-myyyy! The commercials are trying to sell me things I *don't need!*")

Sharon (mom to June, 7), Massachusetts:

> "I have explained marketing to June," Sharon says. "Once, she wanted a Cinderella ball at the store. It cost more than the same ball that was a plain color. I explained that the plain ball worked just as well, but that people put the Cinderella on the ball just to make people buy it. Once she understood that they are trying to trick her into spending more money, it was easier for her to take 'no' for an answer."

Explain "impulse purchases" to your child, as well. Tell her: "Stores put tempting things near the cash register to trick us into buying them. They call that an 'impulse buy,' and those are really tricky."

Amy (mom to Harry, 12, Kurt, 10, and Sophia, 6), Utah:

> "Sophia understands what advertising is and what marketing is," Amy says. "We have conversations every time we step into Target or a similar store with huge displays, where she's likely to say, 'Gosh, I really want all those princess balloons.'

"So, we talk about that before going into the store. I'll explain, 'That's so smart that they put those products by the cash register, because then everybody wants to buy a princess balloon on their way out.'

"Now, those things were not possible to talk about with her when she was two and a half, but at age six, she knows what an impulse buy is. She still has a lot of questions, though, so we have kind of an expanding dialogue about the role of advertising and marketing in people's lives."

Once this vocabulary is in place, you will be in a good position to help your children see through marketers' practices and resist the overwhelming princess marketing they encounter.

Pop Culture Coaching, Step 1: Identify and Communicate Your Family's Values

Stores sell a wide range of princess products. Some of these will suit your family's values, while others will not. After reviewing this book's chapters on body image, gender stereotypes, and race stereotypes, you may find that you object to certain princesses or certain categories of princess toys. It's great if you can make this a conscious decision—one that is rooted in your family's values.

TIP 1: DECIDE WHICH PRINCESS PRODUCTS ARE OKAY FOR YOUR CHILDREN

What kinds of princess toys, videos, and books do you want in the house? Are there certain types you like, and others that you think undercut what you want your children to learn? Spend some time in the toy aisle alone, or browsing princess products for children your daughter's age online, and think about where you would like to draw the line.

For example, some parents draw the line at Barbie-type princess dolls. There are princess dolls with all kinds of shapes, such as plush dolls and toddler dolls, as well as figurines in Polly Pocket style, so some moms, like Amy from Utah, direct their children toward other types of princess dolls.

Amy (mom to Harry, 12, Kurt, 10, and Sophia, 6), Utah:

Amy's daughter, Sophia, loves Disney Princesses. She has Disney Princess movies, coloring books, storybooks, and stickers—but she does not have any of the Barbie-style dolls. That's where her mom, Amy, draws the line. The reason? Amy explains: "I don't approve of Barbie dolls because they send such a negative message about body image. And just like Barbie dolls, the Disney Princess dolls have super long legs and large breasts."

She explains her objections to Sophia in a straightforward way. "I tell her, 'Their bodies just aren't normally shaped.' Now Sophia knows why I don't like Barbie-type dolls, and that if she asks for one, I'm going to say no. She doesn't throw a tantrum. She expects me to say no, and she understands my reasons."

You can also think through your take on licensed products, or products with trademarked characters or logos on them. Some people object to these because they are basically advertisements for the brand. Which licensed products fit your family's values, if any, and which do not?

- Are Disney Princess T-shirts okay?
- What about bedding?
- Wall art?
- Underwear and socks?
- Kitchen items?
- …Paint?

Alesandra (mom to Marisol, 6, and Gabriela, 3), New York:

"The Disney Princess brand is in your face constantly," says Alesandra, "so it's important to find some alternative—striking some kind of balance with all the princess products."

Although Marisol and Gabriela enjoy princess toys and videos, Alesandra and her husband, Mark, made a conscious choice to avoid letting other princess purchases consume their family. "For example, my husband and I decided that we would not buy princess cups or princess plates at all," Alesandra says. "That stuff is everywhere, and it's an easy thing to give in to—to think, 'Oh, it's just a plate. It's not a big deal.'

"But we felt that if we could limit the impact of the marketing in our house in terms of decorations—whether it be pillows or toothbrushes with characters on it—the girls wouldn't see it constantly, so they wouldn't grow to expect it. Every now and then, they'll be like, 'Oh, can I have this princess thing?'

"A quick 'No' is always our answer, and they're used to that. They never really put up a fight about it. So we consciously limit companies' ability to do marketing in our house through everyday household products—and I think we'll get through the princess-dominated years."

TIP 2: OFFER REWARDS AND TEACH DELAYED GRATIFICATION

When shopping, reward your children for behavior that you value—for being polite and reasonable. Come up with a reward system that positively reinforces the behaviors you've been coaching them on.

- If whining during shopping trips has been an ongoing problem, and you would be willing to buy a toy as a reward for good behavior, set some parameters. Be specific about what and why. "If you are good at the store, I will buy you one princess toy. Do you know what being good means? It means no begging for toys and listening to me and staying with me—no running away. If you are good, I will let you choose one toy when we are all done."

Also, help your children practice delayed gratification. Respond to their (nonwhiny) requests with a conversation about how and when they might receive a coveted princess item. For example, you can suggest that the child...

- Save up money to earn the item.
- Complete household chores to earn the item.
- Add the item to his or her birthday wish list.
- Add the item to a holiday wish list.

Pop Culture Coaching, Step 2: Establish a Healthy Media Diet

As your child's pop culture coach, you want to ensure that your child has a balanced media diet, with limitations placed on how much screen time they have and with attention given to the content they consume. So, think about princess products as a type of *media*. You can make sure your daughter neither spends too much time with princess toys nor fixates on princess products to the exclusion of other interesting options. After all, diverse interests are healthy.

TIP 3: SET PARAMETERS FOR PRINCESS BUYS

Use your values to coach your children as they interact with pop culture products, devising value-based guidelines. You can be formal or informal about this. Are the guidelines general and committed to memory, or will you turn them into written house rules? Do what feels right for your family and your parenting style.

Whatever your approach, the key is to talk about your values regularly with your children. Most children will embrace (or at least respect) rules that they know come from values shared by the entire family.

- *Share your rationales with your kids.* For example, you might say, "We don't buy clothes with princesses and other cartoon characters on them, because we don't want to be walking advertisements."

Kelly (mom to Susie, 4, and Bobby, 3), Massachusetts:

Kelly doesn't hesitate in explaining to her children that princesses don't fit with her values. "I tell them, 'Mommy doesn't like princesses,' and I won't buy them anything princess. The older one gets it—she's always asking me to explain why I don't like the princesses' 'messages.' I tell her my honest opinions—but I also add, 'That doesn't mean that you have to agree with me.'" In this way, while Kelly communicates her values, she also communicates respect for her daughter as an individual with her own opinions.

- *Talk with family and friends about your preferences.* Let them know which kinds of princess gifts, if any, your daughter would enjoy. Keep a list of good suggestions (including plenty of nonprincess options) handy as holidays and birthdays approach—building toys, craft items, toy vehicles, stuffed animals, board games, puppets, realistic animal figurines by companies like Schleich, and so on. Don't be afraid to direct friends and family members to other purchases. Most of them want to buy children items they will enjoy, and often, "princess" is a default—an easy gift to give a girl when you're not sure what else to get.

Ann (mom to Lise, 6, and Rosalie, 3), Massachusetts:

"We are a princess-free household, but we have received princess gifts in the past," Ann recalls. "Lise was maybe two or three when we talked with the grandparents about our dislike for them. We pepper our conversations with friends and family about the things that the girls really like and enjoy using, and we make sure that photos get sent of them with their favorite nonjunk toys.

"The positive reinforcement has seemed to work! I think grandparents want their gifts to be loved. Princess seems to be an easy guess, but if they have other options that they know will go over well, it helps them choose wisely."

- *How will you handle unwanted princess gifts?* Will you keep them, allowing gifts as the exception to the rule? Will you exchange them? Hide them in the closet? Regift them to families that would appreciate them?

Delmar (dad to Kaneasha, 3), New York:

Delmar and his wife, Janice, have let their immediate family know that they try to keep princess items to a minimum. They also circulate suggested gift lists before the holidays. If a gift they receive is really contrary to their values and guidelines, they have let their families know that they will return the gift.

"For example," Delmar recalls, "when Kaneasha needed a toy bench, my wife found what she figured we wanted, and she posted it on a gift list. Then my mom went and found a toy bench for Kaneasha—but it was a purple and green princess toy bench."

Delmar sighs. "I thought I had been clear, but I guess not. I was like, 'No.' Like, we had to send that back. I like to think that my mom and I have the kind of relationship where if I have a case to make, I'm going to lay my case. I don't tiptoe around my mother with stuff like that."

TIP 4: AVOID WATCHING MORE COMMERCIALS THAN NECESSARY

Can you watch favorite shows on the Internet or through Netflix or Amazon Prime, rather than on television? If so, you and your children will see fewer ads, which could lead to fewer impulsive requests for the latest princess products, as well as other junk foods and junk toys.

TIP 5: STRIKE A BALANCE BETWEEN PRINCESS PRODUCTS AND OTHER ITEMS

Give your girls much, much more than princess toys. Even if all they ask for are princess-themed items, offer alternative toy options that can be played with in many ways. Play scarves, building blocks, trucks, pirates—the options are endless!

Kelly (mom to Susie, 4, and Bobby, 3), Massachusetts:

"The princess stuff can be detrimental to kids, so my husband and I are really intentional about getting basic toys," Kelly reflects. "My daughter owns a lot of Disney Princess products. We've offered our daughter lots of cars and trains, which she likes as much as tulle."

Celeste (mom to Sara, 3, and Carter, 3 months), Massachusetts:

Celeste agrees that in addition to saying no, it's critical to offer alternatives. "I've found that offering alternatives really helps," she explains. "Diversify, diversify, diversify! We've subtly pushed Sara toward other interests. Explaining what real princesses do—cut ribbons at the opening of new flats and wave at crowds—didn't hurt. We didn't want her to think princessing was all fairy godmothers, ball gowns, and singing animalia."

Also, if possible, weed out the excess princess stuff. Keep only the best, healthiest toys. You could even set a one-in, one-out policy. If your daughter really wants that new princess wand, remind her that she'll need to choose an old princess toy to give to charity. This will keep the princess clutter from taking over the house and keep the variety of toys she owns in a healthy balance.

Pop Culture Coaching, Step 3: Watch and Talk about Media Content with Your Kids

It's important to talk with children about the media content they encounter, such as advertising. Advertisements are everywhere, so keep an eye out for opportunities! And if you think about children's toys as forms of media, then you can also use toys as creative opportunities for pop culture coaching.

TIP 6: STAY ON TOP OF ADS AND TOYS AT HOME

Call out the tricky commercials. If an ad comes on-screen that you think makes a toy look better than it is, say, "I bet that toy isn't that interesting. They're just trying to trick us!"

TIP 7: ENFORCE LIMITS WHILE SHOPPING

Shopping trips are full of minicommercials. Store signage and product packaging are vying for your children's attention, pleading with them (and you) to make a purchase. So, treat these items like advertisements—persuasive pieces that can be resisted.

- *Coach your children before shopping trips.* On the way to the store, remind them what they're up against. "The store is going to try to trick you into asking me for toys or candy, but we are not buying any today. Do you understand?"
- *Avoid stores known to prompt nagging bouts.* Does the toy aisle of Target make your children beg and plead for the latest princess fad? Skip it.
- *Never reward your children's badgering.* Ever. (Really, *ever*.) Ignore their whining—but be sure to tell your little ones exactly what you are doing, and why. "You will never get something you want by whining for it." Then, ignore them—don't give in. In time, this can be turned into a question. You can ask, "Have you ever gotten what you want by whining?" If you've stuck to your guns, they are likely to pause and say or think, "No." In most cases, this should nip a whining session in the bud. With any

luck, the request will be made again in a polite way, which you can reason with.

Celeste (mom to Sara, 3, and Carter, 3 months), Massachusetts:

"Sara has a few princess things and is interested in the genre," explains Celeste, but by saying "no," Celeste has kept princesses from taking over their household. "Saying 'no' has been effective in keeping things like princess Band-Aids or bath soaps from being a huge draw," she says.

- *Remind your child of your values.* Starting at age four, in addition to saying "no," explain why you're saying no from time to time. This will familiarize your child with your family's values. For example, you could say, "No, you can't have a princess T-shirt. Our family doesn't wear clothes with movie characters on them, because clothes with movie characters are like advertisements. We don't want to be advertisements."
- *Don't ask "Okay?" after explaining or restating your family values.* This implies the decision is really theirs. Try replacing "Okay?" with "Do you understand?"

TIP 8: COACH YOUR CHILDREN'S PLAY

Just as co-viewing media with your child benefits them, so does co-play. Play is a major way children learn, so try modeling fun, new, creative ideas—such as using princess toys in unexpected ways.

Bill (dad to Ashley, 4), Illinois:

For Ashley's fourth birthday, she only wanted two things: a Cinderella castle for her princess figurines to play in, and a fire truck.

Bill and his wife, Laura, have tried to limit princess products in their home, but Bill remembers, "We were actually okay with getting her the Cinderella castle because she was also asking for the fire truck."

For the next few months, the family had a blast playing Princess Firefighters. "We would say, 'Oh my gosh, the castle is on fire!'" Bill recalls.

"Next thing we knew, the princesses were driving the truck. I would tell Ashley, 'Wow, I think those princesses are really good firemen.'"

Ashley would reply with confidence: "Yeah, they're very good. Ariel is really good with the water because she's from the water, so she gets to use the hose."

"We loved encouraging that," Bill chuckles.

Pop Culture Coaching, Step 4: Teach Children about Media Creation

Children don't often think about how media are created. After all, they only see the end result. But when children understand that advertisements are created by people, and that those people are looking to influence people's behavior, they feel empowered.

TIP 9: DISCUSS HOW ADVERTISEMENTS ARE MADE

At the beginning of this how-to section, I suggested teaching your children some simple definitions, such as "commercials" and "impulse purchase." Once children understand those concepts, they can also be taught that commercials are created by people called "advertisers," and that these advertisers work very hard to create ads that will persuade people to buy the products they are paid to promote. This means that ads often make products look better than they are in real life to convince us that we should buy them.

Children who are of grade-school age might enjoy watching the videos in the series *Buy Me That! A Kids' Survival Guide to TV Advertising*. These videos can be found on YouTube, but they were released in 1989 as a collaboration between HBO and *Consumer Reports*. Because the videos are old, the examples of TV advertisements are a little dated—but the principles are still the same, and the content itself is still exciting and engaging.

For example, in one segment, the video divulges what happens behind the scenes in a hamburger commercial, with an emphasis on how the people who make commercials style the food to make it look better than it does in real life. Kids viewing the segment may be shocked to see the extent to which products are altered on-screen to make them look more appealing to viewers.

Look for the videos online, and consider sharing them with your children.

READ BOOKS TOGETHER THAT REINFORCE YOUR VALUES ABOUT CONSUMERISM

Books are a great way to show your children that your family's values about consumerism are shared by others. There are plenty of books that you can read together on the topics of resisting materialism and consumerism, which you can then refer back to when princess products and other items rear their heads. Here are some suggestions.

BOOKS FOR PRESCHOOLERS...

...On Resisting Ads

Arthur's TV Trouble by Marc Brown. Arthur learns that the products on television commercials aren't always what they're cracked up to be! A good prompt for conversations about ads.

The Berenstain Bears and the Trouble with Commercials by Stan and Jan Berenstain. Mama Bear teaches her cubs not to believe everything they see advertised on TV.

...On Shopping and Collecting

The Berenstain Bears Get the Gimmies. The cubs throw temper tantrums when they can't get what they want, so their parents teach about budgeting and appreciating what they already have.

The Berenstain Bears' Mad, Mad Toy Craze. The cubs become obsessed with collecting Bearie Bubbies. A story of passing fads.

It's Not What You've Got by Wayne W. Dyer. The book teaches children that their belongings don't make them who they are, and that you can't buy happiness.

More by I. C. Springman. A magpie collects more, more, more. On realizing you have enough.

Nothing by Jon Agee. The wealthiest lady in town starts a strange new trend—paying money to buy nothing from stores. A witty parody of must-have shopping trends.

Those Shoes by Maribeth Boelts. Jeremy wants the trendy shoes that all his friends have. Teaches the difference between needs and wants.

...On De-Cluttering

The Berenstain Bears Think of Those in Need. The Bear family has too much stuff everywhere, so they de-clutter to free up space and benefit those in need.

Too Many Toys by David Shannon. Spencer has too many toys, so he decides to give some away. At first, he doesn't want to. But in the end, he fills a box, then decides the one toy he can't part with is the box.

...On Saving and Spending Money

Alexander, Who Used to Be Rich Last Sunday by Judith Viorst. Alexander goes from feeling rich to poor in only a week, spending the dollar his grandparents gave him much too quickly.

The Berenstain Bears' Trouble with Money. How to strike a balance between being a miser and a spendthrift.

Just Saving My Money by Mercer Mayer. Little Critter learns about saving up to buy an expensive toy. A good lesson on delayed gratification.

...On Alternatives to Spending

The Gift of Nothing by Patrick McDonnell. What do you get for someone who has everything? Nothing! Time together is more important than material gifts.

Joseph Had a Little Overcoat by Simms Taback. When Joseph's overcoat gets old and holey, he refashions it into a jacket. When the jacket wears out, he turns it into a vest—and so on. Promotes the idea of repurposing and reusing old things instead of throwing them away.

Sam and the Lucky Money by Karen Chinn. Everything Sam would like to buy costs more than he can afford, so he decides to give his New Year's money to a homeless man, instead—realizing that helping someone in need is the best possible way he could use that money.

When I Was Young in the Mountains by Cynthia Rylant. Memories of a low-tech, nonmaterialistic childhood in the Appalachians.

CHAPTER FOUR
The Problem with the Pretty Princess Mandate

It is winter in Salem, Massachusetts, and three-year-old Ava refuses to dress warmly enough to leave for preschool. Sobbing indignantly, she cries, "Princesses don't wear sleeves!"

This daily battle between Ava and her mother, Cindy, leaves both exhausted. Ava wants to look just like the pretty princesses she adores, and to her, that means she *must* go sleeveless.

The desire to be as pretty as a princess runs strong among many little girls. Princesses are so appealing: they wear gorgeous, glittering gowns and tiaras! They have tiny waists and long, lithe limbs. They have mounds of luxurious, perfectly coiffed hair. Their shoes are so shiny! Their wide eyes sparkle.

Why *would* Ava want to wear anything but princess attire? Ava is a beautiful child, with waist-length blond hair and large blue eyes. When she wears a princess costume, everyone tells her how beautiful she looks—because she does, in fact, look beautiful. The praise is positive reinforcement, and it's persuasive. From Ava's perspective, it makes complete sense to dress as similarly to a princess as she can, even when she's not in costume. She knows that people *really* like the way she looks as a princess. So if she can't wear a princess gown to school, she'll wear the next best thing—sleeveless dresses or tops. Even though it's winter.

"Ava is fully princess-obsessed," Cindy laments. "We're talking full-blown obsession. And I don't know what to do about it." Cindy feels guilty about it, too. She has always loved princesses and fairy tales, so she introduced the Disney Princesses to Ava at an early age. She had no idea that Ava would cling to the idea of being a princess so passionately. "Now I don't know how to get out of this situation. Princesses are everywhere you go, you know? That's the thing."

Cindy's right. Princesses are everywhere—and not just on TV and in stores. Countless little girls want to spend their days dressed like princesses. Ava is not alone.

Day has seen this firsthand in her work with children. Girls are so obsessed with princess culture that some of them actually wear their dress-up clothes as regular clothes everywhere they go—around town, to the grocery store, and, yes, to preschool.

"When kids go to school in their Disney Princess costumes," Day explains, "I notice that it's taking their imaginary play time and extending it from twenty minutes to all day. It extends the period of time that people can comment to these girls about their appearance: 'You're so pretty.' 'What a beautiful dress.' 'Look at your shoes.' It can go on all day, and it's a self-perpetuating cycle. It makes girls want to continue wearing clothes that get them attention."

This is discouraging because what girls *should* hear at school is praise for their interests and abilities, Day explains. "Instead of, 'How smart you are,' or 'What a good reader you are,' the costume draws the comments," she says.

Cindy has been trying to counteract Ava's fixation with looking like a princess by talking about the importance of intelligence, kindness, and other traits—the exact types of things Day says girls should be hearing. "I tell her that it's a lot more important to be smart than beautiful, and that being a nice person is what makes you really beautiful," Cindy says.

Cindy is doing a great job. But in teaching Ava that beauty is found on the inside, Cindy is fighting an uphill battle. Girls learn at ever-younger ages that if you're a girl, you are valued for one thing above all else: your appearance.

For example, think about the slogans found on little girls' clothing nowadays. So many of them emphasize the girls' appearances: "Cute." "Cutie pie." "Super cute." "Totally adorable." "Daddy's princess." "All about glitter." "Most likely to be a princess." "Little fashion diva." Clothing for tween girls is even worse, with controversy arising from slogans like "Too pretty for homework," "Too pretty to do math," and "Boys are better than books." Meanwhile, there are no comparable shirts for boys. (Thank goodness.) Although the occasional baby boy shirt might say "Handsome" or "Little cutie," the vast majority of boys' tees focus on interests and activities—not physical appearance.

Girls receive the same messages from video games, apps, and toys. For example, Disney offers a Disney Fairies app for iPhone and iPad. Although the Disney Fairies movies are about friendship and nurturing one's own interests—for example, Tinker Bell learns she is gifted in "tinkering," or fixing things—the app is all about giving fairies makeovers. As the app's description says: "With just the right amount of pixie know-how, you too might have what it takes to be a Fairy fashionista! Become the ultimate Fairy style star and build your fashion empire today!"

Likewise, Bratz dolls were the first fashion dolls to really give Barbie a run for her money about a decade ago. Unlike Barbies, who at least comes in astronaut and teacher editions, the Bratz only have a "passion for fashion." Their looks are everything.

Another example may be found in LEGO, which makes separate offerings for boys and girls. LEGO markets many lines of action-oriented toys toward boys and the appearance-oriented LEGO Friends line toward girls. The popular LEGO City line that targets boys features emergency vehicles, fire stations, and coast guard patrols. Meanwhile, the LEGO Friends for girls offers sets such as a beauty shop full of makeup and hair accessories; a city pool whose accompanying characters, Andrea and Isabella, wear bikini tops; and a performing stage whose accompanying character, Stephanie, wears a tiara.

It is also becoming increasingly common for toys to emphasize appearance, even when there's no good reason for them to do so. For example, when Hasbro released a talking Princess Celestia doll from its hit series *My Little Pony: Friendship Is Magic*, they completely changed her character. On-screen, Celestia is a powerful leader and a mentor to the younger ponies—but in talking toy form, she's fixated on beauty. The toy was programmed to say twelve different things, as follows:

Appearance (5)
I love when you comb my hair!
Oh, my hair looks beautiful.
My wings are so pretty!
My barrettes look so pretty!
You're beautiful!

Friendship (2)
I love to make new friends!
You're my best friend!

Princess (2)

I am Princess Celestia.

I'm a princess! Are you a princess, too?

Activity (2)

Let's fly to the castle.

I will light the way.

Exclamation (1)

Spectacular!

In other words, five of twelve of this toy's sayings are appearance-centric—possibly more, depending on your interpretation of the phrases "Spectacular!" and "I'm a princess! Are you a princess, too?" So if a child plays with this Princess Celestia toy, about half of the time, he or she will be subjected to pretty princess rhetoric—the kind of vanity discourse that the show, happily, is free of. For parents who appreciate the show's generally informed approach to girly-girl stuff and its alternative approach to princess culture, this toy can be an unpleasant surprise.

But for those who are aware of broader patterns in princess culture, it's not that surprising. In a study of children's animated films, including many of Disney's princess films such as *Cinderella*, *The Little Mermaid*, and *Beauty and the Beast*, researchers at the University of South Florida found the films focused too much on their female characters' appearances. More than 72 percent of the films they sampled emphasized physical attractiveness, and 84 percent associated a woman's good looks with her sociability, kindness, happiness, or success.

A common message is that a woman's physical appearance is the first reason a man would love her—rather than other traits. The male characters often fell for a woman's beauty before learning anything else about her, even though in real life, attraction is more complex and does take personality into account.

Because of these problems, experts Diane Levin and Jean Kilbourne argue in their book *So Sexy So Soon: The New Sexualized Childhood and What Parents Can Do to Protect Their Kids* that the Disney Princess line can be damaging to girls—priming them to focus to an unhealthy degree on being pretty, sexy, and sexually appealing. For this reason, they say that Disney Princess is a "lion in lamb's clothing" contributing to the sexualization of girls in subtle but pervasive ways.

Media studies expert Gigi Durham echoes these concerns about Disney's role in the sexualization of young girls. In her book *The Lolita Effect: The Media Sexualization of Young Girls and What We Can Do About It*, Durham notes that several Disney princess films—*The Little Mermaid*, *Aladdin*, and *Pocahontas*—feature buxom, curvaceous, scantily clad heroines alongside fully clothed men. Regarding this pattern, Durham argues, "The core message is not hard to recognize: if you're female, your desirability is contingent on blatant body display." (It's almost like a tamer version of the controversial Miley Cyrus/Robin Thicke performance at the 2013 MTV Video Music Awards where Cyrus twerked in her underwear while Thicke sang fully dressed in a suit. The sexualization of Cyrus is much more intense than anything found in a princess film—but the messages about men, women, and power are the same.)

Like Durham, psychologist Jennifer Hartstein believes girls' princess obsessions can lead them to fixate on appearance. Although she notes in her book *Princess Recovery: A How-to Guide to Raising Strong,*

Empowered Girls Who Can Create Their Own Happily Ever Afters that sometimes princess play is perfectly harmless, she agrees that many girls who develop an unhealthy fixation on "pretty toys and dresses" become obsessed with their appearances.

Such girls battle their parents in the same way as little Ava. They want to dress up even at times when they are supposed to run about freely, thus they focus on *appearing* rather than *playing*. Hartstein argues that this is a contributing factor in girls' problems with body image and self-esteem. Without early interventions, she reports, the consequences can last even into adulthood.

Day agrees. She foresees long-term psychological consequences for girls growing up in today's princess culture. Drawing upon twenty-five years of experience in the field, she believes no previous generation of preschoolers has surveilled their own appearances so relentlessly.

"It's troubling, because while it seems innocent, it isn't," Day explains. "Girls are becoming hooked on constant comments about their appearances, which walking around town in princess play clothes definitely solicits. But once they've outgrown the cute stylings of princesses at age six, there's nowhere to go but sexy." Indeed, as Levin and Kilbourne explain in *So Sexy So Soon*: "The overwhelming message the princesses convey is to look pretty, aka sexy, so they can hook their prince. Everything else is secondary."

In short, our culture teaches girls that their appearance is *everything*. And that's a problem.

MOMS ON THE DISNEY PRINCESSES AND BEING PRETTY

It bothers me that princess stories revolve around the idea that the goal in life is to score a man. They push the idea that looks and a sweet nature are the most important attributes. They also make it clear that women are judged by—and their success is dependent upon—their beauty.

—Belinda, Washington, DC; mother
of two girls, ages three and five.

I think that the Disney princesses are very unrealistic. They give girls all these high expectations of how perfect they need to look, and how skinny they need to look. I do not think that is what children should grow up with, but that is how a lot of children think they have to be, because of the images of these princesses. They believe that they can only be pretty if they're dressed up and have their hair perfectly done. Every child wishes she was a princess and could meet her Prince Charming, but not every princess has blond hair with blue eyes and a perfect figure. It's not like that.

—Louisa, York County, Pennsylvania;
mother of a three-year-old daughter.

The Pretty Princess Mandate

I call the message that being pretty is everything "the Pretty Princess Mandate." The Pretty Princess Mandate is part of a larger problem in our society: we are biased to favor attractive people in general, men and women alike—but women in particular are led to believe that how they look truly, deeply matters.

If we take the time to understand the source of the Pretty Princess Mandate, we can better understand its implications for little girls like Ava—and do a better job at using pop culture coaching techniques to guide our daughters through a range of potential body-image pitfalls.

So, here are three points that can help us better understand the Pretty Princess Mandate and why it sinks its talons into young girls so easily.

1. **Our society is heavily biased toward attractive people, and we believe (mistakenly) that attractive people are happier.**

   It's a sad truth: Western society favors attractive people, men and women alike. When we are raised in the United States, we grow up believing that what is beautiful is good. We assume— without thinking critically about it—that outward appearance tells us truths about a person's life: that attractive people have happier marriages and better jobs, are better parents, have better social lives, and in general have better prospects in life. In other words, we believe we *can* tell a book by its cover.

   Because we buy into these stereotypes with little thought, we also believe that if we could become more attractive, our lives would change in overwhelmingly positive ways. If only we looked more like the beautiful people on TV, we would be so much happier! For this reason, the cosmetics and diet industries earn profits of tens of billions of dollars a year—and the cosmetic surgery industry isn't too far behind.

   But in actuality, our physical appearances have strikingly little to do with our happiness and satisfaction in life. In fact, research shows that people who are deemed unattractive are approximately as happy and satisfied with their lives as those who are rated very attractive. It turns out you *can't* tell a book by its cover, after all.

   So why do our beliefs that *beauty = good* and *beauty = happiness* persist? Psychologists claim that two things strongly influence our beliefs about the lives of attractive people: what we observe in everyday life and the stories told to us by the media. In the first area, we witness that attractive people are more popular than their peers and receive preferential treatment. We cannot witness attractive people's internal lives, however, so we simply *assume* that the preferential treatment they receive results in greater happiness. But this is not the case.

In the second area, we learn from stories in books and on-screen that good things are associated with beauty, and bad things are associated with ugliness—for example, that "the wicked witch and giant are ugly, and the heroic prince and virtuous princess are attractive." And such stories invariably end with the good, attractive people living happily ever after, as illustrated by pretty much every princess story ever.

BIAS IN THE CLASSROOM: TEACHERS FAVOR ATTRACTIVE CHILDREN

Our biases toward attractive people influence the way we treat those around us—even children. For example, in a classic study, professors Margaret Clifford and Elaine Walster—researchers from the University of Iowa and the University of Washington—did an experiment to see if teachers would favor attractive children over unattractive children. Clifford and Walster felt this was an important question to investigate, because teachers' expectations of the children they teach can have a tremendous impact on the children's success in school.

Previous studies had shown that when a teacher is told a random child is an early bloomer (even when he or she actually has not been identified by any tests as such), that child will make greater gains in school than his or her peers. The teacher's belief in the child becomes a self-fulfilling prophecy, made true by the way the teacher interacts with that child.

So, Clifford and Walster decided to give teachers a set of children's academic records, accompanied by photographs of the children. They asked the teachers to review the records and rate each child's intelligence and how far he or she was likely to progress in school. They also asked the teachers to say how interested the child's parents likely were in his or her education, and how popular the teacher believed the child would be with his or her peers.

The result? The teachers' assessments of the more attractive children were significantly more favorable than those of the less attractive children. "Attractive children appear to have a sizeable advantage over unattractive children," Clifford and Walster reported.

Day has witnessed this pattern in many schools over the years. "This is something you can actually observe working in schools," she comments. "It is always noticeable to me, and sometimes teachers even discuss which children are the cutest and which aren't. It's troubling. From an early age, you can see the cutest children being the most popular *and* being favored by teachers, and those two things reinforce each other."

It's not very fair, is it? But our biases toward attractive people are so deeply ingrained in us that even educators, who have children's best interests at heart, unwittingly buy into them.

2. **The pressure to appear attractive is especially intense for women, but cultural standards of female beauty are largely unattainable. This can lead to harmful behaviors—not happiness.**

   Although we are biased to favor attractive people in general, the consequences of these biases are especially intense for women and girls—so intense that being pretty feels like a mandate. In our culture, women are constantly objectified. Our physical appearances are constantly evaluated. Stereotypical female beauty encompasses many traits: nice hair and smooth skin that are as light as possible, reflecting a bias toward white beauty standards; large eyes, high cheekbones, and full lips; and an extremely thin but curvaceous body. There are not many variations on what's considered beautiful. It's a narrow, narrow standard.

   Most women are physically unable to meet these cultural beauty ideals, although a small percentage of women do so naturally (and others work to achieve the same results with plastic surgery). But when we fail to even approximate stereotypical beauty, we are judged more harshly by those around us than nonconforming men are. It's a double standard.

   Television programming illustrates this. The media are dominated by images of young women who are tall and exceptionally thin, and the media almost never offer diverse ideas about what constitutes beauty. Women in lead roles are so lean and svelte that exceptions like Melissa McCarthy and Rebel Wilson really stand out. It's harder for them to "make it" in the business. Consider that Oprah's struggles with dieting and her fluctuating weight are common knowledge. Meanwhile, the bodies of male actors and comedians don't face nearly as much scrutiny. This is lucky for them, because the consequences on the psyche of having one's physical appearance constantly evaluated are quite serious.

In fact, because most women are aware of constantly being judged, many consciously or unconsciously attempt to preempt negative judgments by turning a critical eye inward. We compare our own bodies with the images around us, internalizing the ideal as a personal goal. But inevitably, when we compare our appearances to those of celebrities, to the ideal glamorized by advertisements everywhere we look, we fall short. The ideal is nearly impossible to achieve and is ever-shifting.

As a result of our constant self-surveillance, we are generally more critical of our own bodies than our male counterparts are of theirs *or ours*. This dissatisfaction leads to a host of psychological consequences, including lower social self-esteem, more social anxiety, lower feelings of motivation, and greater feelings of shame. These consequences are far from trivial. In our quest for happiness by way of idealized attractiveness, we can make ourselves utterly miserable.

As evidenced by the success of the diet industry, the beauty trait that our culture tends to fixate upon the most is *thinness*. We believe that thin = beautiful, and so if we believe that beautiful = happy, we also believe that thin = happy. But unhappily, the thinness the media present as the ideal is quite extreme—often falling well below what doctors would consider a healthy weight for women. This means that in most cases, when women wish they could be prettier, thinner, and happier, the thinness they strive for cannot be attained without self-harm. As a result, women who have internalized the ideal of extreme thinness are at risk for serious body-image problems, including eating disorders.

3. **Girls are attuned to these messages and beliefs about physical appearance, and they begin to agree with them from an early age—sometimes with detrimental results by late adolescence.**

Young girls are aware that thinness and beauty are highly valued in our society. They can see that to be considered desirable, women must look a very specific way. After all, messages about beauty and attractiveness can be seen everywhere— television, magazine covers, billboards, toys, video games, apps. Girls learn about the beauty ideal interpersonally, as well—from their peers and from adults, too. How many little girls have heard their mothers say, "Ugh, I feel so fat today!" or "Honey, does this outfit make me look fat?"

This interpersonal dimension cannot be overstated. For example, as one study of five-year-old girls and their mothers found, if a mother has recently been on a diet, that simple fact makes it twice as likely that her daughter will have ideas about dieting herself. Furthermore, if mothers feel critical about their daughters' bodies, even if they have kept those critical feelings to themselves, the daughters are significantly more likely to have poor body esteem. When it comes to girls' body images, moms are their daughters' role models and influencers—whether they know it or not. Study after study shows that children mirror their mothers on body-image issues. (We'll talk about how dads can influence their daughters' body image later.)

Likewise, when girls go to school with older girls, they learn quickly—through their older peers' example—that it is "normal" to be dissatisfied with their bodies. According to one striking study, when nine- to eleven-year-old girls simply attended the same school as older girls, they had higher rates of body-image issues. They had internalized a thinner female body ideal and perceived themselves as being more overweight than peers who attended schools with a smaller age range of students.

And, of course, the lack of diversity in the media's representations of beauty is a major factor. The media portray only *one* body type (exceedingly thin, with ample breasts and curvy hips) as beautiful, and it promotes *one* coloration (blond hair and white skin) as superior to all other hair colors and skin tones.

So, the majority of girls are aspiring to a body type that can never be theirs, and a significant percentage of girls in the United States are furthermore greeted with images of white-skinned beauties of a race that can never be theirs. In fact, according to the U.S. Census Bureau, 49.9 percent of children younger than five are categorized as minorities—of nonwhite or Hispanic background, or both. "The population of children younger than five is close to becoming majority-minority nationally," the Census Bureau reports.

The fact that girls are attuned to messages and beliefs about female physical appearance surfaces in a variety of ways and can be seen in girls of all ages. Thanks to media, parents, and peers, most girls feel that policing their own and other girls' appearances is "normal."

Sadly, girls can begin making judgments about others' appearances before the age of six. According to one experiment, three- to five-year-old girls were already using negative adjectives to describe fat body types and positive adjectives to describe thin body types. Despite their tender ages, these girls also said they would prefer to have best friends and playmates whose body types are thin, rather than fat or average—showing that biases about body weight begin early.

When the researchers asked the preschool girls to play a board game with them, they witnessed the strength of young girls' feelings about fat. In the game, the girls could choose one of three board-game pieces to play: a character with a thin body type, an average body type, or a fat body type. The girls were so emotionally invested in the idea of being thin that nearly all refused to navigate the game using a character with a fat body type. When asked why, their replies included statements like, "I don't want to be her. She is fat and ugly," and "I hate her because she has a fat stomach."

When girls develop the ability to judge others, they often deploy these skills in cruel ways, teasing and bullying their peers about weight, beauty, and fashion. "This happens at younger and younger ages," Day explains. "Girls internalize it and begin to fear what their peers will think of them, or what the queen bees will say to them."

Bullying, it turned out, was a major factor in Ava's insistence that she only wear sleeveless dresses to school. Months after our first conversation, Cindy learned that Ava hadn't come up with the idea that princesses don't wear sleeves on her own. The idea originated with another girl at her day care who used the idea to bully classmates.

"I heard about this from one of my good friend's sisters," Cindy explains. "Her daughter goes to the same day care as Ava. She was being taunted by this little girl because she was wearing sleeves. The little girl had said something like, 'Princesses don't wear sleeves.' And so Ava didn't want to wear sleeves because she didn't want to be tormented.

"I can't believe that at three years old, she has already dealt with mean girl stuff," Cindy adds incredulously.

Unfortunately, one in ten children between the ages of four and six is bullied, and in consequence, bullying experts suggest that children need to begin learning about bullying at the age of three. Girls who are bullied about their appearances deal with many consequences, including depression, anger, fear, and negative feelings about themselves and their bodies.

Coping strategies are frequently unhealthy. One study of teen girls who have been bullied about their weight found that many girls coped by avoidance (such as skipping gym class), by overeating, or by engaging in unhealthy binge-eating episodes. Children who have been bullied have a reduced quality of life—as do children who have a negative body image, which means that being bullied or teased about appearance is a double whammy for kids.

Soon after girls begin judging others, they turn those judgments inward, establishing a pattern that can last throughout the rest of their lives. At about five or six years of age—not in adolescence, as previously thought—girls begin expressing dissatisfaction with their own bodies. In recent years, some girls in this age group have even begun showing signs of eating disorders. In the long term, girls who are concerned about their weight at this age are significantly more likely to diet or have problem eating behaviors by the age of nine.

Sadly, girls' self-worth tends to decrease when others make negative assessments of their appearance. This means that the earlier girls begin internalizing biases that favor the Pretty Princess Mandate, the more chances there are for girls to feel worse about themselves as they are judged to be inadequate, to be too fat to be included in a peer group.

Self-esteem expert and counselor Marci Warhaft-Nadler, author of *The Body Image Survival Guide for Parents: Helping Toddlers, Tweens, and Teens Thrive*, has seen girls exclude other girls based on their body sizes. For example, she shared the story of one nine-year-old girl whose friend was holding a fashion show–themed birthday party. The invitation asked each guest to bring an outfit. During the party, each girl would try on someone else's outfit and wear it.

"Well, the girl was bigger than her friends," Warhaft-Nadler explains, "so she knew she wasn't going to fit into the outfits and couldn't go to the party"—which Warhaft-Nadler astutely notes was a thoughtless (though unintended) oversight on the part of the birthday girl's parent.

At other times, she has heard of more deliberate, mean-spirited exclusion, like the first-grade girls at a school local to her in Canada who began a "Size One Club." "If a girl can't show a clothing label that says 'size one,'" she explains, "she can't be part of the club."

As girls grow older, these kinds of exclusionary behaviors rooted in physical appearance can become more marked. Studies suggest that for a girl to be considered "popular," her characteristics must include being very pretty, very fashionable, popular with boys, stylish in makeup and hair, and quite thin—with these standards used, conversely, as a basis for teasing or excluding girls deemed unpopular. And when a girl is teased on the basis of her appearance, studies show the effects are more marked than when she is teased about other attributes, such as intelligence—a sad commentary on girls' eventual internalization of the societal message that their physical appearance is the most important thing about them.

In addition to peers, media and toys matter—so much so that some experts claim that popular culture is the most powerful influence in the areas of beauty and the hyper-thin ideal, trumping even the effects of interpersonal influences. In fact, in experimental settings, the results of exposure to popular culture images of thinness can have dramatic and immediate effects on girls.

For example, in one study, researchers gave six- to ten-year-old girls dolls of varying sizes to play with. Afterward, the girls were offered some food to eat. The researchers found that the girls who played with thin dolls ate significantly less food than girls who played with average-sized dolls! The authors were certain this was cause and effect: "The dolls directly affected actual food intake in these young girls," they wrote. Being cued to think about the idealized hyper-thin female body was, disturbingly, enough to prompt preadolescent girls to eat less.

When girls internalize the ideal of extreme thinness prior to adolescence, they are especially at risk later for chronic dissatisfaction with their bodies and eating disorders. After all, when girls reach puberty, their bodies typically change in ways that take them even further from the hyper-thin ideal female body. (This is markedly different from boys' experiences, for in puberty, their bodies move closer to the muscular ideal male body.)

During adolescence, girls' dissatisfaction with their bodies increases, and girls are more likely to experience lowered self-esteem and depression. No wonder girls who develop eating disorders usually do so in adolescence, when their bodies—in what *should* be understood as developing in natural, healthy ways—depart further from the unhealthy ideal upheld by our culture.

Princesses and the Pretty Princess Mandate

Unfortunately, the majority of the characters and dolls created for girls perpetuate the Pretty Princess Mandate. Marketers know that young girls are aware of our culture's valorization of beauty and extreme thinness. In fact, studies show that girls will only identify with female characters if they consider them attractive—unlike boys, who mainly identify with male characters they perceive as intelligent.

As a result, nearly all the female characters in children's television and films—and nearly all the fashion-type dolls produced for girls— are stereotypically attractive. They have exaggeratedly tall and thin bodies, copious amounts of long hair, never-ending legs, and facial features dominated by extremely large eyes. Whether it's Barbie, Bratz, Monster High, or the Disney Princesses, they're all making the same visual appeal to girls—and research suggests that early exposure to unrealistically thin dolls can be detrimental to girls' body image, putting them at greater risk of eating disorders.

These facts help us better understand why the princesses served up to little girls embody all of the stereotypical traits of female beauty. It's a requirement for nearly *any* female character's success in the marketplace. If the princesses did not have the look that is idealized by society at large, little girls in the target audience would not find them attractive. They would not want to play with them. They would not want to buy them.

But what's good for the marketplace—what we vote for with our dollars—isn't always good for us as individuals. Beth Mayer notes that many parents of little boys understand this. They'll ban toy weapons, like swords and guns, from the house. "But many parents who are okay with saying, 'No weapons in the house!' will have princess dolls in their homes," she reflects. "Why are we so much more comfortable taking a stance on weapons than we are with princess dolls, when a princess doll is—in some ways—like a weapon?"

This is a good point. When a child plays with a toy weapon, he or she is generally aware that it's fantasy. They know that what they're doing isn't going to hurt somebody. But when a girl is playing princess, she's encouraged to live up to that unhealthy ideal—as Disney's ad campaign "I Am a Princess," which features many little girls expressing their own identities as princesses, makes clear.

Note that the beauty standards set by the Disney Princesses are exclusionary of girls who are on the larger size in any way (weight or height). That can be very hurtful. In particular, Disney's princess dresses—which are so beloved by Ava and countless other girls—come only in "regular" sizes, 2 through 10 (XXS through L), in the Disney Store.

For sizes larger than that (up to a size 16, or XXL), families must purchase the dresses sold in the Disney theme parks. But these are two to three times as expensive as those from the Disney Store, and purchasing them requires an expensive trip to a Disney park for most families. And even these are not offered in plus sizes! It surprises and disappoints many parents to learn that although the average child is larger than he or she was a generation ago, the Disney Store doesn't sell dresses for all girls.

Ashley is a former Disney employee who worked in the Disney Store and, later, in the Bibbidi Bobbidi Boutique at Walt Disney

World, where families spend between $54.95 and $189.95 for princess makeovers for their daughters (plus an extra $32.95 for photos). In both the Disney Store and the boutique, the dresses that are available for sale are huge sellers that drive families to visit, because many girls want an authentic Disney Princess gown—not a knockoff.

There, Ashley and her coworkers frequently saw little girls whose hopes were dashed by the limited availability of sizes. "For example," Ashley says, "one bride came in with two little girls who were going to be her flower girls. One was slender and the other was heavier. They were there to purchase a pair of limited-edition Rapunzel dresses for them to wear in the wedding. But the heavier girl could not fit in our dresses, and she was just devastated."

Ashley also recalls helping grandparents find a dress for their five-year-old granddaughter who was big for her age. "The granddaughter loved princess dresses so much, but for any of them to fit around her waist, she needed a size ten. That meant they were way too long on her." Although neither the Disney Store nor the boutique does alterations, Ashley knows how to sew, so she offered tips.

"I explained to the grandparents—like I did to all guests in this position—that to shorten the dress, they could lift the top layer of tulle up, gather it in just a few places, and do a few stitches to tack it, bringing the tulle up to the same level as the underskirt, which was shorter. That way, they didn't have to fully hem the dress; they could just ruche it in a U-shape." That worked well enough that the grandparents soon returned for a second dress—but on their third visit, they were out of luck. The five-year-old girl had outgrown the Disney Store's dresses completely. "She was so, so upset," Ashley recalls.

"What does that little girl feel like," asks Mayer, "who walks into the Disney store and knows that when she tries to get a dress—which is a perfectly normal thing to do—she can't get one? That's horrifying." And when that girl gets invited to a birthday party where all the other girls are going to be wearing Disney Princess dresses?

"That's a really shaming experience," Mayer says. "In this day and age, if that happened to my child, I would call in all the moms and say, 'Can we have something that's different? My kid is going to be unbelievably shamed by this. What do you guys think?' You can challenge other women, other mothers, to think about that—to remember that this is a group, and when kids are in first grade, second grade, and you have to invite the entire class to the party, you don't want those two kids who are heavier to be shamed." (Not to mention that princess parties exclude boys, too!)

Warhaft-Nadler offered a succinct response to Disney's limited dress sizes: "That's a failure from a moral or a humane kind of perspective," she said. "I don't understand that."

Similar stories are not too hard to find. Meg is the mother of Sophie, a five-year-old girl on the autism spectrum who loves the Disney Princesses "in every way, shape, and form." Meg sees Sophie's delight in the Disney Princesses, as children on the spectrum often struggle with fantasy play—but the princess script is simple enough to engage Sophie. So despite some reservations about the princess brand and its messages, Meg supports Sophie in this interest.

A broad-shouldered girl who is tall for her age, Sophie is already wearing a size eight, so Disney Princess dresses won't fit her much longer. Already, her mother has to alter them to make them work: "She's mostly torso," Meg says. "The dresses are made for much ganglier kids. It's tricky. They're always too long when they fit her around the chest. She doesn't fit the stereotypical Disney Princess mold."

Meg finds princess culture frustrating. "I think it would be wonderful to see princesses that are young and have age-appropriate body shapes," she says. "Sophie made a comment the other day that she doesn't like that she has a big belly. She said she didn't like how her belly stuck out, and I had to nip that right in the bud by saying, 'You look exactly how you should look as a kindergartener.' But she's bombarded: the media messages are everywhere, saying you're supposed to be skinny and ultrafeminine. We have to fight against that."

To their credit, Disney now produces a line of Disney Princess dolls under the label "Disney Animators' Collection," which imagine what the princesses might have looked like in their preschool years—and they even have round bellies like kindergarteners do. At 16 inches in size, the Animators' Collection dolls are just a little smaller than an American Girl doll (which is 18 inches), but appear to be of similar quality—and at $24.95 each are a fraction of the cost.

The dolls have sold well, and it's great that girls have this alternative form of Disney Princess to play with—one that is not a buxom, long-limbed, extremely thin fashion doll. But when I asked Ashley how her customers at the Disney Store and Walt Disney World reacted upon the release of these dolls, her comments showed how ingrained the Pretty Princess Mandate is in so many young girls. She explained, "Little girls would come up to me with one of the dolls and say, 'Why doesn't she have boobs?' or 'Her belly's not flat!' I would explain, 'She's a little girl. She's not a big girl.'" They just weren't used to seeing princesses that looked like themselves.

The Pressures of Princess Performance

Within the princess culture industry, many women face the same pressures that young children experience—especially those who are employed to perform as princesses. Disney and other smaller, independent companies have thousands of women working for them to portray princess characters—either the Disney versions (at Disney) or their generic counterparts. (For example, only Disney can offer its guests costumed performers portraying Ariel, because Ariel is a trademarked name, but anyone can be the Little Mermaid, which is a public domain character.)

But unfortunately, for the average adult woman, passing for a princess can be a rather tall order. When I worked as a birthday party princess, I spent as much time getting dressed and made up as I spent at the birthday parties—even though I only got paid the same as the men who could don their superhero attire in five minutes (*ahem*).

Applying princess-perfect makeup was a painstaking process, and the wigs were tough to secure over my own long, thick hair (which I cut to chin length for the first time in years to make the process easier). The Spanx-like undergarments were a struggle to squeeze into—and for someone who doesn't even wear a bikini at the beach, that mermaid costume was uncomfortably revealing. (This was especially so at the occasional party when dads who had been drinking beers all afternoon would leer at me when their wives weren't looking. Ick.)

During my time as a birthday party princess, the princess gowns I was supposed to wear were not always easy to fit into. They were made to one preexisting set of measurements—based on those of the birthday party company owner's teenage daughter. And I'm no teenager! In fact, most of the performers the owner hired were adults like me—not the high school or college students you might expect. ("I find adults to be more reliable than most teenagers," the owner, Mike, explained.) He just looked me up and down at my interview and said approvingly, "Yeah, the costumes should fit you."

This meant that one day, when I tried on a brand-new Rapunzel costume, I felt anxious. I could squeeze into it, but just barely. The construction was so odd; the darts came up over my bust, not under it, and the waist was much too high. It was a tight enough fit that I could not stretch enough to raise my arms over my head while wearing it, which was a necessary action for some of the party games I was supposed to lead (like the ones with a parachute).

I *needed* to fit into this costume to work this job. There was no alternative costume available, so I would have to lose weight to perform as Rapunzel. I had done a lot of work to improve my body image over the past decade, and I was happy with the way I looked. My weight was in the middle to high end of a good, healthy weight for me. So reluctantly I set a goal of losing five pounds, just to gain some wiggle room in a birthday party costume.

But I did it—and in addition to fitting into the Rapunzel costume better at subsequent parties, I also received lots of positive feedback from family and friends. People asked: "Have you lost a little weight? You look great!" "How did you do it? What's your trick?" "I wish I could drop some weight like that! You look amazing!" The thin ideal is so ingrained in us that "Oh, you've lost weight!" seems to be the biggest compliment anyone could give a woman.

But for princess performers, slimming down—even if you already look great—is par for the course. For example, Jennifer—a former princess performer for Disney—vividly recalls when a casting director suggested that she lose a few pounds. "I was nineteen years old," Jennifer recalls, "and I was being considered to play Alice in Wonderland and Cinderella. I was dressed for a dance audition, wearing nice shorts and a little 'tankini' kind of top and a little dance skirt over it, just to do my routine. And after the dance audition, they asked some of us to stay—and a casting director asked, 'Can you take off your skirt?'"

Jennifer felt incredibly embarrassed by the request. "Now, I was dressed. I had spandex shorts underneath my skirt. But I had *never* felt so naked as when they asked me to take off my skirt so they could stare at my body. I just wanted to hide, but I had to stand there and stare straight ahead. Finally, they said, 'Okay, thank you,' and I got to walk away. And that's when I promised myself, 'Rain or shine, snow, sleet or hell, whether or not I got this role, I am going for ice cream right after,' because I needed it really badly.

"But," Jennifer recalls, "I didn't end up keeping that promise to myself because on the way out the door, they asked me to lose five pounds. They pulled me aside privately and were very quiet and said, 'Hey, I want you to know, you look great, there's nothing wrong with that, but, um, you know, it wouldn't hurt to lose five pounds.'"

She lost the weight—and she got the job.

How did she like it? Well, she didn't feel very good about herself: "I felt like I was exactly halfway between a model and prostitute," Jennifer says. "As a face character, you are praised. You have fans. You sign autographs. People literally go crazy as soon as they see you, like you're a supermodel.

"But you are treated like a self-moving prop by the supervisors, assigned to stand in certain places at certain times, which felt a bit like working your corner," she continues. "I had people feel me up, like reach up and squeeze my breasts. One man walked up to me, picked me up, and carried me over to his daughter so he could get the picture he wanted—and the supervisors didn't do anything."

She only spent a year in the position, then moved on.

★ ★ ★

A few months later, during a visit to Orlando, I spoke with Will, a former casting director and manager for the Walt Disney World resorts in Florida. He worked for Walt Disney World for more than a decade and had a lot of experience working with the performers.

Will said that during his tenure at Disney, it was fairly common for performers to lose their jobs at the end of their contracts because they had gained too much weight for their costumes. But the executives didn't want to see well-trained, successful performers go because they had gained weight. After all, training them in the first place had been an investment. So did they create larger costumes? Of course not; princesses are as thin as possible. Instead, when performers began to gain weight midcontract, they began sending them to see a nutritionist, who asked them to do weekly weigh-ins.

Although that seemed like a good idea on the surface, Will said, "That crossed a line." The new fixation on the scale backfired, and people started getting eating disorders. So Disney cut the performers' nutritionist program.

Will also recalled the extremes to which some young women went as they tried to secure work as a Magic Kingdom princess in the first place. He explained that a crucial part of the casting process was determining whether an auditionee's facial features resembled those of a specific animated character. They would hold "fittings," in which people who had made it through callbacks were dressed in costume, and then the casting directors would try to figure out if they really worked as that character.

"We would look closely at people and compare their faces to the animators' drawings," he said. "And originally, we gave them specific feedback when they'd come in for fittings. Like, 'Your eyes are too close together,' or 'Your nose is not the right shape for this.'"

But soon enough, the casting directors were no longer allowed to offer any feedback as to why individuals weren't right for the role. The reason? "We started having girls who were going out and having plastic surgery, and then they would come back six months later and ask, 'Okay, well, how do I look now?'"

At the time, performing as a Disney Princess in the Magic Kingdom paid only $9.80 an hour. But the allure of being a princess was so strong that aspiring performers would get plastic surgery—changing their faces in hopes of getting the part.

In most cases, the plastic surgery didn't even work out. "Most people, they would do it, and then we would have to tell them, 'You're still not the right look.' The thing is, it's all subjective. It depends on who is sitting behind the table at casting. I like my Mary Poppins to look a little bit more mature than my Cinderellas, because Mary Poppins was Julie Andrews—she was a nanny, not a sixteen-year-old girl. But another stage manager liked really young-looking Mary Poppins. So it was all subjective.

"And I don't think that people understood that it's all subjective," Will added. "It's not that you're not pretty, that you're not good enough. It's that you don't look like what somebody drew on a piece of paper thirty years ago." But some of the young women they encountered took it incredibly personally.

Did they ever have similar problems with the men who auditioned?

"Oh, no," Will says. "For boys, it was like, 'Okay, I didn't get the part, no big deal.' But for girls…they would be devastated."

But once on the job, the Disney Princess characters sometimes fixated on their role as a validation of their beauty. Jennifer recalls: "There were times where my fellow performers were like, 'Can you believe twelve thousand people across the United States auditioned for these parts, and we were the most beautiful of all of them?' And I literally said, 'No, we just look the most like the animations.' But there's no way to avoid taking it to heart in some way," she conceded. "You can't have a crew of people assigned specifically to make sure your clothes look perfect and this other crew specifically assigned to make sure your wigs look perfect and not feel like you must be the most beautiful person in the world."

It's telling that so many harmful body-image issues exist within the ranks of Disney's employees, mirroring what then happens outside the Magic Kingdom. It shows up in the sizes of dresses sold in the Disney Store. It surfaces in the experiences of birthday party performers. It is both a reflection of and a contributor to the unattainable body-image ideal. For so many girls—and for the women they later become—the Pretty Princess Mandate is inescapable and unavoidable.

In this context, how can parents help girls develop resilience? What can we do to lessen the Pretty Princess Mandate's grip on girls' self-image, to foster their critical-thinking skills, and to nurture a self-esteem that is holistic—based on the whole girl, not just her physical appearance?

How to...
Help Girls Beat the Pretty Princess Mandate

As our children's pop culture coaches, we can help them to understand how unrealistic the beauty ideal found in media and popular culture is. But in addition to exposing the Pretty Princess Mandate's complete split from reality, a parent can serve as his or her daughter's role model, mentor, and advocate.

Pop Culture Coaching, Step 1: Identify and Communicate Your Family's Values

What are your family's values about the beauty ideal and body image? If you're reading this chapter, you are probably either feeling conflicted about the Pretty Princess Mandate or are against it. The following tips, based on solid research and expert advice, may help you develop and articulate your perspective.

TIP 1: START WITH THE MOM IN THE MIRROR: DEVELOP AND MODEL YOUR OWN HEALTHY BODY ESTEEM FOR YOUR DAUGHTER

The research is clear: When a mother is critical of her own body, her children pick up on it. Unfortunately, most adult women *are* dissatisfied with their physical appearances, as proven by the massive successes of the cosmetics, dieting, and plastic surgery industries. If encouraging your daughter to have a healthy body image is one of your family's values, one of the most important things we as mothers can do is to work on our own body image—to work at becoming more comfortable in our own skin. It's a value worth prioritizing.

Think about it this way: Young children love their mothers unconditionally. They think we mamas are beautiful. They love to snuggle up against our squishy tummies; they see nothing wrong with our bodies' softness, which is a source of physical comfort to children.

I vividly recall being a small child and adoring my own Memere's softness, her wrinkly skin—loose arms, crinkly toes, the lines around her eyes, freckles and all: everything about her body. It never occurs to small children that we, the family they love, are anything but beautiful! How touching that their esteem for us is so much higher than our own.

And yet it's easy to feel mixed emotions about our children's praise for us, knowing that despite their adoration, we fall short of the beauty ideal in some way or other. When we reveal those mixed feelings to our children, it shocks them. They notice. I remember that experience of shock firsthand. I was perhaps four or five and told my parents that I was going to draw a picture of them.

My mom—who I now know had struggled with substantial weight gain for several years after my baby sister was born, but I had not noticed it at the time—fretted aloud: "I hope I don't look too fat in your picture." *Fat?* I was baffled. My parents were perfect! *Fat* was never on my radar…until then.

Perhaps we parents should all be a bit radical when it comes to our self-images and believe our *children*, rather than the media.

Nancy Gruver—founder of *New Moon: The Magazine for Girls*, author of *How to Say It to Girls: Communicating with Your Growing Daughter*, and a nationally recognized leader in the girl empowerment movement— advocates for this mind-set. "Our children are a huge mirror for our self-growth," she explains. "They reflect us back with pure love. They *love* us. And what we see coming back from them is honest. If we tune in and we are willing to believe them, it can help us see ourselves more clearly. It's wonderful—a huge, huge gift of being a parent."

Moms and dads alike can work on developing a healthy body image and modeling it for their children.

- *Be quiet about your diet, and in family conversations, focus on healthiness—not thinness.* Are you dieting or worried about your weight? Be as positive about your body as you can. If you work out a lot or don't eat certain things, your children will notice. Consider framing your activities in terms of healthiness and fitness—not in terms of pursuing a number on a scale.

Jessica (mom to Shara, 7), Massachusetts:

"I don't say the D word (diet) in front of my daughter. And I make sure she sees me getting exercise—not to lose weight, but to be healthy. I also make sure she sees me eat a lot of normal food. I'm quite a big person, and she is likely to be as well. She's very tall and strong for her age, and her doctor says she will hit six feet. So it is important for her to be healthy, active, and positive. I tell her that Mommy is so very tall and strong because I am an 'Amazon.'"

Celeste (mom to Sara, 3, and Carter, 3 months), Massachusetts:

"I try to never, ever put down my body in front of her. Anna often likes to play with my squishy belly, and I will never say anything about it being fat. I usually say, 'Do you like playing with Mama's belly? I grew both you and your brother in there. Isn't that awesome?' I will often compliment myself in front of her. And we talk about how we're big and strong (and promptly flex our muscles). For me, I think showing her what healthy behavior is like by having a healthy attitude toward myself is the biggest thing."

Angela (mom to Lizbet, age 8), California:

"I never fat-shame myself or complain about my body in front of her. When I go to my Pilates classes, I talk about how they will make me healthier and stronger. I never talk about losing weight or calorie counts or diets. I don't hide my body from her or say bad things about my stretch marks. I'd be healthier if I lost about thirty pounds, but I refuse to let her see me run myself down for it, and I think that has helped my own attitude about my body."

Olivia (mom to Ben, 9, and Cara, 6), Pennsylvania:

"When the kids have dessert and I don't, they ask why. So instead of saying 'because I'm fat,' I say, 'I'm not hungry anymore. I stop eating when I am not hungry. But later, if I get hungry, I might have some!' That way, I am making it about how I am feeling, and not how I think I look. I'm also sending a subtle message that there's no need to eat just because something is there."

Linda (mom to Hannah, 8, and Michael, 6), New Hampshire:

"My husband and I focus a lot on doing the things we do to help ourselves be and stay healthy: eating well, being active, getting enough sleep, hygiene."

• *Don't be afraid of the word "fat" when it comes to nutrition.* "'Fat' has become a really bad word—like another f-word," Warhaft-Nadler says. "We talk about fat in our diet as a negative, but fat is an essential nutrient. We need it to protect our organs. It makes our nails strong and our skin clear and our hair shiny. It's a *positive* thing. Body-image issues and eating disorders reflect a terrible fear of fat. I had an eating disorder for years, and I was afraid of even healthy fats. I wouldn't eat avocado or olive oil—things that were healthy for me—because they were high in fat. Instead, I would go for foods that were sugar-free, fat-free, full of chemicals and unhealthy, because they were fat-free. They were bad for me, but I was so afraid of 'fat' that I thought fat-free was better. And that's how we're conditioned: 'Fat is bad.' We need to bring it into our lives in a positive way."

- *Put down the magazines and look for photos of real women online.* While working on your own body esteem, it might help to peruse online image collections like Mybodygallery.com and The Fourth Trimester Bodies Project. They are enlightening. They share photos of real women of all shapes and sizes. The former's goal is to help us see "what real women look like." The latter's goal is "embracing the beauty inherent in the changes brought to our bodies by motherhood, childbirth, and breastfeeding."

- *Focus on your best features.* What do you love about your body? Talk about your best features in front of your children.

- *Want to be really radical? Throw away the scale.* Gruver threw away her scale before her daughters turned five, and despite the shocked reactions from incredulous family and friends, she never looked back. "I did not want my daughters to see me using it as a way to measure myself—and I didn't want them using it, either. Just getting rid of it was easier."

DADS AND BODY IMAGE

In this chapter I've emphasized the connection between the body images of moms and their daughters, and although Tip 1 is specifically for moms, the rest of the tips in this chapter are of equal relevance to moms and dads. It's important to remember that dads' words and deeds shape their daughters' body images and self-esteem, too.

Children notice how their fathers talk about their own bodies and their attitudes toward food and healthy activities such as exercise. They also notice their fathers' attitudes toward women's bodies. Therefore, as a dad, it's important for you to make it clear to your daughter that you value women for much more than simply their appearances. In doing so, you can contradict the message girls receive from the surrounding culture that physical appearance is the most important attribute of a girl or woman.

In *Father Hunger: Fathers, Daughters, and the Pursuit of Thinness*, Margo Maine, PhD offers many suggestions to fathers who want to help their daughters develop healthy body images. For example:

- Don't discuss women's bodies around your daughters. Think a woman is fat? Think she's gorgeous? Keep a lid on those thoughts for your daughter's sake. You may not realize it, but your comments about women's bodies and appearances send a powerful message to your daughters.
- Demonstrate admiration for the achievements of real women. Talk about how much you admire their accomplishments (in arenas that have nothing to do with physical beauty).
- Be respectful toward women of all sizes. If you notice fat-shaming, call it out. Make it clear that beauty is found within.
- Call out men around you who make comments that objectify women or sexist remarks.

- Think about starting with the dad in the mirror. How is your own body image? Being kind to yourself shows your daughter how to be kind to herself regarding her own body, too.

  For more suggestions, see the list of items for further reading at the end of this chapter. In the list, you'll find books and articles that are written specifically for fathers.

TIP 2: NO APPEARANCE SHAMING. BE KIND ABOUT OTHER PEOPLE, TOO

Children are quick studies. If your kids see or hear you judging the way others look—from friends and family to celebrities on-screen—they will quickly learn that appearance does matter, that you value how people look, no matter what else you are doing to teach them otherwise. So be kind to others and put a moratorium on gabbing about how other people look.

Gruver recalls growing up in a family that put a lot of focus on women's appearances, as did her husband. She said that all the talk about how people looked, and how thin they were (or weren't), impacted her personally in negative ways. "When my girls were young, my husband and I agreed to never again make comments about other people's appearances or weight, even to each other. We realized we had a very skewed mind-set from the way we were raised," she explained, "and we needed to break that cycle. They now have far healthier relationships with food than I did at their age."

Amy (mom to Carter, 7, and Samantha, 5), Massachusetts:

"In our home, my husband and I show our kids how to make

thoughtful food and activity choices by going to farmers markets and exercising regularly. But we try to never criticize choices others make, as we want them to realize priorities depend on very specific circumstances. People eat all sorts of food. People do all sorts of things with their bodies. It's not a good-and-evil distinction. Live and let live."

Katha (mom to Gabriella, 4, and Harrison, 1), New York:

"I don't criticize my body or anyone else's body in front of her. She knows because she has been told that people come in all shapes and sizes, and that's okay. We're active as a family but don't connect activity to weight or body image."

TIP 3: SUPPORT AND PRAISE YOUR DAUGHTER'S INTERESTS AND ABILITIES

Want to raise a daughter who isn't obsessed with her appearance? Give her plenty of other things to focus on. Make it utterly clear that you value her for her interests and abilities. Help her grow as a musician or athlete.

"It's really important to get your kids involved in *something*," Warhaft-Nadler says. "Everybody has something special about themselves—everybody. And as parents, it's our job to help kids figure out what that is. Nothing feels better than doing something that you love and that you're good at. And everybody has something, whether it's music or sports or dance or writing. Expose your kids to everything. Support them in figuring out what they like. When you feel good about who you are and what you can do, it puts a lot less pressure about how you look."

Warhaft-Nadler speaks to the importance of developing strong interests from her own early struggles with an eating disorder. "When I went through my issues, I didn't feel that I was smart enough, that I was interesting enough, that I was funny enough. I wasn't anything *enough*. So I thought, I'd better damned well be skinny enough and pretty enough, because I had nothing else. When I got older, I realized there was more to me than how I looked. It didn't take everything over anymore and keep me from living my life. With today's kids, it's become so big that they don't even know to look inside for something else. It's such an important thing to help your kid find that spark!"

Mayer agrees. "We can look toward our children's strengths and really build those strengths. If we give them enough diversity in their experiences, they can feel good about more aspects of themselves."

TIP 4: IT *IS* OKAY TO PRAISE YOUR DAUGHTER'S APPEARANCE! JUST BE CAREFUL HOW YOU DO IT, AND BE SURE TO BALANCE WITH OTHER FORMS OF PRAISE

Despite all the other things we've discussed in this chapter, you probably *do* value how beautiful your children are. That's okay! There's nothing wrong with admiring our children's appearances. It's as natural as their admiration for us. In fact, as parents, we're hardwired to admire our children from the day they are born. (Think of how hard it is for new parents to take their eyes off their baby.) It's okay to tell your daughter she's beautiful. Our children *are* beautiful, and it's a normal impulse to want to share these loving feelings with them.

The problem arises when girls receive the message that their appearance is *the* most important thing about them. So, be sure to praise her appearance in moderation, balanced out with praise for all the other terrific things about her—her interests, skills, abilities, and so on.

One helpful tactic: Make your compliments about how she looks *more* than just about how she looks.

"When parents talk about their children's appearance," Mayer suggests, "they should do so in very specific ways that are about the child's interests and choices. For example 'I love the color you chose for your shirt' makes the compliment about who the child is."

Pop Culture Coaching, Step 2: Establish a Healthy Media Diet

In the media, it's really difficult to find images of girls and women that don't perpetuate the Pretty Princess Mandate. But as a parent, you can do your best to direct your child to alternative images, even if that means looking beyond mainstream media.

TIP 5: DIVERSIFY! OFFER YOUR DAUGHTER LOTS OF ALTERNATIVE IMAGES OF GIRLS AND WOMEN, AND TEACH HER THAT NO ONE IS PERFECT

Present your daughter with images of diverse images of girls and women. Girls need to see that girls and women come in all shapes, sizes, and colors—not just those dished up and idealized by the media. Mayer argues that the lack of diversity in media culture is a major problem for girls.

"Princesses teach little girls to idealize thinness. They don't have a big princess, do they?" Mayer asks rhetorically. "That gives girls the perception that they should want to be like that—a *little* princess. This is really dangerous in our world. Little girls want to emulate what they consider perfect, and a princess is perfect to them. The image of a princess as a skinny, magical, beautiful woman is not healthy for any young girl to emulate."

Day adds, "Princesses really should be one item on the menu along with other things. When a child plays princess 24/7, it is going to have the effect of turning her very appearance conscious and passive. Parents shouldn't feel like people are harshly saying to them, 'No, no, no. No princess.' Diverse play experiences are important."

Emulating princess perfection, Gruver adds, can cause girls to limit their ideas of who they are, what they can do, and what's possible for them in life. "Perfectionism limits the level of risk girls are willing to take," Gruver explains. "Perfection is essentially something that is static and doesn't change. It's not something that is alive and growing! Wanting to be perfect can be totally disabling. Girls can come to feel they can't do *anything* because they can't do it *perfectly*."

"Whether its princesses or Barbies or any kind of doll or figure, if it's not diversified, it's *dangerous*," Mayer says. "We need more diversified skin colors, more diversified body sizes."

- *Show your children what real princesses look like.* "You can go online with your daughter and look at images of all the real princesses in the world," Mayer suggests. "They're not all gorgeous. You can bring some reality to your child. Teach them that the way toy companies have developed the idea of the princess is not how reality is. There are many, many real princesses in our world, and they're from many different countries." You could even make a collage together featuring images of real princesses, past and present.
- *Buy diverse dolls for your children.* Make sure your daughters have dolls that look like them—as well as dolls that don't look like them. Mayer says, "As much as possible, get diversified dolls for your kids. That would be helpful. Do you bring home more

diversity to your children?" And if you can find dolls that don't have an exaggeratedly thin body type—like the Disney Princess Animators' Collection dolls, the Go! Go! Sports Girls dolls, the Groovie Girls dolls, and the Lottie dolls, which are modeled after the proportions of an average nine-year-old girl? Buy those, too.

- *For a compassionate reality check, admire family photos together.* Do you have photos of your extended family or of grandparents, great-grandparents, and so on? Exploring family photo albums together can give your children a much different outlook than what they get from dolls, magazines, and television. Conversations around photos of beloved family members can help your daughter consciously understand that her genetics play a substantial role in her appearance—everything from skin tone to eye color and size to hair texture to body shape—and that this is something to be proud of. While looking at family photos, in a loving way, you might talk about who looks like whom. Warhaft-Nadler explains, "Kids have to realize that your body is your body. Thanks to genetics, there are certain things you can change, and certain things you can't." Owning your heritage can be empowering.

- *Seek out real-life role models from your community as a counterpoint to popular culture.* For example, "take your girls to your local fire station or police station," Warhaft-Nadler suggests. "If you're expecting to see firefighters who look like the men and women who play firefighters on TV, brace yourself! They don't look like that. They're in all shapes, sizes, and colors. Let kids can see what real people look like who are doing amazing things—that they look just like regular people. It reaffirms that they can be special, too, and they don't have to look a certain way."

- *For another compassionate reality check, go people-watching together.* Talk about how wonderful and interesting it is that we *don't* all look the same. Warhaft-Nadler explains: "One of my favorite things to do is to go to a mall with my child and say, 'Let's stop for a minute. Let's watch all the people going by. We really all do look so different.' We really do! It's amazing when you see that people come in so many different shapes and forms—but we forget that, because we're so used to seeing one size, one type of beauty that's acceptable. It's amazing!"

Sandra (mom to Miranda, age 3), Massachusetts:

"I try to excite my daughter about differences between people. I tell her there are so many ways people can look, and they are all good in one way or another."

- *Fight back against perfectionism.* Gruver says that she finds the saying "Excellence is not perfection" to be quite helpful. Remind your daughter that she doesn't have to be perfect—that, in fact, no one can be. You can also help your child develop a more flexible mind-set by introducing new things into her life. "Parents can change up their daughters' routines, change up the things their daughters eat," Gruver says. Encourage your girl to try things out and see how they are. Don't expect her to like all of them, or to feel like she's good at everything she tries doing—but let her know that it's worth trying.
- *Watch women's sports together.* See what strong women who use

their bodies to engage in physical activities really look like. Top athletes are in peak physical shape—but they often have body types that are quite different from those of models, celebrities, and cartoon girls. Make it clear that these are great examples of what it means for a woman to be strong and fit. And if your daughter expresses any interest in trying a new sport herself, help her to do so! Sports participation is widely recognized as a terrific way for girls to develop healthy body images and self-esteem—and therefore a great antidote to the problem of our culture's beauty ideal.

TIP 6: READ BOOKS TOGETHER THAT EMPHASIZE DIVERSE BODIES AND NURTURE A HEALTHY SELF-ESTEEM
Ages Three to Five

It's Okay to Be Different by Todd Parr. Bold, silly scenes encourage children to accept and celebrate the differences between people.

A Rainbow of Friends by P. K. Hallinan. A book about the value of friendships with people of all races, sizes, and abilities. Our differences make us special.

Shades of People by Shelley Rotner and Sheila Kelly. Vibrant photographs of happy children with a wide range of different skin tones.

We're Different, We're The Same (Sesame Street) by Bobbi Kates and Joe Matieu. This book shows diversity in race and body types but underscores that despite these differences, we all have a lot in common.

What Is Beautiful? by Maryjean Avery and David Avery. This picture book has one sentence per page describing what is beautiful about the person illustrated—showing that beauty can be found in every person, regardless of gender, age, or race. A mirror on the last page reflects the child's own image back at him or her.

Ages Four to Eight

Grandma Has Wings by Mary Murray Bosrock. An older woman has soft, squishy arms. Her six granddaughters learn an exciting secret: Grandma's arms are wings! A warm message about body image, self-acceptance, and the way older family members can be positive role models for young girls.

I Like Myself! by Karen Beaumont. This book is about an African American girl who has great self-esteem. It encourages children to like everything about themselves, inside and out, with engaging silliness and humor.

Impatient Pamela Asks: Why Are My Feet So Huge? by Mary Koski. Pamela thinks her feet are too big until she realizes how useful they are. She learns that what she can do is more important than how she looks.

Shaped with Love by Megan Osborne. A Christian counselor's approach to teaching children that everyone is shaped differently.

Shapesville by Andy Mills, Becky Osborn, and Erica Neitz. This picture book features five friends of different shapes, sizes, and colors. Readers learn that talents and interests are more important than appearance.

Pop Culture Coaching, Step 3: Watch and Talk about Media Content with Your Kids

Studies show that when mothers instruct their daughters on media content, their daughters are less likely to sexualize themselves; and, conversely, they are more likely to have better critical-viewing skills, better body esteem, and better self-esteem. So, it's important to discuss aspects of the Pretty Princess Mandate when they show up onscreen. Explain what's realistic and healthy, and explain what's not.

TIP 7: TALK WITH YOUR CHILDREN ABOUT THE BEAUTY IDEAL FOUND IN MEDIA AND POP CULTURE

Use your best pop culture coaching techniques to talk with your children about what you see on television, in apps, in toys, and beyond. Warhaft-Nadler has been talking back at the screen for her children's benefit for years. "Ever since my kids were little, when I would see a weight-loss ad on TV, I would say something to voice my opinion. That way, they would hear my messages. We don't always recognize it, but it really does sink in."

- *Is a story in a book, film, app, or TV program emphasizing a character's appearance? Call it out.* "I wonder why it's so important to Gaston to marry whomever he thinks is the most beautiful girl in town. He hardly even knows Belle. There's so much more to her than how she looks!" "It's too bad this Disney Fairies app is only about fashion. Doesn't Tinker Bell like to fix things, too?"
- *Are commercials hawking weight-loss regimens? Talk back.* "Ugh, so many commercials try to trick people into thinking they'd be happier if they weighed less. They're really after their money. I'm glad we are happy the way we are!"
- *Is your daughter interested in dolls that are unhealthily thin?* Let her know your concerns. "That doll is extremely thin. If she were a real person, do you think she could be that size and still be healthy?"

Mayer also advocates for arming children with facts about the unhealthy dieting and beauty practices that the media glorifies. Mayer offers the show *The Biggest Loser* as an example. "If a kid is watching *The Biggest Loser*, I would say, 'Do you understand what's really going on here? First of all, I know for a fact that people on *The Biggest Loser* have ended up getting eating disorders. And even though they promote this show for the masses,'" she adds, "'losing that amount of weight can be very dangerous. Do you know that?'" By giving young viewers facts about that level of weight loss, parents can provide a dose of reality in response to an unrealistic "reality" program.

- *Want to contradict a show's unhealthy messages? Google is your friend.* If something about a show is bothering you, and you want to provide counter-messages to your children, remember: you can always look up the facts.

Pop Culture Coaching, Step 4: Teach Children about Media Creation

An important part of pop culture coaching is teaching our children how media are created. If children understand authorship—that media are created by people—they can understand that *choices* were made about what types of female bodies to show in the media.

TIP 8: TEACH YOUR CHILDREN HOW THE BEAUTY IMAGES IN POP CULTURE ARE CREATED.

The female bodies shown in the media are often pure fantasy. Even when they appear to be images of real people, they've been heavily edited. When it comes to images of beauty, the Internet provides us with many opportunities to learn about *image editing* and to share that knowledge with our children.

Introduce your kids to the tricks of the trade. Go online and peruse professional Photoshop portfolios (for example, www.gregapodaca. com/portfolio/before-apple/), or look at image galleries of celebrities before and after they've been altered with Photoshop (like www.chill outpoint.com/misc/celebrities-before-and-after-photoshop.html).

After you've found some images that you feel are age-appropriate (images of celebrities can be risqué, of course), share them with your children. Let them know that Photoshop isn't just about brightening teeth and removing freckles—it's used to entirely change the shape of women's faces and bodies, too.

Warhaft-Nadler demonstrates the extremes of professional photo retouching to children regularly in workshops. Kids are invariably amazed by what she shows them—which tells her that even though our kids may be tech savvy, there's a lot they don't know.

"What's amazing is that even at the high school level, where the kids learn Photoshop in class, the kids think Photoshop is just about retouching wrinkles and cellulite," Warhaft-Nadler explains. "They don't realize that sometimes, they actually take one person's head and put it on a different person's body. The kids are blown away by that. One girl a couple months ago was *mad*. She said, 'So we're basically being brainwashed! Everybody has to know about this!'" Warhaft-Nadler replied, "That's why I'm here."

BONUS TIP FOR RAISING SONS: HELP OUR SONS TO UNDERSTAND THAT GIRLS ARE MORE THAN JUST PRETTY

Helping girls become resilient to the Pretty Princess Mandate is important, but only one piece of the puzzle. Our sons need to be raised to respect girls, as well—to understand that how girls are portrayed by the media is damaging and disgusting.

Let your sons know that it's not okay to comment on girls' bodies in either positive or negative ways. Praise from boys sets girls up in a feedback loop, in which their body esteem is to some extent dependent on what boys say about them—and this is unhealthy.

Boys' negative judgments can have a lasting impact, as well. Day recalls, "In seventh grade, a boy said to me, 'You're a pirate's dream—a sunken chest.' I was devastated for months!"

We must teach our sons compassion for girls' situations. We can help them understand that girls' obsessions with their appearances—and, when they get older, their self-sexualization—is prompted by a toxic culture, one that teaches girls their whole value is based on their beauty. Boys need to understand that this is a lie—that girls are so much more than the way they look, and that there are many valid ways of being a girl. We must teach our sons to always respect girls—to regard them as complex human beings, too.

For Further Reading

101 Ways to Help Your Daughter Love Her Body by Brenda Lane Richardson and Elane Rehr.

The Body Image Survival Guide for Parents: Helping Toddlers, Tweens, and Teens Thrive by Marci Warhaft-Nadler.

Dads and Daughters: How to Inspire, Understand, and Support Your Daughter by Joe Kelly.

Father Hunger: Fathers, Daughters, and the Pursuit of Thinness by Margo Maine.

"How to Talk to Little Girls" by Lisa Bloom. *Huffington Post.* www.huffingtonpost.com/lisa-bloom/how-to-talk-to-little-gir_b_882510.html.

Good Girls Don't Get Fat: How Weight Obsession Is Messing Up Our Girls and How We Can Help Them Thrive Despite It by Robyn Silverman.

"Habits of Body-Positive Dads: How Fathers Influence Body Image" by August McLaughlin. *The National Eating Disorders Association.* www.nationaleatingdisorders.org/habits-body-positive-dads-how-fathers-influence-body-image.

Her Next Chapter: How Mother-Daughter Book Clubs Can Help Girls Navigate Malicious Media, Risky Relationships, Girl Gossip, and So Much More by Lori Day with Charlotte Kugler.

How to Say It to Girls: Communicating with Your Growing Daughter by Nancy Gruver.

Real Kids Come in All Sizes: Ten Essential Lessons to Build Your Child's Body Esteem by Kathy Kater.

"Talking to Your Daughter About Beauty" by Emily Heist Moss. *The Good Men Project.* goodmenproject.com/families/talking-to-your-daughter-about-beauty/.

So Sexy So Soon: The New Sexualized Childhood and What Parents Can Do to Protect Their Kids by Diane Levin and Jean Kilbourne.

CHAPTER FIVE

The Problem with Gender Stereotypes

A t the age of two, Caoimhe (pronounced "Keeva") became acquainted with the Disney Princesses—and she quickly came to favor princess over all other types of play. "It just captivated her," her mother, Mary Finucane, explains. "Especially the older, really exaggerated princesses, like Snow White and Cinderella."

One day, Finucane realized something: Caoimhe's play was changing. "Her play went from leaping over our couches and climbing on things, being very rambunctious, to sitting on the bottom step of our staircase," Finucane recalls. "I'd just be walking through the house, and I'd find her sitting there for several minutes at a time with her hands in her lap, very patient. I had never seen anything like it before, and when I asked her what she was doing, she said, 'I'm waiting for my prince.'"

Now, some parents might be thrilled to see a previously rambunctious child play quietly. But Finucane is a psychotherapist with professional training in play therapy, and she knew that watching a child play is the best way to learn about a child's worldview. When she witnessed her daughter's play change so dramatically, it was a red flag. Caoimhe was playing at stereotypical princess passivity, which didn't seem normal or healthy to her mother.

Finucane decided to chronicle her quest to reclaim Caoimhe's imagination "after it was hijacked by Disney Princesses" by creating a blog called *Disney Princess Recovery* (disneyprincessrecovery.blogspot .com).

Other parents have made similar observations. For example, Maureen (mom of three children in central Massachusetts) observes, "What bothers me most about the princess role is how it shapes pretend play. So much of a princess's role is about rescue. 'Someone is going to help me; someone is going to do something for me.' Not 'I'm taking charge of my life.'

"And boys' pretend play is all about rescuing somebody and being in charge," she adds. "It certainly is at my house. And for girls, it's so much more passive. I don't think that is okay."

Alexis (mom of Addie, age six, in Maryland) had the same concerns—but when she tried to help her daughter diverge from the passive princess script, Addie just dug in her heels. "I was staying home with her at the time, so we kind of had endless time for princess play. But when we were playing princess, Addie would wait and wait for the prince. So one day, I said, 'Well, how can you save yourself?' She didn't like that at all, because I wasn't following the story."

Not all girls who play princess are rigidly passive. Some girls wear princess dresses and run around excitedly. Others use their princess dolls to imagine fun adventures. But when girls fixate on passive types of play, parents are right to feel concerned.

The Passive Princess Problem

When girls focus on passivity, they miss out on other styles of play that psychologically benefit children. Experts argue that rough-and-tumble play shouldn't just be for boys. It actually enables girls to feel "stronger as individuals and therefore less at the mercy of peer approval and matters of appearance and dress"—an important point, given what we learned about the consequences of the Pretty Princess Mandate in Chapter 4.

Moreover, modern princess culture's encouragement of passivity is part of an ongoing, well-documented problem with children's media. The media have usually cast girls in one of two narrative clichés: princesses in peril or token females (a lone female in a group of males, like Smurfette). For this reason, Disney's *Frozen* is refreshing. It's a tale of two princesses who are sisters, both of whom have fleshed-out characters, and who ultimately do not need a man to rescue them.

But otherwise, stories about princesses—from Cinderella to Snow White to Princess Peach—have long underscored the presumed weakness of females and implied that helplessness is romantically desirable. These tales reflected the way our society encourages girls to learn dependency and helplessness, believing that a man will someday take care of them. The resulting mind-set is called the Cinderella complex, and it is psychologically unhealthy and limiting. In fact, in the long term, it can be economically detrimental to women.

Many princess stories' unflattering depictions of strong-willed, older, single women double down on these problems. These older women are cruel, heartless, threatening figures who are fixated on preserving their youth and beauty at all cost (like the Queen in *Snow White* or Mother Gothel in *Tangled*) or are determined to snare a man in deceitful ways (like Ursula in *The Little Mermaid*). As such, they serve as cautionary tales. A girl must be sweet and demure and helpless to find her prince, or else she might wind up a hateful, villainous old woman someday. It's marriage or bust.

Perhaps for this reason, traditional princess characters never have female friends. (Until *Frozen*, they didn't even have sisters who were more than window dressing, as was the case with Ariel's sisters in *The Little Mermaid*.) The implied message is that other women—like Cinderella's wicked stepsisters—are competition in the quest to win a prince. So princess culture presents girls not just as waiting for a prince, but as waiting alone—isolated—without the support of maternal figures or female friends.

I asked children's media expert Dafna Lemish, PhD, professor of communication at Southern Illinois University Carbondale and editor of the *Journal of Children and Media*, to expand on how princess culture teaches girls that marriage is the be-all and end-all in life. "The princess narrative is strongly related to the bridal narrative," she explained. "It tells girls that you've reached the peak of your life when you are finally chosen for marriage by your dream love. All you're doing is building up toward this huge ceremony where you're a princess for a day, and you are glorious and beautiful and loved and romanced, and it's as if there's no life after that."

Cyndy Scheibe agreed. "Princesses are constructed in a way that is really narrow and manipulative," she argued. "Princesses have to be beautiful; they have to be passive; they have to be feminine; and their only goal is to find somebody to fall in love with and get married and live happily ever. And it's *not* about what they do; what else they do is not particularly important. It's a very narrow construct of what girls should be."

The fact is that this perspective, if not countered by other types of stories and dreams, can limit girls' aspirations. "In order to have aspirations and expectations for yourself, you have to have options," Lemish noted. "If you close down your options to this one possible narrative of happiness, you're closing off other possibilities. That's one of the major concerns I have with the princess narrative: that it blocks off other options for more productive, more equal paths in life."

Overall, then, the stereotypes that princess culture promotes grate on parents who are well-informed and forward-looking. Modern parents don't want to raise girls who are living, breathing stereotypes. They cringe at the thought of young women hooked on the romance narrative, and reading *Cosmopolitan*'s list of the best and worst colleges for meeting men with interest. Today, countless parents want their daughters to be healthy and empowered, with a sense of identity that does not rely on being in a romantic relationship—and with interesting personal goals beyond getting married.

As Brian, a father of a six-year-old girl in Michigan, put it: "Being a guy, it was when I learned I was having a daughter that all of a sudden, gender became this really big thing for me," he explains. "I thought, 'Nobody had better tell you what you can do or can't do because of your gender. I want you to be a kick-ass little girl, and that means you're going to be inquisitive and questioning—but you can do whatever, *whatever* it is that you want.'"

This was my conclusion after conducting a study of parents' thoughts about princess culture. For this study, my research team (a graduate student, Krista Andberg, and three undergraduates, Morgan Grogan, Jenna Burpee, and Nadine Solomine) and I interviewed fifty-five parents (fifty-three moms and two dads) about princess culture's role in their families' lives. Our conversations usually focused on the Disney Princesses, since that franchise has the widest reach of any princess property.

During our interviews, we asked the parents what they liked about princess culture, including the Disney Princesses, and what they disliked. A pattern quickly emerged. What the parents *disliked* revolved around stereotypical princess behavior and attitudes—being passive, being overly fixated on romance, and so on.

Interestingly, what the parents most often *liked* were examples of bucked stereotypes—princesses displaying intelligence, strength, and self-reliance. Though princess culture teems with regressive stereotypes, proactive behaviors and progressive attitudes are becoming more common in princess characters.

Consider that the earliest princesses (Snow White, Cinderella, and Sleeping Beauty) were victims. Horrible circumstances beyond their control shaped their lives. The Queen wanted Snow White dead; Cinderella's stepmother made her little more than a slave; and Maleficent cast a horrible curse upon Aurora. As a result of the actions of these evil women, the princess characters spent most of their films simply reacting to the situations in which they found themselves, with limited agency, requiring the help of others. Reflecting the attitudes of these princesses' times, their problems were ultimately solved through romance and marriage.

Decades later, in the aftermath of the second wave of feminism in the 1970s, the next generation of princesses (Ariel, Belle, Jasmine) appeared. They were modernized in ways that reflected women's new opportunities in life. Each wanted something more from their world, something different from what they knew. They sought adventure and excitement—and they had more agency than their predecessors. Ariel saved Prince Eric from drowning; Belle saved her father from the Beast; and Jasmine escaped the confines of her palace to see her kingdom firsthand, breaking the rules.

Ultimately, though, each girl's story presented details that give modern viewers pause. For example, Ariel literally gave up her voice; Belle fell in love with a Beast that had abused her; and Jasmine acted as a seductress to distract the villain Jafar. And like their predecessors, all their problems were solved by romance and marriage, rather than any other of the myriad possibilities that life presents to modern women.

In contrast, the heroines of newer Disney Princess films such as *The Princess and the Frog*, *Tangled*, *Brave*, and *Frozen* are more self-directed than the early princesses were. Tiana wanted to run her own restaurant. Rapunzel wanted to leave her tower and see the display of lights that occurs each year on her birthday. Merida wanted to change her future and avoid an arranged marriage. Romance was only an afterthought for Tiana and Rapunzel, and Merida eschewed it entirely. And *Frozen* can be taken as a condemnation of the very concept of true love at first sight—an argument that getting to know the person you plan to marry is an important and healthy part of life.

Taken as a whole, the stories told in princess culture are becoming increasingly modern, moving further from passivity and romance, or least decentralizing it to some extent. Why are parents still concerned, then?

Well, a significant challenge is that the Disney Princesses are marketed as a cohesive unit. Within the brand, old-fashioned, classic princesses like Snow White and Cinderella are on equal (or superior!) footing compared with princesses like Tiana, Rapunzel, Merida, Anna, and Elsa, who bring more modern values to the franchise. So when little girls love princesses, they become exposed to the princess behaviors and attitudes that hearken back to the social norms of the 1930s, '40s, and '50s. And in the princess toys and other products that exist beyond the confines of the screen, princess culture's dial is still set firmly on the "pretty and passive" setting—even for the newest of princesses.

Parents Speak Out

Here's a more detailed rundown of what the parents in our study had to say about the stories told in princess culture.

1. **A lot of parents disliked the message that princesses are passive damsels in distress.**

- "I think the main problem is the passivity of the princesses. A lot of them are placed in a position where they need to be rescued, where they end up in the damsel-in-distress role."
- "There are just so many princesses that are passive. That whole 'a man's going to rescue you' thing just grosses me out."
- "My daughter watches *The Little Mermaid* and the *Barbie Rapunzel* story, and they are both equally annoying to me. It's the same standard story line of the damsel in distress with her zero-inch waistline—she's so, so pretty and it's questionable how smart she is."
- "Why are you waiting for a prince? Why can't you go be the hero of your own adventure? You're a princess. You can do it yourself. I mean, look at Snow White. She's *dead* and the prince comes along and brings her back to life. That's the damaging stuff—waiting for the prince, waiting for the guy to come solve your problems."

2. **Snow White was frequently singled out—for having a story that is especially dated, for being of dubious intelligence, for having a childish voice that grates, and so on.**

- "I can't stand the airheadedness of the princesses that act brainless. Snow White, for me, typifies that. She just seems like she doesn't have any kind of intelligence. She's willing to be led in any direction and doesn't really have the capability to think."
- "Snow White I hate. I think maybe it's just because she was one of the original ones, so she's even more archaic, but—ugh. I can't watch it. I don't like her voice. I don't like how she seems like a little girl. She's just a child, and yet this child is supposed to somehow be old enough to get married to someone that she doesn't even know who rescues her with a kiss."
- "Snow White—what a horrible voice that princess has got."
- "Snow White kind of bothered me just because she was always the victim. She has a lilting voice, and coming into the dwarfs' house and cleaning up after men? You know, that's so stereotypical."

3. **Parents disliked the message that in being rescued by a man, girls can be rewarded with wealth and a life of leisure.**

- "Cinderella's story tells girls, 'If you dream hard enough, you can escape the confines of housework and find a very rich man who has servants. And he can give you his last name and you will be fine.'"
- "Even though my daughter thinks of herself as a princess, I have taught her that she'll be working in life. Things aren't going to be handed to her when she is a grown-up. For me, there's nothing worse than someone who is entitled."

4. **Parents also felt that princess culture portrays relationships in superficial, unhealthy ways (for example, the idea of love at first sight).**

- "The Disney Princesses really push the theme that superficial things are important. I don't want my daughter growing up thinking that her worth is based on how she looks and whether she finds the perfect guy based on how *he* looks in a chance meeting. I want her to understand that real love and romance is based on something deeper and friendship."

- "A lot of what disturbs me is that it portrays Prince Charming as a perfect man with no flaws at all. A relationship is give and take; no one is perfect. You have to take the good with the bad. There is no one out there that's perfect."

5. **One of the most common complaints was about the princesses' subservient, self-sacrificing, unhealthy behaviors.** For parents who want their daughters to someday be strong partners in egalitarian relationships built on both love and mutual respect, the idea that the girl should subordinate herself is off-putting:

- "You very rarely see the prince conform. Because in a real relationship, everyday, a partner makes different decisions. No one is going to *always* agree in a working relationship; it alternates. People give in to the other person. But the princes almost never give in to what the female wants. It's a bad image. That's damaging."

- "I think, 'Long range, what damage is this doing?' The princesses are so shallow. They just want to wear pretty dresses and cook and clean for their man."

- "We got a collection of princess books, and the tip of the iceberg was waiting for the man and all of the stress on outward beauty and being ladylike—which often meant being quiet or being second."
- "With Ariel, the fact that she's willing to trade her voice to marry a prince is not the best message."
- "*Beauty and the Beast* is actually a movie about an abused woman. Most of the time, when people are mean, they don't change. That really sets women up for abusive relationships."

6. **Some parents were concerned that even the modern characters' strength was undercut when they were forced into a romance narrative, either at a film's end or in its sequel.**

- "In *The Princess and the Frog*, the whole narrative was a big letdown. You have this strong, independent princess who is supposed to be a diversion from what we've seen in the past, and then she goes and falls for this total loser."
- "We refuse to buy the second movies because of the weddings. The *Rapunzel* sequel and the *Mulan* sequel where they actually get married? We don't have those."

So, What about the Positives?

Because the parents were concerned about princess culture promoting stereotypical behaviors and beliefs (which many had seen their daughters embrace), what they *liked* the most were the ways Disney's modern princesses buck stereotypes.

Tiana, Rapunzel, and Merida were all described as strong and goal-oriented:

- "I like the way Tiana is portrayed as a strong character."
- "Tiana worked, and she made an effort. She didn't have a goal of marrying a prince; she had a goal of working to accomplish something. And she didn't set out to change another individual or change for him. When they did get married, it was sort of this unexpected thing that happened at the end—and then they showed them in their life afterward doing things together and still being equals."
- "In *The Princess and the Frog*, there's more than just a princess being saved by a prince. I do think newer Disney movies are a lot less reliant on the Snow White kind of story, where a princess makes mistakes and then a boy comes and saves the day."
- "I thought that Tiana from *Princess and the Frog* and Rapunzel from *Tangled* were both strong women that were shown taking care of themselves, or at least trying to take care of themselves. Rapunzel needs a little help, but I thought those were positive attributes. Whereas some of the earlier ones, like Sleeping Beauty and Snow White, don't have many redeeming qualities."
- "What I liked about Rapunzel is that she also had goals. She had things she wanted to do. Her goal was not to get a man. Her goal was to do something for herself."
- "Merida was brave, strong, and independent. She took care of herself. She admitted her mistakes. She took care of her family. She defended those who need defending. I mean, there were so many amazing qualities about her."
- "I love that Merida's plotline doesn't surround her getting married."

A couple of parents singled out Belle for her intelligence, calling her "smart" and "literary," and commenting, "I want that library!"

Interestingly, Mulan—who is included in the Disney Princess franchise even though she is not actually a princess—was praised by a notable number of parents, even though she was not a favorite of their daughters:

- "Mulan is really good. I like that fairy tale. She has to parade as a man to be a warrior to cover for her father, but at least she's strong and brave and tough. She's not a girly girl—that's what I actually like about that character."
- "Mulan, in fact, was actually the only hard-core, cool princess of all the princesses."
- "I like that Mulan struggles with the fact that she's not like other girls, but she comes to realize that who she is is all right. And she accomplishes amazing things with her strength."
- "I think Mulan is a go-to for parents who are feeling like, you know…You might as well take the best of the package and show that one to your kids."

Disney's *Frozen* Is a Blast of Fresh Air

Disney released *Frozen* at the end of 2013, after I had completed my study with parents. At the time of its release, Disney revealed that *Frozen*'s protagonists, princesses Anna and Elsa, were destined to become part of the official Disney Princess brand. This meant that *Frozen* was the first Walt Disney Studios film to be released since Orenstein's *Cinderella Ate My Daughter* hit bookstores in 2011 (remember that Pixar produced *Brave*—and though Disney owns them, it's still a separate studio), prompting a nationwide critique of princess culture.

And judging from *Frozen*'s contents, Disney execs were listening. *Frozen* does a great job of addressing several of the problems that plagued Disney's prior princess films. Although they make no progress regarding the Pretty Princess Mandate—more on that later—*Frozen* does two things really, really well.

First, *Frozen* rejects the ideas that princesses are passive damsels in distress who need men to rescue them. Anna and Elsa are active, dynamic characters with individual personalities. The elegant older sister, Elsa, has magical powers over ice and snow, but as she unwittingly transforms everything she touches into ice, she lives in fear.

While she struggles to gain control over her powers, Elsa retreats from nearly every relationship she has, including that with her sister, Anna. She wishes to keep the powers secret and protect others from accidental harm by them. In contrast, younger sister Anna is effusive, charmingly awkward and quirky, but lonely. Her royal family has cut itself off from the outside world to keep Elsa's powers a secret, and she longs for more human connections. She also longs desperately to reconnect with her sister, whose powers are unknown to her.

As Elsa's powers continue to grow, they spiral out of control and plunge the kingdom of Arendelle into deep winter. Everyone but Anna misunderstands Elsa and believes she cursed the kingdom. They don't realize it was an accident. (In a different Disney film, Elsa could easily have been cast as a villain for this. In fact, this was Disney's original plan for the character.)

Elsa flees into the mountains. When the sisters eventually find themselves in a perilous situation with both of their lives on the line, Anna's selfless actions—driven by a sisterly love never previously depicted in a Disney Princess film—save both Elsa and herself.

Second, *Frozen* deliberately undercuts the unhealthy romance narrative of true love at first sight. Early in the film, Anna meets handsome Prince Hans, who visits from a neighboring kingdom on the occasion of Elsa's coronation. Because she is so lonely, she falls for him quickly. She even agrees to marry him on the day they first meet!

In the typical princess story, love at first sight is presented as dreamily romantic. But in *Frozen*, Anna's dedication to it is called into question twice: first by her sister, Elsa, who—horrified—tells Anna, "You can't marry a man you just met," and then by her new acquaintance Kristoff, a young mountain man, who is flabbergasted.

He says, "Wait, you got engaged to someone you just met that day? Didn't your parents ever warn you about strangers?" After asking her some questions about Hans to drive home the point that she really doesn't know much about him, Kristoff states outright that he doesn't trust her judgment because of this—then asks again: "Who marries a man they just met?"

By the film's end, Anna needs an act of true love to save her from a curse that Elsa accidentally placed upon her, freezing her heart, but when she approaches Hans for a kiss, she discovers that he was only using her to gain power in her kingdom. He scoffs at her, saying: "You were so desperate for love, you were willing to marry me, just like that!" and leaves her to die—proving the points that Elsa and Kristoff had made to Anna. And so this sets the stage for what happens next: Anna's act of love for Elsa saves both of the sisters, as I mentioned above.

This made the film a winner in the eyes of many parents. One pleased mom told me, "I liked that they made fun of the concept of meet, fall in love, and get engaged on the same day." And as a Disney Store employee revealed to me, "Every mother I have talked to loves that the plot doesn't have to do with a love interest. And moms love the sister connection," she added.

It was a real positive, then, that romance didn't concern Elsa in any way. As another parent explained to me: "I did like that Elsa not only had no love interest, but her lack of a love interest wasn't important to the plot, either."

Some parents are still critical, however, and raise an interesting, valid point. Couldn't the film have eschewed romance entirely? One mom who offered me this opinion argued: "I am just so frustrated with Disney that there always has to be a love interest. You could have removed the love interest and ended up with the same, or a stronger, message. Stop already."

In discussing these positive attributes of *Frozen*, something about its director is worthy of mentioning. A woman, Jennifer Lee, codirected the film. This marks the first time in Disney's history that a woman received directing credit on a feature-length Disney animated film (of which there are now fifty-three). According to the *Los Angeles Times*, Lee helped break *Frozen* out of the one-leading-girl-only rut found in the rest of the Disney Princess films.

After joining the team, Lee quickly had an impact on the sister story line, which hadn't been in previous iterations of the film, according to visual development artist Brittney Lee. "As soon as Jen came on, I suddenly saw my sister and me in the sisters," Brittney Lee said. "I recognized these two are real girls. Once a female perspective was present in the writing, it was so much easier to get behind it."

Jennifer Lee said she attempted to humanize Anna, who may be the first Disney princess to have gas.

Of course, not everyone was happy with *Frozen*'s disruptions to the typical princess script. Media critic Akash Nicholas, writing for the *Atlantic*, offered a rather strange argument that *Frozen* was wrong to challenge the standard Prince Charming story line because doing so "shames" young girls' fantasies. And according to my source at the Disney Store, a little boy approached him in the store one day with a complaint. "He didn't like that a girl saved the day," my source explained, "and he said that it should have been a guy who saved the day at the end of the movie. I told him that girls need to stand up for themselves, too, but he was unconvinced."

Furthermore, as I mentioned earlier, the film did fail to redress the Pretty Princess Mandate. The princesses' appearances were so over-the-top stereotypical that many parents and critics were exasperated. Writing for *Slate*, Amanda Marcotte complained that Elsa and Anna's eyes were larger than their wrists, and *Boston Globe* columnist Joanna Weiss lamented (while quoting me on the matter):

> *In a movie with stunning artwork, the guys are original creations, with varied shapes and varied personalities to match. In contrast, the princesses are standard-issue Disney, from their flowing hair to their pinched-in waists to their tiny pug noses ("vestigial at best," in the words of my friend Rebecca Hains, who teaches media studies at Salem State). [...] At this point, I'd prefer a disempowered female lead who at least didn't look like a human version of Bambi.*

While I don't agree with Weiss that a disempowered female lead would be preferable, a lot of parents agree with our mutual assessments of Anna and Elsa's looks. One mom complained to me, "Even when Elsa and Anna were tween-ish, they had huge chests and tiny waists." Another pointed out, "I didn't like when the girl turns into the frost princess and her dress becomes lower cut and has a higher slit in the skirt. Why did she need to become über sexy?"

Artist David Trumble agreed. He has given a lot of thought to the stereotypical appearances of Disney Princesses. He once created a satirical set of cartoons on the subject, redesigning powerful women like Hillary Clinton and Rosa Parks in Disney Princess style, and the project became a viral Internet sensation in 2013. (You can see his art and read my interview with him about his project on my blog, at rebeccahains.wordpress.com/2013/11/04/role-models-reimagined/.)

"The only thing I would say about the reveal of Frost Queen Elsa," Trumble told me, "is that it's hard for me to imagine a girl celebrating finally being free and unrestricted by getting *into* high heels. The thing that bugged me about that 'transformation' was that she went from a traditional symbol of female objectification (buttoned-down corset and tied-back hair) to a modern symbol of the exact same thing (the beauty pageant winner with the red lipstick, sparkly low-cut dress, and high heels). Essentially she swapped one cage for…another cage."

Trumble added, "If it were me, she'd have been barefoot, with a similar dress but less leg, easier to move in, and her hair would be wild and unfettered. She'd be naturalized, wilder…and that can *also* be sexy! That's the weirdest thing: a less contrived way of making her look free and uninhibited does *not* mean she won't be unappealing."

Media critic Amy Jussel, a former writer, producer, and creative director who is now the executive director of Shaping Youth (shapingyouth.org), agreed. "The transformation of Elsa landed on me as a predictable segue of extremes," she explained on her blog, "transitioning from being covered up head to toe in a Puritan fashion statement to protect her powerful persona, to emerging as a loosened-up, smokin' hot, sexy, off-the-shoulder sparkling-gown femme fatale. I found myself thinking, *Was that really necessary?*

"Why do we need to impart to five-year-olds that sheroes

transform into 'hotties' with come-hither Mae West struts, perfect figures, and tumble-down long tresses," Jussel added, "especially when body-image bias and dissatisfaction are surfacing in preschoolers?"

Other than these issues, however, *Frozen* represents some great progress for Disney. By undoing the idea that princesses are passive people who cannot be heroes in their own right, and by disrupting the dominance of the romance narrative in princess media, Disney's *Frozen* is a great choice for girls.

> Parents: You can use pop culture coaching techniques to help your daughters focus on the positive aspects of *Frozen* and think critically about the role of the Pretty Princess Mandate within it. Check out the parent-child discussion guide for *Frozen* in the section Talking about Princess Films.

Lost in Translation: Strong Princesses in the Marketplace

Unfortunately, the best aspects of princesses' stories—those that the parents we interviewed praised—are often lost in the marketplace. When the princesses get translated into toys, clothing, and other products, they are split off from their story lines. The princesses are presented in a more uniform way: glamorously decked out in their fanciest dresses and accessories. In other words, the progressive content found on-screen is often undercut by the merchandising. The products based on the movies are almost always about beauty and romance, to the exclusion of other attributes.

For example, the fact that Mulan is a war hero is inspiring, but it is literally impossible to find Mulan dolls wearing the battle armor in which she spends most of her movie. Instead, she's always in the *hanfu* (Chinese dress) that she was uncomfortable in during the scene with the matchmaker.

As one mom complained, "I scoured Disney World to find a Mulan doll that is actually in her soldier outfit, but I couldn't find one anywhere. And my daughter is well aware that Mulan didn't like her bride's outfit—but that's the only way she's ever dressed."

Likewise, the fact that Belle reads a lot is great—but do any of the toy manufacturers sell a "Belle's Library Set"? No.

Instead, they sell a Disney Princess Make Up Center with five separate palettes—one each for Belle and four other princesses. You can also buy Belle-branded products including tiaras, magic wands, purses, tea sets, and toy cell phones.

In fact, what happens in the marketplace is this: the newer Disney Princesses, who usually are improvements in some ways over their predecessors, are redesigned to fit in with the line of princesses that came before them in the collection. The Disney Princess *brand* is held in a higher position than any of the individual princesses' stories and unique characteristics, because as a brand, Disney Princess is worth far more than the sum of its parts.

This branding logic means that the Mulan doll *must* wear that dress, because otherwise, she won't fit in with the other princesses. Imagine one girl in armor, surrounded by girls in ball gowns. The parents I spoke with might find this brilliant, but from a marketing standpoint, it would never do. A brand needs a cohesive identity—one that is readily identifiable. And the Princess brand is all about glitz and glamour, regardless of the stories.

The logic of the Disney Princess brand has also meant trouble for products based on Merida of *Brave*.

Brave presents Merida as a natural, unruly beauty, with wild red curls and no makeup. Her appearance suits her character as a girl who will not be constrained—who prefers to run free through the wilds of Scotland on horseback with her bow and arrow than to engage in princess-like pursuits.

When *Brave* debuted, Merida dolls were available from two sources: the Disney Store and Mattel. The Disney Store's Merida dolls featured Merida in the dark-hued outfit and cape that she wore in the wilderness. Her pose was strong and powerful—ready to wield the bow and arrow she carried in her hands. Although most Disney Store dolls wear a lot of eye makeup, the Merida doll's designer used a light touch around the eyes. She also displayed a crooked smile, rather than a stereotypically demure and pretty one.

But the Mattel dolls—which were more widely available through multiple retailers, such as Target and Toys R Us—were an entirely different story. Completely ignoring the movie's plot, Mattel glammed Merida up with incredibly long eyelashes, impeccably groomed eyebrows, rosebud lips, a gentle expression, and dainty body language. They also dressed Merida in the light blue dress that, in the movie, she is depicted as hating for constraining her movements.

Even more incongruously, one of Mattel's Merida dolls was a "Gem Styling Merida Doll." Although this doll carried her bow and arrow, she also came with a vibrant floral cape over her blue dress and sparkly gems. The gems were meant as decorations for Merida's hair and outfit. Fun for girls, to be sure—but a complete break with the character. Go online and compare these dolls to any image of Merida from the film or its publicity materials, and you'll see that Mattel feminized Merida, making her much more stereotypically girly and much more conventionally beautiful than she is in the film—totally in line with the passive princess type.

Redesigning Merida: *Et Tu*, Disney?

Unfortunately, a year later, in May 2013, Disney's Consumer Product Division also feminized and weakened Merida. On the eve of Merida's "coronation"—her official induction into the Disney Princess lineup—Disney released a 2D version of Merida that fit stylistically with that of her princess peers. This 2D version would be found on new products featuring Merida grouped with other princesses.

But Disney's 2D version of Merida didn't really look much like the computer-animated (CGI) version or even the doll that had been available in the Disney Store for the past year. Instead, the new cartoon version of Merida glammed her up and feminized her so much that parents and critics referred to her as "Sexy Merida."

Compared with her film counterpart, Sexy Merida was slimmer and bustier. She wore makeup, and her hair's characteristic wildness was gone: It looked volumized and restyled with a softer texture. Furthermore, she was missing her signature bow, arrow, and quiver, and she wore a sparkly, off-the-shoulder gown. (As Orenstein noted when she broke the news of the redesign, "Moms tell me all the time that their preschool daughters are pitching fits and destroying their T-shirts because 'princesses don't cover their shoulders.'" As you know from Chapter 4, I've heard the same.)

Now, it bears mentioning that Disney has been routinely redesigning its older princesses, as well. Visit the Disney Princess website and you'll see an updated Cinderella who bears a striking resemblance to pop star Taylor Swift; a Belle whose hair is tousled and who has a come-hither gaze; a Mulan whose hair has been volumized and who appears to wear heavy makeup; and so on. Their appearances are tweaked every year or so and always made to work together as an ensemble. The redesigns emphasize commonalities between the princesses—beautiful hair, beautiful eyes, beautiful clothes, and sparkles (oh, my, *so* much glitter)—rather than celebrating their differences.

But Merida is a different kind of princess, embraced by a certain set of parents as a more worthy role model for girls than her predecessors. *Brave* garnered positive publicity for depicting a princess who wasn't all about beauty and romance. The movie is actually a tale about a mother-daughter relationship—a rare thing in today's media. And unlike all the other Disney Princesses, Merida was created by a woman, Brenda Chapman, who also directed *Brave*. Working with her own five-year-old daughter in mind, Chapman intended Merida to be an alternative kind of princess—one who "breaks the mold."

As a result, when Disney Consumer Products Division redesigned Merida into a princess that *fits* the mold, a tremendous backlash arose from parents. More than 250,000 people signed a petition created by A Mighty Girl, a pro-girl shopping site and blog, asking Disney to withdraw the new Merida. The petition stated, in part:

> *We write to you on behalf of all the young girls who embraced Merida as a role model, who learned from her that they too could go off on an adventure and save the day, that it's not how you look that matters but who you are. For them and for all the children—both girls and boys—who benefit from seeing depictions of strong, courageous, and independent-minded girls and women that are so scarce in animated movies, we ask you to return to the original Merida that we all know and love.*

When Disney execs responded to the petition, they dismissed these concerns, saying the redesign had been "blown out of proportion."

According to Disney fan site Inside the Magic, which obtained an exclusive interview with Disney execs:

> [Disney] had no intention of changing who Merida is. [...] They noted Disney uses different styles of art on characters regularly, changing them to fit their needs at the time.
>
> And in this case, that time was the coronation. Noting that Merida wanted to "dress up" for her coronation ceremony, the new 2D artwork was created, first debuting on the official invitation that was sent out to the media.

When I read this, my immediate thought was: What a disingenuous response. Merida "wanted to dress up"? She is a fictional character. She doesn't *want* anything!

So I asked Chapman for her thoughts. After all, she created Merida—she dreamed her up, pitched a film about her to Pixar, and directed it. Chapman should know better than anyone: Would Merida have chosen to present herself like that for her coronation ceremony?

"No!" Chapman laughed. "Oh, she wouldn't wear that dress. They stuck her in the dress that she hates!"

And of course, the outcry was because of more than just the dress—a fact which, in their response to the petition, Disney studiously ignored. In fact, some bloggers and commenters who took Disney's side argued that Merida's look *had* to change when they switched the character from CGI to 2D—but Chapman insisted that's not the case. "That's how we design her, as a 2D character. We create the 3D model from there." She added, "That kind of excuse is coming from people who don't know anything about drawing cartoons or animated characters."

Chapman then quickly rattled off several ways in which the redesigned Merida strayed from the original. "They gave her bigger breasts," she said. "They gave her a smaller waist. They put a lot of makeup on her and changed the shape of her eyes to look more seductive. They cleaned up her hair. They took away her bow and arrow, one of her symbols of strength. Some people couldn't see the difference, but for the people who love that character for who she was—they could see right away that it wasn't the same character. They had totally stripped her of her personality and put a sort of 'come-hither,' heavily mascara'ed look on her face."

Chapman added, "She looked about fifteen years older, you know?"

So why did this happen?

"It's the shallowness of marketing and the superficiality of Consumer Products," Chapman explained, referring to Disney's Consumer Products Division. "They think they already know what girls want. They should instead be thinking about who this character is and how it has affected little girls. Girls love this character! Instead of changing it, they should embrace it and market what girls love about it."

Scheibe makes a similar point. "You know, the ultimate thing is they think it will make more money for them," she argued. "That's the ultimate. But also it comes from their narrow view of what a princess is. It's the people in charge—mostly men—who have made this decision."

By squeezing a character so widely regarded as a barrier-breaking role model into a cookie-cutter mold, Disney's Consumer Products Division sent the message that in the end, looks are all that matter— bringing us full circle to where we started with Snow White, whose status as "the fairest of them all" was so pivotal to the story. It's a regression to the mean, and in a world full of stereotypes, it's unfair to girls.

. . . .

INTERVIEW: BRENDA CHAPMAN ON *BRAVE*

Brenda Chapman created and directed the 2012 film *Brave* for Disney/Pixar Studios. She is considered a pioneer in the animation field. In her early career, she worked for Disney on films such as *Who Framed Roger Rabbit*, *The Little Mermaid*, and *Beauty and the Beast*. She was later the head of story for *The Lion King*—the first woman to serve in that capacity at Disney. Then she helped launch DreamWorks Animation Studios, where she directed *The Prince of Egypt*—making her the first woman to ever direct a full-length, animated feature film for a major Hollywood studio.

She joined Pixar Animation Studios in 2003, working on *Cars*, and then she proposed making the film *Brave*, which was based on her own relationship with her daughter. The project was green-lighted. Disney purchased Pixar in 2006, and *Brave* was ultimately released in 2012 as a Disney/Pixar production.

Unfortunately, Chapman was let go as *Brave*'s creative director in 2011 after six years working on the film, due to what she called "creative differences." (This is apparently not uncommon in the animation industry.) Chapman's firing made headlines, however, as a decision that "hurt not only her but her female colleagues in animation," according to outlets such as the *Los Angeles Times*.

In the summer of 2013, Chapman spoke candidly with me about her take on princess culture and her goals for the film *Brave*.

Rebecca Hains: I know that you were working at Disney on *The Little Mermaid*, and that you were very involved with the story for *Beauty and the Beast*. What did you learn about princess culture during your Disney years, and what was your take on the kinds of stories about princesses that were being told prior to your work at Pixar on *Brave*?

Brenda Chapman: Well, you know, I was young and just excited to be working at Disney and doing what I love to do! At first, I didn't think a lot about it because I loved the fairy tales when I was a child growing up. Two of my favorites were *The Little Mermaid* and *Beauty and the Beast*, so I was thrilled to get to work on those two.

But the big problem with all the princesses is that they needed a man to come and save them for them to be complete. With *Beauty and the Beast*, they sort of tried to shift that a little bit, where she saves the Beast in the end—not only magically by telling him she loves him, but by coming back and helping him.

In contrast, in the princess films that were done in the '30s, '40s, and '50s—*Snow White, Sleeping Beauty, Cinderella*—the princess characters seemed very passive. All of them were very reactionary. They were sweet, nice girls and all that, but they didn't have a lot of forward thinking. They were sort of *waiting*. Cinderella was sweet and beautiful and had a really good heart and was very optimistic—which I think is a really good quality—but how could she have done things differently?

In *The Little Mermaid*, Ariel is a very active character. She goes after what she wants. She doesn't wait around for the prince to come and rescue her; she rescues the prince. And she falls in love, and that's what she really wants—and she goes through a lot. In the real fairy tale, she *doesn't* get what she wants, because the lesson of that fairy tale is don't go above your station; you need to stay in your own world. So we gave it a happier ending than having her turn into sea foam.

So Ariel was proactive, which made her a much more interesting character. It was the same with Belle. She wasn't waiting around. She went after her father to find out what was wrong, and she sacrificed herself for him. I know people accuse Belle of having Stockholm syndrome, but I don't look at it that way. She doesn't succumb to Beast's way of thinking. She doesn't just accept the life that he's presented to her; she changes him. She pulls the good out of him.

But yet again, at the end, the big prize was the man and the sense that, "Oh, life is complete now."

With *Brave*, I wanted to break away from that and say, "Here's a character who is very complete as an individual." She is confident in who she is.

Hains: A lot of people have commented on how nice it is, too, that Merida has an intact family.

Chapman: Yes. All those other fairy tales didn't have a family relationship. It was always just a father and a daughter. The mothers were all dead or who knows where, and I wanted to create a totally different type of fairy tale. The most important relationship in a young woman's life is with her mother. Merida breaks away from her mother but still learns the wisdom that her mother has to offer. She has a lot to learn, and the mother has a lot to learn as well.

I wouldn't say this makes *Brave* more realistic, but I think it has a more real quality than the others because princesses were working people. Being a princess was kind of a job. And the queens were working moms. They were the diplomats. They were the ones who tried to smooth things out. It was a stressful job—and in *Brave*, the mother's grooming her daughter for a job.

Hains: Those things that Merida and Elinor fight about as Elinor is trying to groom her to take on that job of princess, I find interesting: they are the stereotypes found in other princess movies, from appearance to behavior to romance. Because of that, I think that many people who love *Brave* see it as this alternative kind of princess story, as a response to the princess films that preceded it.

Chapman: Yes, it was a response to those—and on top of that, all of those other princess movies were put forth and directed by men. I wanted to put a more female point of view on a princess story. Something that we could relate to.

Also, because of marketing, the princess stories have turned into the "girly-girl" movies. When I was a kid, boys and girls went to see the princess movies: *Cinderella, Sleeping Beauty, Snow White*, you know—whenever Disney would rerelease them, every kid in my class would want to go. It wasn't just a girly thing. Boys loved the dragons and the dwarves and the witch. It was something that everyone enjoyed.

But marketing has turned them into these pansy, girly, sort of unsubstantial airhead kind of characters. I wanted to do something different. I used to say that when little girls want to dress up as Merida, I want the moms to go, "Yeah!" as opposed to, "Oh, she wants to dress up like a princess." I wanted moms to feel like their daughters were trying to emulate another female with strength and character.

"P" Is for "Pushback"

With concern growing over the stereotypical behaviors found in princess culture, pushback is on the rise—not just from parents, but from children's media creators and others working in the children's culture industry.

For example, Lena is a twenty-five-year-old professional actress who, on weekends, works as a birthday party princess. She plays Sleeping Beauty, the Little Mermaid, Cinderella, and Beauty (a generic version of Belle), and she also appears as Tinker Bell. Not being affiliated with Disney, her performances are not restricted to the Disney versions of these classic characters. She can put her own spin on them. And being aware of the problems with princess culture, Lena delights in bringing these characters to life in ways that make them better role models for girls.

"I make a special effort to be articulate and to have opinions on things," Lena explains. "I think it's so easy to be like, "Oh, I'm playing a fairy-tale princess. I'll just be an airhead and smile.' Instead, I try to really push intelligent stuff on the kids.

"Like, sometimes they'll ask me where Prince Charming is, and I'll say, 'Oh, he decided to stay at home. He wanted to help clean the castle, which I really appreciate.'"

Lena also explains that when children compliment her on stereotypical things, such as her beautiful dress, she will often reply, "This is my party dress because I'm at your birthday and I wanted to dress up," and perhaps additionally comment, "I certainly wouldn't be wearing this dress if I was going to be exercising!"

Lena also engages older children in conversations about the political power and responsibilities of princesses. She has given a lot of thought to what a princess does in real life, and—like Chapman—she bears in mind that being a princess actually involves tangible responsibilities. "I've thought about it a lot," she says. "The fact is that in real life, a princess is a political party—part of a monarchy."

Lena even works to undercut the "love at first sight" narrative that dominates princess culture, arguing that Disney's vision "isn't a practical portrayal of relationships." Thus, when children asked if her prince was handsome, she responded: "He is very handsome to me. What people think is attractive is different to every person, and it's always been important to me that, you know, a guy is intelligent and thoughtful."

And Lena is not alone in this. Camille, a thirty-four-year-old marketing professional, spent several years working as a birthday party princess on the weekends, most often playing Cinderella, Beauty, and the Little Mermaid. Like Lena, she tried her best to disrupt the passive princess stereotype. Camille explained, "I would try to infuse a bit more self-initiative and strength of character into the dialogue to show that I, as Cinderella, didn't just sit around waiting to be rescued. For example, I would talk about going out and doing volunteer work, or leading a park cleanup crew while Prince Charming would be home in the castle kitchen making dinner.

"Who knows if the kids got the message," she adds, "but I got an appreciative laugh from many moms."

Of course, birthday party performances happen at the local level, with one princess performer in one home. Though women like Lena and Camille stand to make a major impact on the girls at their parties—who are usually wowed by the opportunity to meet their favorite princesses in real life—they are promoting new ideas about princesses at the individual level, rather than in the mass media. (And of course, not all birthday party performers bring this outlook to their work, either, so unless parents make a special request when hiring a performer, it's hit or miss.)

That's why it's good to see that pushback is also happening among media producers. *Sesame Street* has done some great work in this area. For example, *Sesame Street* runs a segment called "Word on the Street" that teaches children new vocabulary words. In one episode, when the day's vocabulary word is "career," Supreme Court Justice Sonia Sotomayor teaches Abby Cadabby the meaning of the word "career."

When Abby, a fairy-in-training, replies that she would like to have a career as a princess, Sotomayor gently teaches Abby that she cannot grow up to be a princess, because princess "is definitely not a career." Sotomayor reminds Abby that a career is a job that involves schooling and preparation, and then offers Abby some examples of real careers (such as being a teacher, lawyer, or scientist). By the end of the segment, Abby—a favorite of many children in the *Sesame Street* viewing audience—has cast off her princess gown and is wearing judicial robes, just like Sotomayor. She understands that pretending to be a princess is fun, but being a judge is a career that she could study and prepare for.

Better still, in February 2010—during its fortieth season—*Sesame Street* debuted a ten-minute segment called "The Prince and the Penguin" (which is also available on the DVD *P is for Princess*). *Sesame Street*'s Rosemarie Truglio, PhD, senior vice president for curriculum and content at Sesame Workshop, told me that they created this segment to teach girls that despite the trope of princesses as damsels in distress, they don't need rescuing.

"We try not to typecast our characters," Truglio explains. "Just because you're a male character versus a female character doesn't mean you have to act in certain ways. Television is all about modeling. You learn through modeling—we know that. So when it comes to children's programming, you're planting seeds. We're trying to model for girls and boys that there is a range of behaviors and options for you, and you should not be limited because you are a boy or a girl."

In the episode, guest star Paul Rudd plays the Handsome Prince, who repeatedly tries to rescue three girls who are dressed in princess outfits and playing princess: Abby; her friend Rosita, a young monster; and a penguin the girls call Princess Penguin. During the course of their play, Princess Penguin finds herself in trouble three times: first, when she jumps too high and can't get down from a balcony; second, when the girls decide to roller skate, but one of Princess Penguin's skates is missing; and third, when Princess Penguin skates so fast that she crashes and gets stuck in a mailbox.

Every time Princess Penguin gets into trouble, the Handsome Prince appears. Accompanied by regal trumpets, he sings in a loud baritone voice: "Have no fear, your prince is here!" and then intones, "Do not worry, fair princess, I have come to your rescue."

And every time, he fails to rescue Princess Penguin. As he panics and cries melodramatically, wailing, "Oh, woe. Woe is me," Abby and Rosita resolve the problem themselves, instead.

The Handsome Prince is upset. "I'm supposed to save the day! I'm the Handsome Prince!"

Abby and Rosita explain to the Handsome Prince: "Just because we're dressed like princesses doesn't mean we need you to rescue us all the time!" The third time around, the girls offer to work with the Handsome Prince and, joining forces, pull Princess Penguin out of the mailbox together.

As the segment ends, the Handsome Prince is impressed. "You

are very strong maidens indeed!" He leaves them to play their "dainty princess games," and the girls reveal that they are about to play "Princess Football"—and recruit him to join the team.

"Girls don't need rescuing," Truglio insists. "On *Sesame Street*, we expose children to counter-stereotypes in our portrayals to model for our young audience that there are endless possibilities for both boys and girls," she says. "It's like the Geena Davis Institute on Gender in Media has been arguing: Don't typecast girls!"

Children's authors have also been providing children with more empowered takes on princess culture for many years. For example, *The Paper Bag Princess*, written by Robert Munsch and illustrated by Michael Martchenko, was first published in 1980. It had its beginnings in a day-care setting, where Munsch frequently told the children stories of a prince saving a princess from peril.

One day, in the mid–1970s, his wife asked him, "How come you always have the prince save the princess? Why can't the princess save the prince?" So reversing the traditional roles, Munsch told a story in which Princess Elizabeth saved Prince Ronald from the dragon. After he published this story as a book, it garnered critical acclaim and an endorsement from the National Organization of Women.

More recent children's books that attempt to disrupt princess stereotypes include:

- *The Guardian Princess* series, independently published in 2014 thanks to a successful Indiegogo campaign that netted $12,545.
- *Princess Smartypants* (1997) by Babette Cole.
- *Do Princesses Wear Hiking Boots?* (2003) by Carmela LaVigna Coyle.
- *Do Princesses Scrape Their Knees?* (2006) by Carmela LaVigna Coyle.
- *Not One Damsel in Distress* (2000) by Jane Yolen.

- *Not All Princesses Dress in Pink* (2010) by Jane Yolen and Heidi E. Y. Stemple.

For example, in *Not All Princesses Dress in Pink,* Yolen and Stemple—a mother-daughter team—offer page after page of princesses playing sports, dancing in the rain, getting their hands dirty while farming, and so on—breaking the passive princess stereotype. And the princesses wear not gowns, but attire that is appropriate for those activities: sports jerseys, jeans and sneakers, and overalls.

When I asked Yolen about her decision to create a book that pushes back against princess culture, she explained that she is a "not-Disney person." As a grandmother to five young girls who are dynamic, interesting people, she was eager to work with her daughter to buck the stereotypes promoted by Disney-style princess culture.

"I feel that the Disney retellings are—as all retellings are—such a mirror of a time and culture," Yolen explained. "But with their enormous power to cross international datelines, they have imposed their particular cultural ethos far beyond their time and place. The dumbing down of the great stories, where strong girls like Cinderella have their power subsumed by singing mice and pigeons, for example, carries with it a message of misogyny and girl helplessness not in the original tales.

"It's an uphill battle against all those pink Disney Princesses," Yolen adds, "but we feel equal to it."

How to...
Help Girls See through the Gender Stereotypes

As our children's pop culture coaches, we can help them to see through the gender stereotypes—to understand that gender roles are not requirements. With a little guidance, girls can grow up with a healthy perspective on our world and their place within it.

Pop Culture Coaching, Step 1: Identify and Communicate Your Family's Values

Think about your family's position on gender stereotypes. Which gender stereotypes do you disagree with? Do you object to traditional gender roles? Be conscious of your values regarding gender roles, and be sure that your actions and conversations show your children where you stand.

TIP 1: OVERTHROW GENDER STEREOTYPES AT HOME

If you are married or living with a partner of the opposite sex, think about what you already do that disproves gender stereotypes. Who does the dishes, the laundry, the cooking and cleaning? Who does the yard work? Mix things up. Show your children that household chores are not assigned based on sex. No Cinderellas and Snow Whites here!

Try to make ignoring gender stereotypes a casual, everyday thing in your home. Don't remark on what is "man's work" or "woman's work." Share household duties in an equitable way.

As Tara, a successful young veterinarian, notes, "My parents are somewhat nontraditional. My sister and I were encouraged to help out both our parents. We helped put the roof on the house as tweens with both parents, helped Mom and Gram can vegetables, and worked with Dad building stuff," she recalls. "Dad did most of the cleaning. Mom was the one that fixed anything with an engine or electric connections. Mom and Dad never had women's or men's job in our household. They were just *jobs*, and the person with the most talent or time for the job did it."

Martin, father to three young women, recalls: "Growing up, my daughters all built things such as birdhouses—so they learned how to use a hammer and saw. They helped mow the lawn and learned how to use a clutch. We spent time at the science museum, learning how to make and fly paper airplanes and making Cartesian divers, so that they learned that science is fun."

"A lot of the toys I was given as a child were gender-neutral or even what people would think of as 'boys' toys,'" my friend Mindi reflects. "Games like Chinese checkers and Pick-Up Sticks, a Lionel train layout, and my favorite, a box of architectural blocks made of real stone, with columns and turrets and arches. When I got a little older and had some more manual dexterity, I was handed tools to help with home repairs."

TIP 2: CHOOSE YOUR WORDS CAREFULLY

It's easy for even the most progressive families to use language in ways that suggest certain duties are for males or for females. For example, even though both mothers and fathers *parent* their children, it's easy for families to talk about dads "babysitting" their children. But they're not babysitting—they're *watching* the kids, or *parenting*.

Likewise, even though everyone in a household needs to learn to be responsible for themselves, it's easy for families to talk about cleaning and other chores as "helping Mom." But it's not helping—it's *doing their share*.

Also avoid gendered terms for careers, like "firemen," "police-men," and "mailmen." After all, small children are literal. They know "men" are not "women." To help them be open-minded about roles and responsibilities, use the neutral forms—*firefighters*, *police officers*, and *mail carriers*—instead.

In other words, pay attention to the language you use and make changes as needed.

TIP 3: MODEL OPEN-MINDEDNESS

When faced with stereotypes, show your children that you are open-minded. As Andrea, mom to a four-year-old boy and a three-year-old girl in Massachusetts, explains: "I try to model curiosity, to teach them how not to make assumptions and how to keep an open mind. So, for example, my son once made a comment that boys can't be nurses, and I responded by seeming confused.

"I said things like: 'Really? Are you sure? I have never heard that before! That seems silly. Why couldn't anyone be a nurse if they wanted to? I wonder why you're under the impression that only girls and women can be nurses. Where do you think that idea came from? What if a boy wants to be a nurse, what should we tell him?' Obviously, I don't ask all those at once (hello, overload), but those would be the kinds of questions I'd respond with, on an age-appropriate level."

Olivia, mom to nine-year-old Ben and six-year-old Cara in Pennsylvania, agrees. "If my kids come up against a stereotype, I confront it and ask them why. So…'Why do you think girls aren't good at sports? We know some girls who are really good.' They're likely to respond, 'Oh, yeah, that's true.' I also don't belabor the point. I point it out and move on to other things."

TIP 4: AVOID *INTRODUCING* STEREOTYPES

Scheibe points out that it's important to meet kids where they are. Address the stereotypes they've been exposed to without introducing new ones. In developing media literacy curricula, Scheibe says, "Our mantra is 'Do no harm.' So if we are going to have a conversation about gender stereotypes, we're cautious about it. We use examples of content that the kids are likely to be exposed to anyway."

So, follow your child's lead. It may be counterproductive to ask your child if she's heard the stereotype that, say, "only boys are doctors"—but if your daughter brings this up herself, then you can address it.

TIP 5: USE PLAYTIME TO IMAGINE GIRLS AS STRONG AND POWERFUL

During playtime, gently encourage fantasy scenes in which girls— even the princess characters—are strong and active, rather than weak and passive. Play cops and robbers or superheroes or dragons. Play Disney Junior's *Doc McStuffins* and encourage your daughter to act as a doctor for her toys and stuffed animals.

Pop Culture Coaching, Step 2: Establish a Healthy Media Diet

To expand girls' horizons beyond the stereotypes of princess culture, take a two-pronged approach. Share stories about nontraditional princesses, and make sure that their media includes many other characters and story types. In today's media environment, it's easy for girls to consume all princesses, all the time. Make a point of establishing a well-rounded media diet.

TIP 6: PROVIDE STORIES ABOUT ALTERNATIVE PRINCESSES

Seek out stories about princesses who aren't stereotypical—like those found in the books *The Paper Bag Princess*, *Princess Smartypants*, and *Not All Princesses Dress in Pink*. Look also to biographies of real princesses, folktales, and mainstream media.

For example, Finucane of the *Disney Princess Recovery* blog found *Super Why!* helpful in expanding her daughter Caoimhe's horizons. "*Super Why!* is all about figuring out the spelling of words," Finucane explains, "and there are four main characters. One is Princess Presto; she's an African American princess. She wears a long purple dress, and she has a sparkly wand. And there's no prince!" Finucane notes with relief. "Caoimhe fell in love with her, so I even went out and got a doll that we incorporated into some of her play."

According to Finucane, *Super Why!*'s depiction of a princess who loved spelling, rather than romance, helped broaden Caoimhe's ideas about what being a princess means. "It made it a little bit bigger in her mind," she says.

Many parents have also told their daughters the stories of real princesses, like Princess Diana and Kate Middleton; related the real story of Pocahontas, rather than the Disney version; and emphasized the historic versions of fairy tales. Finucane has spent a lot of time on this with Caoimhe during her Disney Princess recovery.

"Through this process, I have found some really interesting real princesses. Like there's a children's book called *The Last Princess: The Story of Princess Ka'iulani of Hawai'i* by Fay Stanley. She was the last princess of Hawaii, and it's got these beautiful illustrations," she adds. "It's historical, and it's got just the right amount of tragedy mixed with adventure. I was blown away by the story.

"I'm really interested in the variations of Cinderella and of those fairy tales, too," Finucane says. "We've read a lot of cultural books, like the Korean Cinderella, the Apache Cinderella, and we've done some comparisons of them. They're stories that don't just belong to us living in the modern day—they have been really around for a long time in different forms. By reading these stories together, instead of constantly talking about the princesses and princes, we end up talking about things like, 'Where is Afghanistan, and where is Korea? What are people like there? How is their country the same as ours?'" These stories help broaden their conversations and Caoimhe's horizons.

Note that some girls may dramatically resist new ideas about princesses. For example, I read *Not All Princesses Dress in Pink* to a group of preschoolers, and some—those girls who the preschool teachers had identified as being extremely interested in princesses— had a hard time believing that all the girls pictured were really princesses. Only the first page of the book depicts a traditional-looking princess in a big, red gown; the rest of the pages show princesses wearing everyday clothes. At the end of the story, the girls wanted to know: "Where's the princess?" They meant the one in the dress. They asked if they could hold the book, and then they flipped through all the pages until they found the "real" princess for me.

Rogow says that this is understandable. "Part of it is going to be, 'I have limited categories to process the world when I am three,'" she explains. "'And so if you are giving me information that doesn't fit into any of my existing categories, I don't know what to do with that.' So, some of it is a developmental learning thing. As adults, instead of trying to blow apart the categories that children know, we can just try to gently expand them."

So, for some girls, characters like Princess Presto—who explores language and spelling while wearing a stereotypically sparkly, purple princess gown—may be an easier sell than books about princesses who don't wear gowns. But it's worth trying both.

TIP 7: PROVIDE PLENTY OF ALTERNATIVES TO PRINCESSES

The experts agree: There's nothing wrong with little girls loving princesses, as long as the girls are well-rounded and enjoy other types of stories and activities, too. It's when girls love princesses *to the exclusion of everything else in life* that problems arise.

Make it a point to introduce your daughter to stories and activities that aren't about princesses, even if she resists at first.

For example, Scheibe notes that her own granddaughter is really into princesses. But, she says, "The big thing for me is not worrying about her being taken with princesses, as long as she also loves playing basketball, which she does, and loves swimming and loves playing other things. She's also got a workbench with all sorts of tools that she *loves* using, pounding as hard as she can, using wrenches. I spend a lot of time helping her help me to fix things."

While you're providing alternatives to princesses, don't forget toys and apps, too. Make sure that for every princess toy or app your daughter receives, she also is provided with other options: spelling apps, board games, superheroes, toy cars, baby dolls, building blocks, open-ended sets of LEGO bricks—the possibilities are endless.

Even imaginative play can be used to invent alternatives. For example, Gruver suggests encouraging girls to imagine all kinds of future careers through their play—especially those in which girls are underrepresented. For example, you might say: "Let's pretend we're pioneers going to live on the moon. You're the captain of the spaceship."

Pop Culture Coaching, Step 3: Watch and Talk about Media Content with Your Kids

When you use media with your kids—watching television together, for example, or playing apps or video games—be observant. Watch with gender stereotypes in mind. What do you see? Are girls being stereotyped, or are they breaking barriers? As your children's pop culture coach, you can help them notice both the problems and the good stuff. Talk about it with them to help them become critical viewers, too. It's always great to model media literacy for our children.

TIP 8: ADDRESS THE GENDER STEREOTYPES YOU SEE ON-SCREEN AND ON THE PAGE

Is a girl character acting brainless? Are you bothered by an on-screen princess who is waiting around for her prince? On family video game night, do you wish that Mario and Luigi weren't always rescuing Princess Peach—that those roles could reverse sometimes? Are you tired of books oversimplifying the roles of female characters?

Go ahead and say so. Call them out.

Also ask questions of your children: "What *don't* they show princesses doing?" "Could princesses wear regular clothes?"

Gruver suggests stating your own opinion and then soliciting your child's perspective. For example, you might say: "I don't like it when the girl needs to be rescued all the time. What do you think?" or "It seems like all the girls in this movie act pretty ridiculous. How do you feel about it?"

As Victoria, mom to a nine-year-old daughter in California, explains: "After many years of calling stereotypes out myself, Juliet often calls them out to me now. I tend to ask questions when I see something that bothers me, like 'What do you notice about the female characters in this movie?' or 'What kind of message does this send to kids? How do you feel about that?' When we went to see *Monsters University*, for example, I knew that there were going to be few viable female characters. We talked about that beforehand, and I asked her after the film what she thought about it. We had a good conversation as a result."

Nicole, mom to a six-year-old daughter and a one-year-old son in Kansas, notes: "I try and ask why there isn't a girl doing certain things, or why the mean girl has brown hair again. Basically I ask her small questions about what she's watching."

With younger children, you can even use play as an opportunity to address stereotypes by imagining how else stories could have gone. Have your daughters' dolls rescue their princes or rescue themselves.

Be creative as you read books, too. For example, when my son and I read a Little Golden Book version of *Cars*, I was annoyed to see that the only description of the female car, Sally, was that Lightning McQueen thought she was pretty. My son wasn't reading yet, so I changed the line about this to instead say, "Sally was a lawyer. Lightning McQueen thought she was smart."

TIP 9: PRAISE THE GOOD STUFF

Conversely, if you notice something good on-screen, be sure to offer your praise. Do you like that, at the end of Disney's *Wreck-It Ralph*, Vanellope von Schweetz declines to act like a princess, and that throughout the movie, Sergeant Tamora Jean Calhoun is a tough-as-nails warrior? Say so.

Think about the princesses' good points, too. Draw attention to their best attributes: that Belle loves to read, that Cinderella has a good work ethic, that Tiana never gives up.

As Scheibe explains, "When I'm reading books to my granddaughter that I feel are verging on stereotypical, I point out other parts of it. I say, 'Look! Look how good she is at flying!' So focus on the characters' capabilities, rather than on the stereotypical stuff."

Angela, mom to a six-year-old girl in California, says: "I interrupt myself reading to her quite often to discuss the story and characters. We talk about the movies and how women are portrayed in them. We talk about how strong or smart or independent the characters are. Most recently, this came up when we were watching *Epic*. She was thrilled to note a female 'Leafman' soldier."

Pop Culture Coaching, Step 4: Teach Children about Media Creation

TIP 10: "REMEMBER: SOMEBODY MADE THIS."

Always remind your children that somebody made the movies, apps, television shows, and books that you're viewing.

Rogow explains, "If you get young children used to asking questions, and used to the idea that storytellers are making choices, then by the time children are eight years old, they can begin to get that there are *motives* and *financial interests* at play."

Note that concrete images make great conversation tools. For example, the Sexy Merida redesign is a terrific talking point for older girls. You can Google Sexy Merida and find a side-by-side comparison of the original Merida and the redesigned version—or see the images on my blog at rebeccahains.wordpress.com/2013/05/13/disney-faces-backlash/. Then, ask your daughter what she notices about the two versions. What's different about Merida? Why does she think someone decided to change her appearance so much? What could the reason have been?

Likewise, you might visit my blog at rebeccahains.wordpress. com/2012/01/28/new-at-the-disney-store/ and show your daughter how the Disney Store redesigned their Mulan doll. Her dress was redesigned to include tulle, making her *hanfu* look more princess-like than ever. You might note that Mulan dolls don't sell as well as other Disney Princess dolls, which is why you probably won't find a Mulan doll at Target. What might the Disney Consumer Products Division employees have been thinking when they added a layer of tulle to Mulan's *hanfu*?

TIP 11: CREATE NEW STORIES TOGETHER

As a reminder that people create media, and that all depictions of girls and boys are the result of choices that media creators have made, create stories with or for your child. Tell stories to one another. Make up bedtime stories about girls having adventures that break stereotypes. Write them down and illustrate them, or take photos of you and your children acting scenes out and use the photos as illustrations. Anything to involve your child in the creative process.

Some parents like to create new stories based on their children's favorite stories—adding epilogues to the traditional fairy tales. Brian, dad to six-year-old Mia in Michigan, says that his wife, Michelle, is especially good at this. For example, Brian said: "After our daughter saw *The Little Mermaid* for the first time, somebody bought her a *Little Mermaid* storybook. And my wife would add this whole addendum on the end, about how Ariel and Eric didn't get married right away because Ariel wanted to get to know him. So Ariel moved into town, and she studied to become a doctor. Then she became a really well-known doctor, and she and Eric saw each other for a couple years. Finally, their friendship got to the right point, they decided to get married."

And another: "For *Snow White*, my wife would do this ending where after she woke up, now that the Queen was gone, Snow White got to go back to her castle and be the queen and rule her own kingdom," Brian recalled. "And so she ruled her kingdom, and the prince ruled his; and eventually the kingdoms got along so well and she was such a good ruler that they decided to combine their kingdoms later."

When Mia was older and could tell that those words weren't part of the actual story, Brian and Michelle explained to Mia that the book was "just the part of the story that people know. There are lots of different stories. There's lot of different ways the stories go."

CHAPTER SIX
The Problems of Race Representation and Racism

R ace representation matters. Children of all colors need to see dolls and on-screen characters who look like themselves. All children deserve validation that they are beautiful and valued by society and worthy of love. And all children benefit from media that depict the diverse world we live in.

But sadly, our popular culture is rarely inclusive enough—which has consequences for children of every race and ethnicity.

Consider the case of four-year-old Amanda, a young Latina girl who loved Barbies and Disney Princesses and other dolls with smooth, straight hair. She played with them every day.

Then, one day, her mother, Angela, realized Amanda had been spending a lot of time in front of the mirror. Amanda kept brushing and brushing her tight, curly hair, but the more she brushed, the frizzier it became.

And her daughter was becoming deeply upset.

"I want to be like *them*," Amanda told her mother tearfully. "I want to be like them and have straight hair. Why can't I have straight hair?"

When Dolls Aren't Diverse

Amanda's question was troubling. Girls often regard their dolls, especially fashion dolls, as perfect beauties. The dolls' long, soft, luxurious hair is incredibly appealing. Girls spend a lot of time styling that hair, making it a focal point of girls' doll play. And whether Barbies or Disney Princesses are meant to be black, white, or another race, the dolls' hair is almost always straight—rarely curly, never coarse. And considering that as of 2012, 49.9 percent of U.S. children younger than five were of a minority background, the fact that parents can rarely offer their girls of color dolls that reflect their heritage is inexcusable. The marketplace needs to catch up to today's diverse society.

For decades, critics have lamented that fashion dolls meant to represent African Americans and other races are too often simply "dye-dipped." For example, black Barbies have the exact same body and facial features as the white Barbie dolls; they're just darker. This means their features conform to white standards of beauty.

Not even Tiana, Disney's African American princess, has curly hair, which of course means that toys made in her image don't, either. This bothers many parents. For example, Nicole, who is the mom of a six-year-old daughter and a one-year-old son in Kansas, observes: "Tiana's hair is pressed, or permed, and it is always pulled back. So even though Tiana is an African American princess, she's an African American princess who has Caucasian beauty ideals."

Nicole herself is Caucasian, but her husband is African American—so her children are of mixed race. She reflects: "I think it shows girls that they are not good enough the way they are. It's so pervasive because it goes back to slave times, when it was a status symbol to be able to look like you're mixed, like you're part of the master's family. It has continued today. That's why they want lighter skin tone and finer hair."

Amanda's mother, Angela, similarly recognized that the problem with the dolls' hair reflected a broader problem in society. In the media as a whole, people of color are underrepresented, marginalized, and stereotyped, and women of color are rarely presented as being as glamorous as their white, blond peers. "When everything around you is predominantly white," Angela mused, "the ideal beauty doesn't reflect the women and girls you see in your life. So there is an absolutely tangible impact on little girls who have curly hair and don't have the flowing hair that's always shown to them."

When girls from diverse backgrounds internalize the white beauty ideal that soft, flowing hair is best, it can affect them throughout life—often with financial consequences. Irene Smalls is an author and historian who launched Hairmath, a website to engage African American and Latina girls with advanced mathematics through hairstyling, and she has studied the issue at length.

Smalls reports that in 2011, African American women spent half a trillion dollars on their hair, and that Latina women spend 43 percent more on brand-name hair-care products than the general population—all money that could be spent on other endeavors, if they weren't conditioned to feel badly about their natural hair. But the beauty industry relies on women of color feeling this way, because it's a source of immense profit.

"A lot of women get hair weaves," she explains. "And to me, that's saying, 'My hair is ugly. My hair is not good enough. So I'm going to spend a thousand dollars on a really good weave to change my hair and to look like a white girl.' Everyone on this planet is trying to do the best they can," she adds—"to succeed, to fit in, to be appreciated and recognized, but the consequences for African American and Latina women are tremendous."

Angela wanted her daughter to understand that real people are more diverse than those found in the media, or even in dolls—and that diversity is actually a really good thing. So she had a conversation with her. ·

"I told her that we're all different," Angela recalls, "and that the company that makes these dolls envisions them this way—that this is the kind of doll they like. I asked her, 'Does this doll look like anyone you know?' and she said, 'No.'"

"This doesn't mean that the doll is ugly," Angela explained to Amanda. "It means that the doll is *different*. Unfortunately, there are no dolls that look like you or your friends.

"You shouldn't want to be like this doll," Angela told her daughter gently. "You just have to be beautiful for yourself and understand that beauty comes in many forms."

"Oh," Amanda replied tentatively, "so my *doll* is really different."

"Yes," her mother explained. "The doll is pretty on her own, but she's not you, and she's not your friends—and she's not the people you see every day. She's so different from us, she's almost like a Martian. She's not real."

Angela felt that the conversation went well. Without disparaging the dolls Amanda loves, Angela had offered her daughter a new perspective on their limitations—on the fact that there is no Latina Disney Princess. "It helps that Tiana from *The Princess and the Frog* had a different flavor than the other princesses," Angela remarks, "but for our Latina girls, the Disney Princess brand is still pretty limited."

"There Are No Black Princesses"

Like Amanda, seven-year-old Taylor loved the Disney Princesses. In fact, because her mother and father always called her their little princess, she identified as a princess herself. But because *The Princess and the Frog* had not yet been released—Disney's film featuring its first black princess—the children at her predominantly white school insisted she wasn't a princess.

"You can't be a princess!" her peers told her on the playground. "You're black! There are no black princesses."

Maybe the little white girls were deliberately trying to be mean. Or maybe they just thought they were being honest because in their popular culture world, they had never seen a person with Taylor's skin tone depicted as a princess—leaving them closed-minded and unimaginative.

Either way, Taylor was crushed. So when her mother saw an article in their local paper about a professional musical production of *Beauty and the Beast* that had opened in a nearby city, she decided she had to take Taylor to see it.

The reason? The actress playing Belle was African American.

The actress, Adriana, recalls: "The whole time the mom was telling me this story, the little girl was just looking up at me with this awe. And I'm trying not to lose it, and the director started crying. She said, 'That's why we do this.' She pointed to the little girl and said, '*You*—you're the reason why Adriana is here and I hired her to do this role. *You* are the reason why.'

"And I gave Taylor a big hug and said, 'You are just so sweet.' And she said, 'You sing so nice! You sing so nice.'" Adriana was touched to be able to validate for little Taylor that, yes, even a little black girl can be a princess. For Adriana, it was the memory of a lifetime—and she hoped it was for Taylor, too.

Why There Aren't More Characters of Color

Although children of color need to see people who look like them in the media, the media are reluctant to create characters of color.

They know that audiences of color will watch media about white people, but they don't believe the inverse is true. They fear that white audiences won't be receptive to diversity—that the majority will be alienated, negatively impacting producers' profit margins.

This plays out in a variety of ways. Studios and networks appear less likely to green-light television programs and movies about people of color than movies about white people, and it can be hard for children's toy designers to get dolls that are truly diverse into the marketplace. (And it doesn't help that the boards of directors that influence decisions in these companies are typically dominated by white men—meaning that they lack diverse voices and perspectives.)

These pressures within the media and toy industries combine in unfortunate ways. When toy manufacturers produce toys based on girls of color from popular television programs, their biases are sometimes evident, with the characters "whitewashed" in toy form—made to look lighter-skinned than they are on-screen.

For example, several toys based on the African American character Princess Presto from PBS's popular show *Super Why!* look incredibly pale compared with their television counterpart. Several years ago, while I was researching my last book, young African American girls made the same complaint about products based on characters they loved, such as Dora the Explorer and the Proud Family.

Meanwhile, authors writing books about characters of color often receive pushback in unexpected places. For example, when *The Hunger Games* was released in theaters, some readers were upset to realize that several of the characters they were familiar with from Suzanne Collins' novels were actually brown-skinned. They had been written that way by Collins herself, but many readers had missed this fact. As a result, when they saw actors of color playing characters such as Rue, they turned to social media to complain—generating controversy online and ample media coverage. Some comments sounded relatively innocuous, like "She's not how I pictured her," but some were overtly racist. For example, one person tweeted, "why does rue have to be black not gonna lie kinda ruined the movie," while another wrote, "call me racist but when I found out rue was black her death wasn't as sad."

Horrible.

Perhaps if these viewers had grown up seeing people of color on-screen as a matter of course, they wouldn't have found *The Hunger Games* so shocking. We should live in a world where diversity is depicted as normal, routine, and expected, because it is—but sadly, we don't.

Because of this, publishers sometimes try to obscure the fact that the main characters in their books are people of color. They white-wash book covers in hopes of broader sales—purchases from not just minorities, but from white audience members, too.

As a result, there was a great deal of controversy when Justine Larbalestier's popular teen novel *Liar*, whose protagonist is a black teenage girl named Micah, was released by Bloomsbury in the United States with a cover featuring…a photo of a white girl. Talk about a firestorm: there was a huge outcry from readers, which led Larbalestier to speak out publicly on the widespread whitewashing of book covers. African American readers spoke eloquently on why they felt betrayed by the cover. As one mother argued in a comment on Larbalestier's website:

> *Bloomsbury was insensitive to the long-standing concern in the black community that children are programmed to wish to be white. There's*

a great (and very old) Whoopi Goldberg comedy routine in which a young girl dons a white pillowcase and pretends to brush her long blond hair. When my daughter was younger, she wanted a specific doll—a Skateboard Ally. They were all sold out except the African American ones. I remember calling every store and finally found a Target thirty miles away. The manager apologized that they had only three left— all African American. I laughed and said, "Perfect, since I am AA." Only my daughter rejected the doll because it wasn't white. See, Disney princesses weren't black. Heroines in novels weren't black. She's a teen now and cringes about those days. But I understood where the need came from, and we worked hard to build her self-esteem in the other direction.

Which is why what Bloomsbury did is unforgiveable. I know, from personal experience, that authors don't have a lot of clout over covers. But they do have means to effect a change. I wish you had fought harder. As is, my teens would find the cover insulting and we can't purchase it.

In other words, when taken all together, the limited race representations in princess culture and beyond—in toys, on television, in games, in movies, and in books—harm the self-esteem of girls of color. In fact, a series of doll studies conducted since the 1940s has repeatedly shown the damage this does to young children. In these studies, when children are presented with a pair of dolls—one white and one black—Caucasian and African American children alike express a strong preference for the white doll. In response to interviewers' questions, the children say that they'd rather play with the white doll; that the white doll is good and that the black doll is bad; that the white doll is nicer; and so on.

Their answers reveal a devastating truth: white children aren't the only ones who buy into the insidious idea that white is better. Thanks to the messages they receive from the culture that surrounds them, black children internalize racism, too, developing feelings of self-hatred from a very early age.

THE GUARDIAN PRINCESSES OFFER GIRLS TRUE DIVERSITY

Setsu Shigematsu, PhD, an associate professor of media and cultural studies at the University of California, Riverside, has a five-year-old daughter. And Shigematsu was so frustrated by the limited, stereotypical nature of princess culture available for her little girl that, as a birthday gift to her daughter, she wrote her own alternative princess story, which she read at the party. The kids loved the story, and the parents' response was really striking. They urged her to publish it.

Recognizing that many girls would benefit if princess culture became more diverse and inclusive, Shigematsu took their suggestion to heart. She came up with a plan that went beyond a single book, however. She created the Guardian Princess Alliance, an organization working to transform the meaning of "princess" in girls' media culture. The group's main focus is the independent creation and publication of a series of princess stories.

The seven princesses in the Alliance are racially and culturally diverse. Unlike the Disney Princesses, who are always in isolation from one another and lack real political power (at least until *Frozen* debuted), the Guardian Princesses work together to protect their people and the planet, appearing in one another's stories. And instead of emphasizing romance and the beauty ideal, these princesses promote diversity and environmentalist ideals.

"Our team currently includes thirty-five educators, parents, artists, scholars, students, activists, feminist lawyers, and professional women who are mostly women of color," Shigematsu notes. "Our aim is to contribute to girls' empowerment by creating more socially conscious children's media that is racially and culturally inclusive and transnational."

Shigematsu and her colleagues launched a campaign on the crowd-funding website Indiegogo.com, seeking to raise $9,500 to fund the production of the first three books in the series. They succeeded beyond their expectations, raising $12,545 in the course of a single month—evidence of parents' strong desire for princess culture to expand beyond stereotypical story lines and characters.

Shigematsu sent me an advance copy of one of the Guardian Princesses' first stories, *Princess Vinnea and the Gulavores*. While at the time of this writing the story line is still under review and subject to change, I was impressed by the fact that Princess Vinnea had real power in her kingdom. Her story is not about romance. It is about using her political power to stand up for her people and protect them from meddlesome outsiders. Furthermore, the book was beautifully illustrated, and the look of Princess Vinnea impressed me: She has very dark skin, long, natural braided hair, and clothing that bucks the typical Western style associated with princesses. Instead, Shigematsu notes, the clothing in this story draws from West African and North African styles.

I asked the author of *Princess Vinnea and the Gulavores*,

Ashanti McMillon (who is also a Guardian Princess Alliance cofounder) to comment on Princess Vinnea's natural hair. "I wanted Vinnea's hair to be in braids because there are too many messages telling black women to alter the unique and beautiful aspects about themselves," McMillon explains. "This has created insecurity and affected the self-esteem of young people. Because of the negative images portraying coarse-textured hair, young black people are transforming their hair to be accepted by society.

"I want to be clear and say there's nothing wrong with straightening your hair or wearing a weave," McMillon adds. "However, there is a need for all young girls to be proud of their hair, no matter what texture it is. I want young black girls to read the Princess Vinnea story and see that an intelligent and brave princess has natural and pretty hair just like they do."

With positive coverage from outlets such as NPR, the *Huffington Post*, and *Forbes*, the Guardian Princess Alliance is worth watching.

Prejudice Is Learned—and So Is Acceptance

Fortunately, young children can become quite open to diversity if they are exposed to it in favorable ways from an early age. Studies show that prejudice is a learned behavior, not an instinctive one, and that what we see in the world around us—from parents and society at large, including media—determines whether we become prejudiced people.

Family, society, and media have their strongest influence on children's development of prejudices when kids are ages eight and under—the exact target audience for princess culture. In fact, when

Caucasian children ages five to seven watch media with diverse characters, or when parents have in-depth discussions of race with their children in this age group, the children's attitudes toward African American people quickly improve.

The anecdotes I heard from African American women like Adriana, who portrayed Belle onstage in the years before *The Princess and the Frog*, support the research. Young children *can* easily accept depictions of people of color. For example, although Taylor heard from her white peers that she couldn't be a princess because she was black, the young white children in Adriana's audience had no trouble with a black Belle. Adriana reports that the children were completely open-minded upon seeing her in the role.

"One of my most memorable moments is when I had to take my place on stage in the dark on opening night," Adriana recalls. "After the narrator tells the story of what happened to the prince and why he was cursed, there's a slow light that comes up on a pin spot on my face as I'm reading a book while leaning against a wall. And there was this little three-year-old in the second row, right in front of me, who gasped and said, 'Oh! Belle!'"

Adriana was touched. "She didn't even notice that my skin was brown, that I had long braids. I was *Belle!* Because of the dress, that little person automatically saw Belle. And I just thought, 'That's just beautiful.'"

She never heard a single complaint about her having been cast in the role.

Naomi, another African American actress who played Belle in a different professional production of *Beauty and the Beast*, reported similar experiences.

"I didn't know, being African American, if the kids would be coming out with their arms crossed after the show," Naomi says with a laugh, revealing her anxiety about whether kids would be upset because she didn't look the part. "You know? But, I was so pleasantly surprised. I'd come out the stage door even dressed in my normal clothes and they'd all be like, 'Oh! Belle!'

"It was really encouraging because I realized, 'Oh, these kids— they don't care. All they want is the story.' All they wanted to do was meet Belle."

It's hard to say exactly why Naomi's young audience members were so open to her portrayal of Belle. Obviously, most of the children in the audience would have seen the film version of *Beauty and the Beast* and known that Belle is a white woman. Perhaps Naomi's performance was so terrific that they were swept away. Perhaps seeing her onstage gave her an aura of authority, which little black girls like Taylor don't have on the playground.

But Naomi has a theory: she thinks that the children in her audience were young enough to have not yet internalized racist ideas. "I really think it just goes to show how open-minded kids are before society puts labels on things and people," Naomi explains. "It was really cool. I never had any kid come up to me and go, 'Why don't you look like the real Belle?' or something—never once. It was amazing."

Even when Naomi did outreach for her stage production at a local bookstore and a local bank, reading the *Beauty and the Beast* story in her Belle costume for children who *hadn't* seen her perform, the children were incredibly accepting of her—giving her more evidence for her theory. "I was like, 'Here I am, holding this book, and I'm dressed as Belle. And clearly the girl in the book does not look like me.' And the kids were just transfixed!" she marvels. "You *could not tell them* that I was not the real Belle."

Disney's Race Problem

Despite children's apparent openness to seeing women with dark skin playing an iconic Disney Princess, Walt Disney Studios has had a race problem for many years. (By contrast, the Disney-ABC Television Group has a good track record. Shows with diverse characters have long been featured on its television networks.) Walt Disney Studios did not offer a film featuring a princess of color until Jasmine's debut in *Aladdin* in 1992—fifty-five years into the company's feature-film history.

The film was a tremendous success, and toys based on the film did incredibly well in the marketplace. But it was also condemned by critics for how it portrayed Middle Eastern people and their culture. For example, the looks of the protagonists, Aladdin and Jasmine, were based on white people. Aladdin's face was modeled after Tom Cruise's, while Jasmine's was modeled after that of supervising animator Mark Henn's sister, Beth. Meanwhile, other characters were presented in stereotypical ways—as dishonest, conniving, unscrupulous, unkind. The film's title song, "Arabian Nights," even included this lyric:

> *Oh, I come from a land,*
> *From a faraway place*
> *Where the caravan camels roam.*
> *Where they cut off your ear*
> *If they don't like your face.*
> *It's barbaric, but hey, it's home!*

The *New York Times* responded with an editorial titled, "It's Racist, But Hey, It's Disney"—deftly summing up a common belief about Disney at the time.

After releasing *Aladdin*, Disney continued working to become more inclusive of diverse cultures, offering up *Pocahontas* in 1995 and *Mulan* in 1998. Their title characters were Native American and Chinese, respectively, so this represented progress in the cultures included within the Disney empire. But given Disney's track record, it wasn't surprising that the films were riddled with problems.

For example, *Mulan* invented a form of female oppression (matchmaking) that did not historically exist in China. This made *Mulan*'s China seem more oppressive of women than it actually was in history—and it also made Western culture seem more enlightened by comparison. *Mulan* also portrayed the Huns in an incredibly racist way. The Huns were the enemies of the army Mulan was in, and in the film, they were grotesquely dehumanized. They appeared gray-skinned and yellow-eyed, with fangs—almost like animals, instead of people.

But on the positive side, at least a Chinese woman was starring in a major Disney film—and she was a strong, powerful character. So although *Mulan* was problematic, in terms of representation, there was progress. Little Asian girls finally had a strong Disney character of their own to look up to, and girls from other backgrounds could only benefit by having their imaginations expanded to include a strong Asian woman like Mulan.

Pocahontas, too, made some major missteps in handling both history and race representation. Historically, Pocahontas was a real person who played an important political role in her society; but in the eponymous film, Disney erased her real political importance. Instead, *Pocahontas* retrofitted its heroine's story into the stereotypical romance narrative mold found in Disney's princess–oriented films.

Pocahontas also included an original song about "savages" that is racist and offensive. It misrepresents the European invasion of Native American culture as a mere *misunderstanding* in which both sides viewed the other as savages. Considering that Native Americans were ultimately the victims of genocide at the hands of European settlers, casting the relationship between the two groups as a misunderstanding is a mind-boggling bit of revisionist history—underscored by the fact that, inexplicably, the film concludes with the English explorers leaving the natives in peace.

For these reasons, Annalyssa Gypsy Murphy, PhD—a sociology professor who teaches a class called "Unmasking Pocahontas: Native American Women from History"—finds the Disney film "sexist, racist—and creepy." Murphy is herself of Native American descent, and she offers the course as a way to correct students' notions of what it means to be Native American, historically and today.

"My college students have this warm, fuzzy connection to Pocahontas based on the Disney movie," Murphy explains. "But in reality, she ended up as a sad, depressed person in the UK who died young, and whose only child also died sad and depressed.

"And this is a serious issue. Native American kids have a suicide rate ten to one hundred times the national average, depending on which study you read," she says. "It's partly because they don't see themselves represented in the culture. They're *invisible*. It's Pocahontas or offensive caricatures, like the logos for the Chiefs and the Redskins. So the last thing we need is the promotion of Pocahontas as the archetype of the Indian—a peaceful, happy person who hugs the animals and sings with the trees."

Because of this, many parents who are aware of the real history of the native people in America have reservations about Pocahontas. "My wife and I have noticed that Pocahontas is more sexualized than some of the other princesses," remarks Brian, dad to six-year-old Mia in Michigan. "She's very statuesque. She does it all. She makes sacrifices for a man she barely knows and for a culture which will eventually come and do very, very bad things to her culture. So even though we allow Mia to watch other Disney Princess films, we don't watch *Pocahontas*."

Tiffany and her husband are a Caucasian couple in Maine with two biological daughters who are in their twenties and an adopted a Chinese daughter who is four years old. Their extended family is diverse, as well. For example, two of Tiffany's Caucasian nieces are married to men who are Asian American and African American, respectively. Therefore, because Tiffany has a family of varied races, she feels it's important that her daughter sees images of love across race lines.

"We're not of the belief that if you're Caucasian, you need to marry a Caucasian," Tiffany explains. "Your skin color doesn't need to be the same. We wouldn't have adopted a Chinese daughter if we felt that strongly about race. I like that *Pocahontas* has an interracial relationship, because you never see that, especially in a Disney movie. You never see racial lines being crossed in young children's videos or storybooks. There is racism in the world, but it doesn't need to stop you or prevent you from living the life you want to live."

In other words, as is often the case in children's culture, *Pocahontas* is a case of one step forward, one step back—a mix of positives and negatives. And parents and critics are divided on if and when the good in the film outweighs the bad.

DIVERSITY FOR PROFIT

Angharad Valdivia is a communications professor at the University of Illinois at Urbana-Champaign who specializes in Latina/Latino studies. At her university, she teaches a class called "Media Business: Disney Studies," and she reports that Disney's inclusion of ever-more races into its Princess line is not a sign of altruism or ethics. "They don't seem to have ethics," she remarks. Instead, it's pure marketing—all about the bottom line.

"Disney has created all these different princesses to increase profit," Valdivia explains. "They want to approach as wide an audience as possible without alienating their mainstream audience. That's their strategy. They realized that in addition to their mainstream audience, there are all these other markets, domestically and globally, that they want to reach out to. So for that reason, they have done a lot of princesses who are coded ethnically, like Jasmine and Esmeralda, then the *Princess and the Frog*. That's their approach: they're reaching out to different segments of the population."

Valdivia says that many people employed at Disney are attuned to the issues of race representation, and these employees have been trying to make interventions for the better. But she says, "Disney is such an old, stodgy industry that it's very, very hard to make interventions. If you're a large, unwieldy corporation, anything you try to do will take decades. It's not because people in it aren't full of great ideas; it's just such a slow-moving institution."

Unfortunately, Disney's approach to appealing to diverse audience segments one at a time—always returning to the "mainstream" white audience in between—is a source of additional problems. Because Disney has many white princesses but only one princess each of other races (Middle Eastern,

Native American, Chinese, and African American), this places a burden on each princess of color.

DISNEY PRINCESSES AND THE BURDEN OF UNDERREPRESENTATION

While viewers can see diverse types of Caucasians on the Disney screen—everything from demure Snow White to bookish Belle to feisty Merida—Disney offers only *one* type of Middle Eastern princess. *One* type of Native American princess. *One* type of Chinese heroine (whom Disney categorizes as a princess for marketing purposes, even though she's not one). *One* type of African American princess.

Each princess of color is implicitly taken to represent an entire group of people, even though each group is at least as diverse in its composition as Caucasians are—which is a problem, as no group of people is a monolith.

So, Valdivia says, "There's a burden of underrepresentation. We know this from African American studies, for example. In the 1980s, there were so few African American characters on television that the few that existed had to represent *all* African Americans. So, Bill Cosby had to be urbane. He had to be upper-middle class, and yet he had to not be disconnected from the working class. He had to be educated, and yet he had to have faced challenges in his history. If he was well-educated, people would say, 'Oh, he sold out.' But if he was poorly educated, people would say, 'Oh, you're reiterating stereotypes that we don't have upward mobility.'

"It's the same with princesses," she remarks, noting that when only one princess of each race exists, their portrayals will never satisfy everyone. People in the viewing audiences are so diverse that what one person considers a positive representation can offend another person from the same racial or ethnic group.

Because of this, "people want everything from their princess characters," Valdivia notes. "It's such a difficult, politically sensitive terrain."

. . . .

Tiana: Disney's First African American Princess

During the same period when Disney released *Mulan* and *Pocahontas*, the studio also released two films set in Africa—*The Lion King* (1994) and *Tarzan* (1999)—without depicting a single African person on-screen. Instead, anthropomorphized animals were proxies for African people—as had been the case in *The Jungle Book* (1967), which was set in India but substituted animals for Indians.

Therefore, audiences were eagerly anticipating a Disney film depicting black people without the racist caricatures found in, say, *The Song of the South* (1946). So it was with much fanfare that Disney released *The Princess and the Frog* in 2009. The film featured a young African American woman, Tiana, who becomes a princess by the film's end. The timing was noteworthy. The film debuted shortly after Barack Obama became the first black president of the United States, bringing two young daughters to the White House who captivated Americans' imaginations. It was a remarkable moment.

Little black girls—the Taylors of the world—finally had a terrific comeback if classmates claimed black girls couldn't be princesses. Tiana was proof that they could. And Sasha and Malia Obama were almost like little princesses themselves, the embodiment of the

American dream: living with a loving, beautiful family in the White House, making a difference in the world around them, proof that our country had changed for the better.

Happily, Tiana has proven to be a popular member of the Disney Princess line. She is beloved by girls of all colors, as I have observed firsthand. On my visits to Walt Disney World, I saw roughly equal numbers of white children and children of color wearing Princess Tiana costumes as they navigated the parks with their families.

And although I stood in line to meet various Disney Princess performers, Princess Tiana's lines were so long that I never made it to the front of the diverse lines of patrons. I just didn't have two to three hours to wait in her queue. ("Tiana is incredibly popular," a staff member said apologetically when I asked him what might be a better time to meet her. "The lines for Princess Tiana are *always* this long.")

The film *The Princess and the Frog* was far from perfect, however. As with Disney's other films about people of color, the fact of their inclusion is regarded as progress, but the details of *how* those people are depicted is cause for concern. For example, some viewers expressed concern that the sinister voodoo magic of Doctor Facilier (or "the Shadow Man") implies that "African people are spooky and scary and have magical powers."

Furthermore, critics complained that Tiana spends too much of the film as a frog. Taken together with Disney's pattern of depicting animals rather than people in its films set in Africa, this is indeed a problem. As author and historian Irene Smalls explained to me, "It bothers me that when there's a black princess, she's a frog. There are all these other princesses, and they're not frogs hopping around, are they? We want the pretty dresses, too. Why does the black woman have to be a frog?"

Smalls even made this argument to Disney personnel when the film was under development. She participated in a focus group they held to gauge audience reception, and she let them know she was offended—but the film went forward with Tiana as an amphibian.

"It was really an insult," Smalls states. "The underlying subliminal message is that black people are animals."

Critics and audience members have also been split over the portrayal of Tiana as a woman who is endlessly working (at least when she is in human form). Tiana's dream is to open a restaurant of her own, so she works long hours at multiple jobs to save money. In the span of just a few minutes in the film, her friends and her own mother alike actually chide her for working too hard.

But many parents I spoke with applauded the portrayal of Tiana as a hard-working person—as a princess who is about more than romance and vanity. For example, in Chapter 5, I shared quotes from parents who liked the way Tiana bucks stereotypes about princesses—saying things like, "I like the way Tiana is portrayed as a strong character" and "Tiana worked, and she made an effort. She didn't have a goal of marrying a prince. She had a goal of working to accomplish something."

Lisa Owen, a mother and popular blogger, agrees with them. Owen, who writes about raising her five children at mysocalledglamorouslife.wordpress.com and blogher.com, is thoughtful on matters of race in her children's lives, and she appreciates that Tiana is industrious. "Wanting to live the fabulous life is a fantasy," Owen told me, "and people need to get over it. I liked the fact that Tiana works hard. My children live pretty comfortable lives, and they need to know that life is hard work. Tiana works hard. I really dug that about the movie! She never lost sight of her goal.

"Think about that," she adds. "Here's a woman who was a frog, who goes through so much to get where she wants to be. And when she falls in love with a prince whose parents have cut him off—yay for the parents, by the way—she keeps her eye on the prize. She doesn't compromise who she is. It's not like Ariel, who gives up her life. Is that really what we want to tell our kids—that it's better to leave your family and give up everything for a man than to work toward real goals?"

But as with Tiana's time in frog form, her relentless focus on work has proven to be a contentious point. For example, Megan Condis—a PhD candidate at the University of Illinois—conducted a scholarly analysis of how Disney films portray girls' labor. In her essay, she argued that in Disney's story lines, white princesses can be said to have attained "a perfect, princessly femininity" when they no longer have to work (as was the case with Cinderella)—while Disney's princesses of color are "glad to continue working even after they've reached their happy ending" (like in Tiana's case). Condis says that Disney films perpetuate a double standard: What it means to be a "good girl" is very different for white people than for people of color. "Good" white girls get to be waited on, while "good" girls of color keep working.

Nicole, mom to a six-year-old daughter and one-year-old son in Kansas, agrees. "I keep talking about how the only African American Disney Princess is the only Disney Princess who has a job. And then the only African American-ish *prince* doesn't even have a single job," she adds. "He is lazy. As the wife of a hard-working African American man, I'm sorry, but I find this racist."

Condis commented to me that even her four-year-old niece had noticed that Tiana was treated differently than the other princesses.

Before Disney had announced that Tiana would become an official part of the Disney Princess brand, Condis had asked her niece: "Do you think that Tiana will be a princess someday, and that they'll put her on backpacks and stuff?" Her niece replied, "I don't think so." Why? Condis asked. "Because she's *different*. She doesn't do the same kinds of things. And she's a *frog* for most of the movie. Are they going to put a frog on with all those pretty girls?"

"So," Condis concludes, "when Disney was making the movie and saying, 'Now, little African American girls finally get to have their own princess,' the actual consumers were noticing that although Tiana is technically a princess, there are 'real' princesses who are princessly. And just because you put them all together on a lunch box doesn't mean they all have equal standing or are equal models of femininity that are interchangeable."

Unfortunately, Disney Princess products make it clear that this is true. The brand's princesses of color often lack an equal footing with their white counterparts. For example, consider Target's Disney Princess toys. The store carries both Mattel's Disney Princess dolls and its own line, licensed directly from Disney for products available exclusively at Target stores. But Target has systematically excluded Pocahontas and Mulan from their collections. In recent years, it has excluded Jasmine, too. The same is true at retailers like Toys R Us and Walmart, creating a pervasive pattern. And when Tiana is included in a collection, she's almost always placed off to the side of the box. She almost never gets a turn in the central position.

The fact that the retailers' Disney Princess doll collections used to include Jasmine but stopped including her once Tiana debuted smacks of tokenism. To be fair, perhaps Target and other licensees have been keeping close tabs on which princesses sell the most, and Jasmine has fallen behind. Perhaps among the people who were buying individual items rather than sets, those who had been buying Jasmine products switched to Tiana after *The Princess and the Frog* debuted.

But when you consider how many dolls are grouped together in some of these sets, it doesn't look good. From a consumers' perspective, it reads as though toy manufacturers see the princesses of color as interchangeable, that as long as one is included, they've made their nod to diversity. Because, after all, the white girls are the *real* princesses.

White Dolls in the Front

Barbie, another major purveyor of princess dolls, has the same problem as Disney: White Barbie is always presented as the brand's main character. When Mattel began making multicultural Barbie dolls, Mattel never had the iconic white, blond Barbie cede center stage. The other dolls are inevitably off to the sides in Barbie advertisements and books, or they're excluded entirely. Rhea and Madison, two nine-year-old African American girls who participated in a study I conducted in 2005, told me that they had noticed this time and again. They explained:

Rhea: When they show Barbie dolls and everything, they always put the white dolls—they always put the white Barbie dolls—

Madison: In the front!

Rhea: I know!

For this reason, Madison said she refused to buy Barbies anymore. Instead, she said, "I buy Bratz dolls because all of them—all the Bratz dolls are treated right."

It's a shame that Disney can't do for their princess line today what Bratz had figured out all the way back in 2005.

★ ★ ★

Mattel has the same problem with its Ever After High line of dolls, which are supposed to be the teenage daughters of fairy-tale royalty. The Ever After High website features cartoon webisodes, or web episodes, that tell the stories of these characters, and a popular book series is available from publisher Little, Brown and Company. It's called *Ever After High: The Storybook of Legends.*

Mattel has released four dolls in its Ever After High collection so far, and all of them look Caucasian. There's Apple White (daughter of Snow White), who is a blond; Briar Beauty (daughter of Sleeping Beauty), a brown-eyed brunette with rosy cheeks; Madeline Hatter (daughter of the Mad Hatter), with blue eyes and blue and purple hair; and Raven Queen (daughter of the Evil Queen), with purple eyes and purple-black hair.

Five additional main characters profiled on EverAfterHigh.com have not yet been released in doll form, but books about them are already on the market. They are Cinderella's daughter, Goldilocks' daughter, Cupid's daughter, Red Riding Hood's daughter, and the Huntsman's son—all of whom look Caucasian, too.

The only character of color I can find on the Ever After High website is Cedar Wood. The daughter of Pinocchio, she appears to be African American. So far, she is not a featured character in her own right. She mainly appears in the Ever After High stories as Madeline Hatter's best friend. Relegating black characters to secondary roles, as friends of primary characters, is common in popular culture. When they lack stories of their own and revolve around a white character, it's a form of tokenism—a way of paying lip service to diversity without taking a real risk.

It's more of the same from competing brand S-K Victory's Fairy

Tale High dolls, which features fairy-tale characters as modern-day teens. The teen versions of the Little Mermaid, Alice in Wonderland, Snow White, Rapunzel, Cinderella, Belle, Sleeping Beauty, and Tinker Bell are all white girls. And the Glimma Girlz and La Dee Da dolls—which also are available in princess versions—all seem meant to be white girls, too (though one of the La Dee Da girls, Sloane, is racially ambiguous, with olive skin, curly brown hair, and green eyes).

Even Hasbro's My Little Pony line, which purveys several princess products (including Princess Celestia, Princess Twilight Sparkle, and Princess Cadence), isn't off the hook for race representation. The ponies themselves do not have races like people do. After all, they're ponies. But in 2013, Hasbro released a movie in theaters called *Equestria Girls*, which features the ponies in human forms. A line of Equestria Girls dolls debuted in stores at the same time. While these human characters are all the color of their pony counterparts—pink, purple, yellow, blue, peach, and (literal) white—the movie takes place in a high school, in which characters of a huge range of colors exist.

Several of *Equestria Girls'* secondary and background characters look very much like Caucasians, which presumably means they're modeled after ponies who are background characters on the *My Little Pony: Friendship is Magic* TV show that are peach or light tan in color, like palominos. Yet not a single character in *Equestria Girls* remotely resembles an African American person or a person from another racial minority, despite the fact that in real life, many brown and black ponies exist.

In fact, when I reviewed the film at home, I paused on a crowd scene at the film's climax, in which every character in the film is present. I could not find a single one that looked like a person of color to me—although several looked like run-of-the-mill Caucasian cartoon characters. It was saddening that in a cartoon fantasy world with a literal rainbow of skin colors, Hasbro didn't create characters with normal human skin tones any darker than beige.

How to...
Help Girls Overcome Stereotypes and Respect All Races and Ethnicities

A PERSONAL NOTE ON ADDRESSING RACE REPRESENTATION AND RACISM

In this section, I offer tips to help parents of various backgrounds address the problems of race representation and racism with their daughters. In preparing these tips, however, I've been conscious of my identity as a white, middle-class woman. In our society, my family and I have privilege—a set of advantages both small and large that people of color do not. And I want to level with my readers about the implications of this.

Many white people are unaware of their privilege, but if we pay attention, we can see it evidenced in many ways. For example, everywhere I look, whether in the media or at people in positions of power in our society, I can see people of my own race. Because of the visibility of respected white people in the United States, strangers are likely to afford me respect and credibility before I have done anything to earn it. Before I even open my mouth to speak, people are likely to assume I am worth listening to—an assumption less frequently made about people of color. How unfair.

Conversely, I will never know firsthand what it is like to be discriminated against in America because of the color of my skin, my accent, or the language I speak. I will never worry that my children will face racist stereotyping at school, in our neighborhood, or in the mall. No one will ever accuse me of being a token racial minority or ask me to be a voice for an entire race or ethnicity—to tell them "what white people think" about an issue.

Why I am bringing this up? Two reasons:

For one thing, I feel it is important for my white readers to be aware of this issue—that white privilege is a real thing. (If you had not previously heard of it, please Google "Peggy McIntosh white privilege checklist" to read up on it.) Once we are aware of our privilege, we can use it in a productive way by calling out racism whenever we see it, and holding people and institutions accountable for perpetuating stereotypes, prejudice, and racism—advocating for racial equality. (As McIntosh argues, "One who writes about having white privilege must ask, 'Having described it, what will I do to lessen or end it?'")

For another, I am conscious that a white person offering tips about race issues to people of color may be accused of hubris or arrogance, or even of victim blaming. People might ask: "Who is she to offer suggestions on racism and race stereotyping to people of color?" I want my readers to know that the advice I offer is not given with the attitude that I know everything, or with a belief that I know as much about these issues as those who live them daily. (I don't.) Instead, I have explored the best research I could access about race, ethnicity, girls, and self-esteem. Not everyone has access to this data, but as a university professor, I do—so I interpret and summarize it here, interspersed with suggestions from other parents and experts.

I do so with full awareness that racism, prejudice, and discrimination are structural issues in our culture. They need to be changed at the societal level. Fixing these problems is not a responsibility that should be shouldered by people of color. But as this book is written for parents, not policy makers, the advice I share focuses on practical ideas at the personal level. Parents can do their best to raise strong, resilient daughters who know the truth. No matter what the media or society convey to them, their value in the world is tremendous. That is essential knowledge for every child.

. . . .

Children learn to be prejudiced from the people and culture around them. They are attuned to their parents' body language, words, and behavior. When they see their parents act in certain ways around people of other races or ethnicities, they pick up on it. They internalize their parents' nonverbalized attitudes. And when they see television shows segregate people of different races and ethnicities, they believe this is the natural order of things—that segregation is normal, and that interracial interactions are unimportant.

But as parents, and as our children's pop culture coaches, we have the power to raise our children to respect people of all backgrounds. This is because until the age of seven or eight, children strongly identify with their parents and want to be like them. Therefore, we can be explicit about the messages we want our children to internalize, model the kinds of behaviors we want them to practice, and expose them to diversity.

Although this advice applies to parents of all backgrounds—any child can become prejudiced—white families are the most reticent to discuss race with their children. According to a 2007 study at Vanderbilt University of 18,950 families with kindergarteners, 75 percent of white families never or almost never discuss race with their children—while families of color were three times more likely to do so.

Why such a difference?

Many white parents are afraid of appearing to be racist and inadvertently fostering prejudice in their children. They fear that even a positive statement like "It's wonderful that a black person can be president" could teach children to see divisions in society, rather than unity.

Simultaneously, many families of color feel they must discuss race to teach their children how to interact with those who are likely to prejudge them. For example, African American families in mixed neighborhoods frequently talk about race relations to prepare their children for discrimination. Pre-arming their children is a survival strategy.

But when white parents don't discuss race with their kids, peer and media influences fill in the gaps—often with terrible consequences. White parents may think it's okay to be silent because they assume their children are color blind, but they're wrong. Children start noticing race at as young as six months of age. Even though they lack racial vocabulary, they quickly begin to categorize people by color, just as they do by sex—drawing upon the most obvious of stereotypes. Because of this, Phyllis Katz, PhD, from the University of Maryland advises parents to talk with children about race from an early age. We mustn't shrink from it.

Meanwhile, parents of children of color have legitimate concerns about media representation, prejudices, and stereotyping that white families just don't face. As a white, middle-class woman, I am conscious of my family's privilege in this regard. While my children grow up seeing themselves reflected in the mediated world around them—they can see positive portrayals of Caucasians nearly everywhere they look—children of color do not. They are marginalized, often left out or portrayed in less than favorable ways.

Many people are fighting to change the culture for the better, but change is all too slow in coming. In the meantime, researchers have been interested in understanding what makes kids strong and resilient in the face of stereotypes—and they've learned that no single approach works for everyone. Best practices vary across (and within) races and ethnicities and can't always be pinpointed.

Girls of color also face a double whammy related to the Pretty Princess Mandate discussed in Chapter 4. The beauty ideal that circulates in Western culture is a *white* beauty ideal. So while all girls struggle with the message that females' looks determine their societal value, the issue is intersectional for girls of color. Our society places girls of color in a lower position in an unspoken hierarchy of beauty, marking them as undesirable "others"—and girls really notice, with definite consequences for their self-esteem.

So, having investigated the research in this area, I'd like to offer ten ways parents can help their children overcome racial and ethnic stereotypes and respect people of all backgrounds.

Pop Culture Coaching, Step 1: Identify and Communicate Your Family's Values

Does your family value the diversity in our world—that it is filled with people from other racial and ethnic backgrounds besides your own? Then tell your children so. Don't expect them to absorb your values through osmosis. Be sure your children know your family's values and that you are against racism and stereotyping.

TIP 1: TELL YOUR CHILDREN YOU VALUE RACIAL DIVERSITY

Children's attitudes toward race are strongly influenced by what they perceive their parents' attitudes to be. For example, studies conducted by researchers at *Sesame Street* showed that most preschoolers liked the idea of having interracial friendships—but fewer than half of the children in the study (who were African American, white, Puerto Rican, Crow Indian, and Chinese American) believed their moms would be happy about it if they actually *had* a friend of another race.

This anticipation of disapproval can have real consequences in children's attitudes and behaviors, even if it's unwarranted—and research with white families, at least, suggests that this is often the case. When parents don't tell their children that they like racially diverse people, kids' assumptions about how their parents feel are way off the mark. Even reading race-themed books to preschoolers is not enough, according to one study. If moms are "color-blind" or "color-mute" during the storytelling, the children fail to understand that their mothers agree with the book's message. The parents in these studies are generally less prejudiced than the kids might expect, and vice versa. Without conversation, neither party really knows what the other believes, and both guess poorly.

The key, then, is to be explicit. Experts such as Brigitte Vittrup, PhD, of Texas Woman's University and George W. Holden, PhD, of Southern Methodist University argue that parents can't be vague. It's not good enough to offer platitudes like "Everybody's equal," "God made all of us," and "Under the skin, we're all the same."

Instead, we must be specific. Vittrup and Holden suggest that parents of children ages five to seven discuss race using clear statements and questions, like this:

> *"Some people on TV or at school have different skin color than us. White children and black children and Mexican children often like the same things even though they come from different backgrounds. They are still good people and you can be their friend. If a child of a different skin color lived in our neighborhood, would you like to be his friend?"*

For maximum effect, though, these conversations should be meaningful—not just a brief mention, but a real dialogue that is age-appropriate. It's worth working at.

TIP 2: HELP YOUR GIRLS DEVELOP A STRONG RACIAL OR ETHNIC IDENTITY

According to the research, children of color who have a strong racial or ethnic identity—meaning that their race or ethnicity is an important part of their self-image—have better self-esteem than those who do not.

For example, Maxine Jones—a former member of the R&B group En Vogue—has given this issue a lot of thought. She left the group to raise her daughter, and she believes that to help girls develop a strong racial identity, parents need to share their history with their daughters. "Knowing our history is important," Jones explains. "Yes, our history of slavery and oppression, but also the successful and history-changing African Americans—from the Buffalo Soldiers of the 10th Calvary in the American West to the Tuskegee Airmen of World War II to George Washington Carver. African Americans have always fought racism, but they haven't made that struggle the only thing in their lives."

Family history is even more important, Jones argues. "Not being afraid to talk about our past, about what happened to us—no matter how painful, shameful, or hurtful it may be—is important," Jones explains. "That's how our daughters learn they're not alone in what is happening to them. These things happened to us, too. Sharing them, and how we felt and what we did, and how we'd respond if it happened today, are critical conversations to have.

"Knowing your history and the outcomes of events helps you and your daughter learn from your past and come up with ways to address your own struggles," she adds. "We are not alone. We build on the broken hearts, bones, and lives of our family and our ancestors."

Meanwhile, what about racial identity and Caucasian children? In general, they don't have any sense of racial identity whatsoever. Lacking the vocabulary to discuss race, instead they use phrases such as "skin like ours" to describe their racial group. White children are socialized into not thinking about race by their families and society, and in consequence, most Caucasians think of themselves as "neutral" or "normal." They tend to assume that only *others* have a racial or ethnic background. (Think about phrases like "ethnic food" or comments like, "She looks more ethnic." These phrases really mean "nonwhite," and they belie a perspective that "white" is neutral.) And when we think of ourselves as "normal" and everyone else as "other," that's a problem.

White parents should work to disrupt this idea, then, by teaching our children some simple concepts about race. For example:

- If your child goes to a diverse school, or if you watch or read books that include people of many races, listen to what your child says. Be on the lookout for opportunities to discuss race. For example, if your child comes home and comments that some kids have brown skin, you can teach basic vocabulary about racial identities by saying: "Did you know that there are many different skin colors in the world? People with light beige skin, like ours, are called 'white.' It's kind of strange because we're not white like pieces of paper are, but that's the word everybody uses. And people with dark brown skin are called 'black.' Again, it's kind of silly because no one is actually black—they're just really dark brown. But those are the correct words, and it's good for you to know them. You might also hear people say the words 'Caucasian' for white people and 'African American' for black people. Those are correct words, too, that are good for you to know."

- Give your child a chance to respond. He or she may ask questions that you can answer, or give you a cue that suggests he or she is looking for more information. Or maybe your child will say something that suggests this was too much information. In that case, you can come back to it at a later date.

- It's also possible that your child might say something like "I'm glad I have light skin" or "I'm glad I'm white." Remember that this kind of preference (for one's own race, sex, hair color, and so on) is developmentally normal in young children, so you can affirm your child's healthy self-image while also broadening his or her horizons. For example, it would be easy to say: "I'm glad you like the way you are. There are so many beautiful skin colors in our world, and that's the way it's supposed to be! It's so much better to have variety. I bet that little kids with dark skin also like the way they look. And they should. Everyone is beautiful exactly the way they are."

- Or your child might say something that is comparative, like "Light skin is better than dark skin," or "White skin is better than black skin." Again, remember that an in-group bias is developmentally normal in young children. You can gently reply: "I'm glad you like our skin color, but did you know that light skin is not actually better than dark skin? All skin colors are great. I am so glad that you have friends of lots of different colors! It's just like on *Sesame Street*—no one is better than anybody else."

We can also teach white children about their own cultural history to make sure it is not invisible to them. Explain to them how race is related to where people or their ancestors came from, and that if they have white skin, it's because their ancestors came to America from Europe. Be specific: Did your grandparents come to America on a boat from Italy in the early 1900s? Tell your children as much of their story as you can.

Try to find and share interesting facts about what people from your culture of origin invented or created in history that your child can be proud of. For example, Wikipedia has a page called "List of Italian Inventions." You could skim a list like this with your child, while also letting them know that other countries also boast amazing inventions.

It's also important to be honest about the downside of white history. For example, Thanksgiving and Columbus Day offer opportunities for gentle but age-appropriate and honest conversations about the European settlement of the Americas. You can set the record straight and make sure your children know that Columbus did not "discover" America. There were already many, many people living here. (The Understanding Prejudice website has a good history of Columbus's expeditions here: www.understandingprejudice.org /nativeiq/weather.htm.)

And you can complicate what Thanksgiving means by bringing up a Native American perspective—letting your child know that many Native American people today (most of whom live alongside us, *not* in reservations) see it as a day of mourning. You can review the ideas and suggestions offered by the Understanding Prejudice website at www.understandingprejudice.org/teach/native.htm and www.understandingprejudice.org/teach/thanksgiv.htm and share some facts, perhaps along these lines:

- "Most Americans celebrate Thanksgiving as a day to give thanks for what we have, and we think back on a time when the Native Americans helped the Pilgrims who had come to America. But it's important to know that for the most part, European settlers and Native Americans did not have a good relationship. The way things went on that first Thanksgiving so long ago is not how things went overall. There were many, many Native Americans living in America, but the European settlers wanted to take their land from them and keep it for themselves.

  "The Europeans had guns and the Native Americans did not, so the Europeans killed a lot of Native Americans in battles. Then, later on, the European settlers forced many Native Americans to leave their own lands and walk far, far away to what they called 'reservations'—new places for Native

Americans to live that weren't very nice. That really was a terrible thing to do.

"So, we celebrate Thanksgiving because we are grateful for so many things in our lives, but we must also remember that a lot of Native Americans who are living in America today feel very sad at Thanksgiving. The way white people treated the Native Americans is a shameful part of white people's history, so it's important today for us to always be respectful toward people of other races. In today's world, everyone is equal, and everyone is important." You could then read books about diversity together as a way to bring this message home. (See Tip 7.)

LOOKING FOR MORE IDEAS?

Murphy recommends oyate.org and cradleboard.org as the best resources for information about Native American children, teaching resources, and so on.

Through conversations like these, we can help our children understand that people who identify as white or Caucasian do indeed have a race—and that all races are equal.

For further reading:

Great Books for African-American Children by Pamela Toussaint (1999, New York: Plume). An annotated bibliography of 250 books that provide uplifting, accurate images of African American culture.

TIP 3: TEACH CHILDREN TO RESPECT OTHER RACIAL GROUPS, TOO

Studies show that when children of color both respect other groups *and* have a strong racial or ethnic identity, they are more resilient when they encounter discrimination. They are also better able to overcome the stereotyping that can damage their academic performance and self-esteem.

For example, in one study conducted by researchers from the City University of New York and Columbia University, African American girls who were "pro-black" and also "pro all racial groups" had higher self-esteem than their peers who weren't. These girls did not use white standards to define themselves. The researchers explained that instead, they were "likely to use other black people as a reference group for their thoughts, feelings, and behaviors," while still respecting people of other backgrounds.

Froswa' Booker-Drew attests to the importance of this. She is a leadership development expert who is currently doing doctoral research on how women build social capital, and she is also the mother of a thirteen-year-old girl. "My daughter has had a really diverse family experience," Booker-Drew notes, "because I'm African American and her father is African American and Japanese." Booker-Drew says she constantly reaffirms her daughter's heritage, letting her know, "It's okay to be you." But she notes that affirming her daughter's racial identity isn't enough. She also pushes her to value diversity—what the researchers might call being "pro all racial groups."

"You have to ground children in who they are," Booker-Drew explains, "but also help them have an appreciation of others. You can't become so ethnocentric that you put other people down. When you are able to accept the fullness and richness of who you are, it's easier to do that with other people, as well."

RAISING EMPATHETIC WHITE CHILDREN WHO RESPECT OTHER RACES

To really respect other people, it helps to adopt an empathetic perspective. Being empathetic involves taking on another person's perspective enough to understand and share their feelings. So, one way to help white children respect other racial and ethnic groups is to help them understand what being in the racial minority is like.

You can ask them questions like: "When we watch television, we are fortunate to always see people who look like us on the screen. Now imagine that there were never people who looked like you on-screen—maybe that there were never people with your hair color or skin color. Wouldn't that make you feel kind of funny, like there was something wrong with you?"

Then, you can link those questions to the idea that this is the actual experience for children from other racial and ethnic groups. "For little African American and Asian American girls, that's what life is really like. They almost never see television shows about people who look like them. That can make them feel sad. Almost half of the little kids in our country are from other backgrounds. It's too bad that there aren't more programs about people like themselves, isn't it?"

Holden suggests that white parents should even take their children to visit safe minority-majority neighborhoods and let them experience firsthand what it's like to be "other." "White parents can take their children to visit an African American church," he suggests, "or a Spanish-speaking neighborhood.

It helps for children to know what it feels like to be in the minority," he explains.

Visiting a mall in a predominantly nonwhite neighborhood could be a good way to do this, too, because in addition to seeing a world full of people who are different than yourselves, you'll also see much different products. For example, when I was a doctoral student at Temple University, my husband and I lived in a predominantly black neighborhood. The mall near our house catered to the people who lived in the area, so in the toy store, black dolls were well represented, and in the CVS, they sold lots of products meant for African American hair.

Once, when some of our friends came to visit us from a neighboring white community, they stopped at that mall on their way over and were caught off guard by its contents. One of them remarked to me afterward: "All the figurines for sale in the Hallmark store were black. It was so weird!" She had never had the experience of walking through a store and not seeing people like herself reflected back at her in the products for sale—a clear marker of white privilege.

A twenty-seven-year-old white woman from Ohio credits her routine childhood visits to black communities as the reason why she is open-minded and not prejudiced, unlike some of her extended family. "My mom was an inner-city tutor when I was very little, so a lot of my earliest memories were of going with her to tutoring sessions," she says. "We were the only white people ever there, and we took the bus to get there, so most of my early memories were of being around black people.

"I don't specifically remember any conversations we had about it," she adds, "but I do remember just thinking of black people as normal people, as indeed they are. And even though I proceeded to go to schools that were 99 percent white as I got older, I never ended up super racist or feeling like black people are some inscrutable alien culture. They're just people."

If you decide to take your children to visit a community that is not predominantly white, the key to success is emphasizing empathy. Make sure that the trips are not about gawking—not about saying, "Wow, look at all those people." It shouldn't be a form of tourism, a means to gawk at others or their surroundings. Instead, it should be about respectful perspective-taking—experiencing being in the minority. The goal should be to develop a better understanding of the feelings of people from other backgrounds who are often underrepresented in pop culture and made to feel of lesser value. In so doing, we can cultivate a genuine antiracist standpoint in our children.

TIP 4: FOSTER GIRLS' INDEPENDENCE

According to the research, internalizing a strong racial or ethnic identity works well for African American girls, but it does not always make a noticeable difference for girls from other backgrounds. For example, Latina girls who have high racial self-esteem nevertheless have low body esteem. In fact, Latino children feel less positive about themselves and the color of their skin than children who are white, African American, and Chinese American. Why might this be?

The research does not answer this question directly, but it hints that the answer might lie in different cultural expectations of Latina and African American girls. (Note: I cannot find comparable studies about girls from other racial and ethnic backgrounds, unfortunately. There is still a lot of work to be done in this area.) While many Latina girls are socialized into *marianismo*—an ideal form of womanhood that values self-sacrifice and submissiveness, many African American girls are raised to value their own independence.

In their book *The Maria Paradox*, psychotherapists Rosa Maria Gil and Carmen Inoa Vazquez argue that as Latinas try to juggle Latina and North American value systems simultaneously, they face significant challenges, for *marianismo* is in direct conflict with the North American value of empowerment (which the authors note does not translate into Spanish or exist as a concept in Hispanic culture). They argue that attitudes and actions that would be condemned in the Old World as selfish—such as self-assertiveness—are actually viewed positively in North America; but when Latinas try to reconcile *marianisimo* with North American values, they question themselves, become alienated, and lose their self-esteem.

In contrast, consider a master's thesis study conducted by Heather Ridolfo at the University of Maryland. Ridolfo reported that a type of mothering prevalent in African American culture may explain why African American girls develop better self-esteem than Caucasian and Latina girls. African American mothers both support their daughters' racial identity *and* encourage high levels of independence in their daughters. When their mothers encourage them to "think, act, and make decisions independently," African American girls develop a strong sense of self-worth.

Given the apparent benefits that independence has for African American girls, perhaps more parents should follow the lead of African American mothers and encourage our daughters' independence.

TIP 5: INTRODUCE YOUR CHILDREN TO DIVERSE ADULTS

Are you friends with people of races and ethnicities other than your own? Not everyone can be, of course. Some people live in areas that are simply not diverse. But if you have friends outside your own racial or ethnic group, make sure your kids see this firsthand. If they do, they are likely to perceive people from other races more positively than they would otherwise.

Vittrup and Holden's study of how parents influence their children's racial attitudes offered support for this point, at least among Caucasian families. (I can't find a comparable study of families from other backgrounds, unfortunately.) They conducted an experiment with ninety-nine white families and learned that although 69 percent of the moms and 78 percent of the dads had friendships with African American people, only 53 percent of the children knew about these friendships. The remaining children either said that their parents didn't have black friends, or that they didn't know whether they did.

When the researchers compared how these children felt about black people, they discovered that the children who *did* know had significantly better impressions of black people than the other kids. Holden says that it's worthwhile for people to travel a distance, if necessary, to connect with people from other backgrounds. "It's pretty hard to find anyplace in America where you can't find some diversity," he told me. "If all parents did this with their children, it would create a much healthier and more harmonious society."

In fact, knowledge of parents' friendships is an even better way of reducing racial biases in children than attending diverse preschools. Although studies have shown that interracial friendships and cooperative learning can help reduce children's biases, doctoral research at the University of Texas at Austin found that children's mothers' friendships were the much more influential factor.

This can be made sense of by remembering that in the preschool years, parents are the major socializing forces in children's lives. Our kids want to be just like us—so they're paying attention to how we actually live our lives. That means we need to pay attention, too, and purposefully expose our children to friends of various backgrounds.

For further reading:

Some of My Best Friends: Writings on Interracial Friendships by Emily Bernard (2005, New York: Harper).

Pop Culture Coaching, Step 2: Establish a Healthy Media Diet

With the media offering limited depictions of diverse people, it's important to seek out alternatives for our children and provide them with images that will nurture a healthy racial identity and self-esteem.

TIP 6: PROVIDE ALTERNATIVES TO THE DOMINANT BEAUTY IDEAL

As discussed in Chapter 4, mainstream standards of beauty are always shifting in subtle ways that keep them virtually unattainable for the vast majority of girls and women. But there's one constant. Even though Caucasians don't typically realize it, the Western beauty ideal is a *white* beauty ideal. This has negative consequences for girls and women of various backgrounds, but it influences girls of different races in different ways.

For example, girls of Asian descent who strongly embrace Western beauty ideals are more prone to eating disorders and may develop a more subservient attitude toward men, while the Latina girls who watch the most television have especially low self-esteem. And if you rank the self-esteem levels of African American, Caucasian, and Latina girls, African American girls have the best self-image and Latina girls have the worst. Because of these differing effects, no one-size-fits-all approach will work in addressing the problem of the white beauty ideal.

That said, a lot of research about beauty standards and race focuses specifically on African American and Caucasian girls, and the studies make it clear: when African American girls reject mainstream beauty standards and focus instead on broader standards, they are happier with their physical appearances. African American women have a long history of recognizing and resisting the white beauty ideal, and this benefits African American girls, who can learn from African American culture that a wide range of physical appearances is beautiful or normal.

When African American girls reject the Western beauty ideal, their self-esteem is substantially better than their Caucasian peers'. One study suggests that young Latina women who embrace Latina beauty standards may not benefit to the same extent—but interestingly, when Latina girls watch black-oriented television, their body image is better than that of Latina girls who watch mainstream television.

No matter what, it's clear that the Western beauty standard is unreasonably narrow, and that broadening girls' horizons can only help them. Therefore, it's important for parents to seek out alternative images and affirm their daughters' own beauty. We must heed the call of scholars such as Tracey Owens Patton, PhD, who argues that women must "create their own standards of beauty" to escape the escape the negative consequences of the Western beauty ideal.

PROVIDING ALTERNATIVES AND AFFIRMATIONS

Betty Bynum is helping parents support their young daughters with her book series and brand, the I'm a Girl Collection. Bynum is a professional actress and author, and her book collection has five titles so far: *I'm a Pretty Little Black Girl*, *I'm an Awesome Asian Girl*, *I'm a Lovely Little Latina!*, *Hooray, I'm a Girl in the USA!*, and *I'm an Incredible Indian Girl!* As the titles indicate, these books are meant to help diverse girls love their own looks.

Bynum got the idea for these books when she saw Julianne Moore on *The Today Show* promoting *Freckleface Strawberry*, a children's book based on Moore's childhood experiences of being taunted and teased for her red hair and freckled skin. Bynum says that when she saw the segment, she thought, "That's really good, but I didn't know any freckleface strawberries in my neighborhood growing up." So she created the *I'm a Pretty Little Black Girl* book to offer girls from her own background affirmations that they, too, are beautiful in all skin tones and hair textures.

Bynum was inspired to expand the book into a series for people of various races and ethnicities when her young son, Joshua, pointed something out to her. What about the girls he was friends with who weren't black? Wouldn't they like a book about themselves, too?

Finding a publisher for the series happened almost immediately, Bynum says. "They knew that there was a huge void," she explains. "With President Obama being in office and having two little girls, the landscape changed. Publishers said, 'Oh, we need to do something for little black girls now!' People became more aware of the void in the children's book area for black girls due to the presence of Sasha and Malia, and more aware of the celebratory nature of the diversity in America because of our newly elected black president."

The series' reception has proven that parents are eager to give their daughters books that fill that void. Her first title, *I'm a Pretty Little Black Girl*, hit number one in its category on Amazon.com.

Bynum's best advice to parents is this: "Purposely get images of beautiful black women and women of color, and paste them all around the house. That way, if you're not going to see those images of beauty in the outside world, you're still going to see them at home."

. . . .

TIP 7: WATCH MEDIA AND READ BOOKS WITH DIVERSE CHARACTERS

Children don't just need to see people like themselves in the media and in books. They also need to see positive depictions of people from other racial and ethnic groups. So, seek them out. Watch movies and television shows about a range of people. And find books that feature stories about people whose backgrounds differ from your family's.

Make a special effort to find picture books featuring cross-ethnic friendships in particular. (This may be especially important if you live in an area lacking in diversity, where cross-ethnic friendships are not an option for your family.) Researchers have noted that children under the age of eight are strongly oriented toward their own racial or ethnic group, so seeing a character who looks like them gives them a character to identify with. Then, when they see that character interact with people from different races, the story functions as a source of indirect cross-ethnic contact for the child—with the potential to improve their racial attitudes.

Just remember that as you and your daughter watch television or read books together, you need to be explicit about your own position. Children of this age range are not very good at making inferences about adults' feelings on race, so as discussed in Tip 1, we have to be clear.

Young children's picture books featuring cross-racial friendships and relationships:

Black Is Brown Is Tan by Arnold Adoff and Emily Arnold McCully was first published in 1973, and it was the first children's book featuring an interracial family. It celebrates the fact that people have different colors.

Black, White, Just Right! by Marguerite W. Davol and Irene Trivas celebrates the differences between an African American mother and a Caucasian father whose daughter is assured that everyone is "just right."

Global Babies by the Global Fund for Children is a series of color photographs of babies from seventeen cultures around the world. Children learn that all babies, no matter how different they look, are beloved.

I'm Like You, You're Like Me by Cindy Gainer and Miki Sakamoto helps children learn respect for others, promoting acceptance, listening, kindness, and understanding. The book shows readers how the diverse children depicted are alike and different from one another.

Me I Am by Jack Prelutsky depicts three diverse and very different children who have a series of mini-adventures. It celebrates individuality and diversity.

One Love by Cedella Marley is based on the Bob Marley song by the same title, and shows people of many colors working together to improve their neighborhood.

Shades of People by Shelley Rotner and Sheila M. Kelly uses photographs of happy children to show that people come in many
skin tones, even within the same family.

The Skin I'm In: A First Look at Racism by Pat Thomas and
Lesley Harker helps children become comfortable with the
visible racial differences among people. It was written by a
psychotherapist and child counselor and includes a guide for
parents on how to best use the book. Illustrations include
kids of color looking at magazines featuring blond-haired,
blue-eyed princesses.

The Skin You Live In by Michael Tyler and David Lee Csicsko
promotes social harmony and the acceptance of diversity.

What I Like about Me by Allia Zobel Nolan and Miki Sakamoto
teaches children that what makes us different is what makes
us special.

Whoever You Are by Mem Fox and Leslie Staub celebrates our
world's diverse cultures.

TIPS FROM THE POWERFUL WORDS CHARACTER DEVELOPMENT SYSTEM

BY ROBYN SILVERMAN, PhD

I've been writing the Powerful Words Character Development
System for after-school programs worldwide since 2005.
Powerful Words is now the number-one character development
system specifically designed for the after-school activity world.

In this program, I like to make "differences" part of the
conversation about "similarities." When we cover the powerful
words "acceptance" or "open-mindedness" or even "respect"

or "empathy," skin color as well as disability or ability, hair and eye color, size, weight, whatever come into play.

For example, as part of my curriculum on "meeting new friends" for children ages four to six, I might ask the children to look around the room and answer some questions about what they see. I know this can be scary for some, but it helps make a strong point.

I ask: "How are we all the same?" And then, "How are we all different (such as hair, height, skin color)?"

Then comes the key question: "Can we be friends with people who are different from us?" Of course!

Parents can do this, too. The key is to make it personal. Ask the child: "Think about one of your friends. How are they the same and different from you? What would you say to someone who told you, 'You can't be friends with that person! They are different from you! They have darker or lighter skin or different colored eyes, or they don't like karate or dance or piano like you. What would you say to them about that?'"

When your child replies, you can affirm their response and say, "Great!" And help them focus on the positives: "What do you like best about your friend?"

Then, you can move to a "meeting" lesson. Ask your child: "Now, think back to when you first met some of your friends. How did you meet them?" After discussing this, you can ask them what they can say or do to meet a new friend. You can coach them to remember these easy steps:

1. Say hello!
2. Tell them your name!

3. Ask a question: How are you? Want to play?
4. Give a compliment: Cool shirt! (Then, "Imagine I'm a new friend. How would you greet me?") (Insert exercise in action.)

You see? With young children, you don't need to hit them over the head with messages about diversity that will encourage open-mindedness. Children are great at picking up what you're putting down.

These same types of conversations easily happen with two books by Todd Parr that I recommend: *We are all Different* and *The Peace Book*. These give ample opportunities to have conversations about differences and similarities. First have your child notice the differences and similarities among people in the books. Then have them make it specific to themselves and their friends and family. Next, challenge them by asking what-if questions about that friendship—and believe me, they'll tell you what's what.

Pop Culture Coaching, Step 3: Watch and Talk about Media Content with Your Kids

Co-viewing and discussing media with our children is a great way to disrupt the stereotypes found on-screen. Call out the racial and ethnic stereotypes that you see. Let your children know you don't think it's fair that the bad guys so often have dark skin, or that the black Barbie is always off to one side in commercials. Make observations, and listen and respond to anything that your kids have to say, too.

TIP 8: SEEK OUT POSITIVE PORTRAYALS OF GIRLS OF COLOR

Help your daughter to seek out television shows and movies that portray girls and women of color in central roles and in a positive light, without resorting to stereotypes. Race doesn't have to be a central issue or theme. The inclusivity is itself a great thing. Check out both shows that are currently airing and those that are off the air but are available on DVD, through Netflix, or from similar services.

Here are some possibilities for your preschooler:

- PBS's *Daniel Tiger's Neighborhood* (Miss Elaina is African American)
- Disney Junior's *Doc McStuffins* (Doc is African American)
- Nick Junior's *Ni Hao, Kai-Lan* (Kai-Lan is Chinese)
- Nick Junior's *Dora the Explorer* (Dora is Latina)
- Disney Junior's *Jake and the Neverland Pirates* (Izzy is of ambiguous race and is voiced by Madison Pettis, a child actress who is of both African American and Caucasian descent)
- PBS's *The Magic School Bus* (Keesha is African American and Wanda is Chinese American)
- PBS's *Sesame Street* (The show always features a diverse cast)
- PBS's *Sid the Science Kid* (The family is ambiguously mixed race)
- PBS's *Wild Kratts* (Aviva is Latina and Koki is African American)
- PBS's *Super Why!* (Princess Presto is African American)

For older girls (ages seven and up), consider shows such as these:

- Nickelodeon's *How to Rock* (featuring African American actress Cymphonique Miller and Ecuadorian American actress Samantha Boscarino)
- Disney's *Shake It Up* (about a black girl, played by biracial actress

Zendaya Coleman, and a white girl, played by Bella Thorne, who are best friends even though they are from different backgrounds)

- Disney's *That's So Raven* (featuring African American actress Raven-Symoné)
- Nickelodeon's *True Jackson, VP* (featuring African American actress Keke Palmer and Filipina actress Ashley Argota)
- Nickelodeon's *Victorious* (featuring a diverse cast led by Victoria Justice, who is half Caucasian and half Puerto Rican)
- Disney's *Wizards of Waverly Place* (depicting a multiethnic family, including Latina superstar Selena Gomez)

TIP 9: DISCUSS RACIAL AND ETHNIC STEREOTYPES IN THE MEDIA

Scheibe suggests that when children are about eight years old, it's possible to discuss racial and ethnic stereotypes with them. When movies or television programs contain stereotypes, you can explain to older children that those stereotypes are the result of decisions made by real people. Scheibe suggests that Pocahontas is a good starting point for conversations about how the stereotypes in media are the results of people's decisions.

"To me," Scheibe says, "Pocahontas is probably the most egregious of all of the Disney Princesses because she was a real person in history, and she could not have had a twelve-inch waist. And she was twelve years old when she met John Smith. She didn't fall in love with him. She didn't marry him, but she did save his life. But the Disneyfication of her story overlays a really skinny, beautiful princess whose goal is to fall in love.

"You can talk about that with your children," Scheibe suggests, "and you can focus on other aspects of who she is. You can point out all sorts of issues, like the way that skin color in Disney movies ties to gender. Females, regardless of the ethnicity, almost always have lighter skin than the males. Jasmine is much lighter in skin tone than Aladdin. Pocahontas is much lighter in skin tone than any of the male Native Americans. Just as a *noticing* thing. You can say, 'That's an interesting thing to notice. Why do you think they did that?' You may not always have the answers, but you can get kids in the habit of noticing that somebody made this film." (See also Tip 9.)

Jean Kilbourne agrees that it's important to talk about race and radicalized beauty with children. "It's hard to be the parent of any girl these days, but to try to be a parent of color raising a girl is incredibly difficult," she notes. "Even the role models, like Beyoncé, have straightened hair. Black models have light skin, and their skin is lightened even more in ads. They almost always have straight hair and relatively Caucasian features. You just don't see very many who aren't like that."

But she says parents can take control by calling out stereotypes and the white beauty ideal when they see it. "Make it conscious," she says. "Talk about it. Bring it up. Talk about how difficult it is, how unfair it is, and how it doesn't have anything to do with real beauty. Try to enlist the help of other parents, too.

"No matter what the problem is," Kilbourne adds, "the answer always seems to be more conversation, and creating the kind of atmosphere where the child feels safe coming to you with questions and knows he or she will get a respectful answer."

Pop Culture Coaching, Step 4: Teach Children about Media Creation

As our children's pop culture coaches, we must always remind them that media are created by people. This knowledge is a fundamental of media literacy. If our children recognize that stereotypes in the media are the result of people's decisions, they can become empowered to resist stereotypical messages, to talk back to media creators, and to internalize the healthier messages we as their parents have provided them.

TIP 10: GO ONLINE TOGETHER AND LOOK UP THE CREW

To demystify authorship with your child, put the Internet Movie Database (IMDb.com) to good use. There, you can look up specific movies and television shows with your child, and under "Quick Links," you can click on "Full Cast and Crew" to see a list of the film or show's directors, writers, and cast members. Most cast and crew members listed will have a hyperlink from their name to a bio page where you can learn more about them.

Click around with your child and you will encounter pictures for many cast and crew members, as well as biographical details such as their age, marital status, and other films or shows they have worked on.

Look for patterns together. Who's represented? Who's missing? Are the directors and most of the writers white men, for example (as is often the case)?

For example, visit the IMDb page for *The Princess and the Frog*, and you'll see that everyone listed has a man's name, except for E. D. Baker, who uses initials instead of a first name. A web search will reveal that E. D. Baker is a Caucasian woman who writes children's books—the only woman given a writing credit because her book, *The Frog Princess*, was used for source material. Disney optioned it to be the basis of *The Princess and the Frog*.

Then, let your child click on the names listed. Of those that have photographs in their bios, how many appear to be Caucasian? (Answer: All of them.)

Once you have discovered these patterns together, you can ask your older child if she thinks it's fair that a movie about an African American woman didn't have any African American women involved in writing it. You can explain in a calm, straightforward way that while the writers surely tried to do the best job they could, maybe the film could have been even better if some of the directors and writers were themselves African American women, with life experiences that would be relate to the movie.

THE IMPORTANCE OF LISTENING

The tips in this section have largely focused on what you, as a parent, can say to your child regarding issues of race, or who and what you can expose them to. But here's one more important bit of advice: Make sure that you really listen to your child, too. By the time they hit adolescence, no matter what their racial or ethnic background, many girls feel they have lost their voice—the ability to speak up for themselves, to be heard and respected.

Elizabeth Iglesias, PhD, and Sherry Cormier, PhD, of West Virginia University argue, "The most important thing adults can do for teenage girls is to validate them." They say that adolescent girls desperately want real communication. They really want to know what adults feel and how they think, and they really want to be listened to.

Parent-child communication patterns should be established early on, because it's tough (though not impossible) to change those patterns during our children's teenage years. So, if we want our teenage daughters to believe we will to listen to them, we have to start when they are young—validating their feelings and respecting their voices throughout their childhoods.

Conclusion

As parents, we want to do right by our children. We want to raise them to be happy, healthy people—confident, secure, loving, and well-loved. And for this reason, we are always looking for the best parenting resources we can find—parenting tools that are flexible and robust and useful in many different situations over time.

As you make use of the ideas from this book, you'll find that pop culture coaching fits that description. It will flexibly accommodate your family's values, even if those values evolve over time. And even though this book focuses on applying pop culture coaching's principles to princess culture, those principles will apply to all kinds of other media, as well—for boys and girls alike. Have a son who's obsessed with superheroes and video games? Follow the four pop culture coaching steps, and you won't be let down.

RECAP: POP CULTURE COACHING IN FOUR STEPS

1. Identify your family's values.
2. Establish a healthy media diet for your children.
3. Watch and talk about media content with your children.
4. Teach your children about media creation.

Remember: By watching and talking about media content with your children in an open-minded manner—one that is respectful of your children's own perspectives—you will do more than raise media-literate children who are good critical viewers and thinkers. You will also keep the lines of communication open within your family, paving the way for dialogue about and beyond the media.

This means that the principles of pop culture coaching will continue to work for you as your family evolves. As your daughters grow up and leave their princess years behind, the core strategies of pop culture coaching will still be relevant—helping you navigate the media and pop culture landscapes that at the moment are still beyond the horizon. But many of the issues your daughters face in their tween and teen years will be familiar to you. Pressures about their physical appearances. Stereotypical ideas about what girls' behavior should and should not be like. Challenges regarding race representation and race relations. And always, always marketing as far as the eye can see.

Fortunately, you're starting conversations on these topics early—working to raise daughters resilient to these cultural forces. And that's the best thing that parents of today's girls can do.

TALKING ABOUT PRINCESS FILMS
Discussion Ideas for Parents

At **RebeccaHains.com**, you will find parent-child discussion guides for each of the Disney Princess films (as well as other types of films, beyond princess themes).

My colleagues and I have prepared these Disney Princess discussion guides for you with the main suggestions from *The Princess Problem* in mind. We've considered each of the major problems with princess media discussed in this book: the Pretty Princess Mandate; the gender stereotypes (including behaviors and the romance narrative); and for some films, issues of race representation.

Then, we've laid out for you how these problems do or don't manifest in each film. So when a film is full of issues, or when a film does a great job countering traditional stereotypes, we let you know. Our goal is to help you coach your child in these areas.

In each guide, we also offer suggestions under the subheading of "Make it real." These provide you with ideas for translating what you have seen on-screen into real-life scenarios with your child.

We end each discussion guide with interesting facts and details meant to help you help your child understand that *media are created by people*, since this knowledge is a pillar of media literacy.

On the pages that follow, I'm including the complete parent-child discussion guide for *Frozen* to give you a sense of what you'll find there. A more detailed synopsis is available on the website as well.

Before you dive in, here are a few tips to help you make the most of the parent–child discussion guides:

- **Let your child be your compass**. You know your child better than anyone else. So, take whatever ideas you like from the discussion guides, but always phrase your comments and questions in whatever way will make the most sense to your little one.

- **Experiment to figure out what conversations are age-appropriate for your child**. In the discussion guides, you'll notice that we group our suggestions by the child's age—but we also know that every child is different. What's age-appropriate for one child might be over the head of another, and vice versa. So, you should experiment to see what kinds of conversations work for your child—how much he or she understands certain types of questions.

- **Don't expect agreement**. These guides offer several examples of ways you might "talk back" to the screen to express approval or disapproval of a film's contents. By talking back to the screen in your child's presence, you are sharing your values with your child. But your child may not always agree with you! That's okay—your child has the right to her own opinion. What's important is for her to know where you stand and for you to model critically engaged viewing.

- **Add your own talking points**. Please note that these discussion guides are meant to be a starting point. They are resources to help you practice pop culture coaching and raise media-literate children, but they are not comprehensive. Different families with different values may wish to emphasize certain points. So feel free to add new content and make different points.

- **Feel free to extrapolate**! As an informed reader, you can extrapolate from one guide to another. If there's something you want to discuss with your children more often or in more than one context, you should be able to do so. For example, we offer tips on discussing race in films featuring white princess characters in *Beauty and the Beast*, *Brave*, and *Frozen*. You could have similar conversations about race regarding, say, *Snow White and the Seven Dwarfs* and *Cinderella*, even though tips on race representation are not offered for those films.

- **Be attentive to your child's responses to the films**. When you watch the princess films with your child, remember to be attentive to anything she has to say. Acknowledge her comments and answer her questions. Always let her know that you are listening to her, and that her ideas are important to you. This will make it clear that you value the opportunity to talk about media with her, establishing healthy patterns of respect and dialogue for your family.

Good luck and have fun pop culture coaching!

Frozen (2013)
Age Range

Common Sense Media recommends *Frozen* for children ages five and older, due to some scary scenes, but notes that it may be appropriate for children as young as age two, depending on the child.

Synopsis

Frozen is the story of the relationship between two sisters, the princesses Elsa and Anna. Elsa has secret powers over snow and ice that she does not know how to control and which she fears. When Elsa inadvertently harms Anna with her ice powers, Anna nearly dies— but Anna saves Elsa from a villain's plot by committing a selfless act of live on her sister's behalf. Through this act, she ultimately saves herself as well.

Discussion Guide

Here are some suggestions for discussion, roughly categorized by age level. Use these as a rough guide: tailor them to your own child's level.

1. THE PRETTY PRINCESS MANDATE

Frozen offers an opportunity to explore the narrowness of the Pretty Princess Mandate because Elsa and Anna's appearances are remarkably similar. Their eyes are incredibly large (larger than their wrists) and their noses are incredibly small. Their waists are diminutive too, which in children's media and toys is always a cause of concern due to the implications for girls' body images. (The princesses' waists are smaller than their heads and only about as wide as their hands are long.)

In contrast, the male lead characters, Hans and Kristoff, are substantially larger—a gross exaggeration of the relatively small average physical differences between real men and women. The underlying message of this dimorphism is that female bodies are most desirable when they take up as little space as possible, while men's bodies are most valued when they are expansive—a message that can promote self-consciousness and body-image issues.

With children ages four and five, parents can address these issues by co-viewing the movie and talking back to the screen, modeling critical viewing. Your child will listen to what you say. Consider making comments such as the following:

- "Anna and Elsa look very similar to one another. Their eyes are very, very big and their noses are very, very small. They are pretty, but there are lots of ways people can be pretty! Sometimes sisters look very different from each other, and that's okay. Everyone is pretty in their own way."

- When Anna tells Hans, "I'm awkward! You're gorgeous," and Hans takes Anna's hand, you can briefly pause the movie to point this out: "Look—in this scene, Anna's eyes are larger than her wrists. Do you see it too? That's so strange! *Nobody* has eyes larger than their wrists. I don't like it when the people who make movies make girls' bodies so unrealistic. It's not healthy for girls. Sometimes it makes girls think their bodies aren't good enough even though they are fine the way they are. That really bothers me."

Make it real: After viewing, you could pull out some albums of family photos, old and new. Explore them with your child, paying special attention to the differences and similarities between siblings in your own extended family. How similar or different do sisters look in comparison to one another? What about brothers?

If your child owns *Frozen* dolls for both male and female characters, you may be able to use them to show your child how extreme Disney's gender dimorphism can be. When I first unpackaged the Disney Store fashion doll versions of Elsa, Anna, and Kristoff, I was shocked at the Kristoff doll's heft and decided to weigh each doll on my kitchen scale. The results: Elsa: $4^3/_8$ oz, Anna: $4^5/_8$ oz, and Kristoff: 11 oz.

In other words, because Elsa and Anna are so wispy and slight in build and Kristoff is so bulky and thick the two sisters *together* weigh less than Kristoff.

If your family owns these toys or similar ones, you might say: "I noticed when we were playing that your Kristoff doll feels much heavier than the Anna and Elsa dolls. It really surprised me. What if we do an experiment with the kitchen scale to see exactly what the difference is between these toys?"

If your results are similar to mine, you could say: "Wow, it is so strange that the two princess dolls *combined* don't weigh as much as the Kristoff doll! That isn't right. It doesn't take two mommies equal the size of one daddy. Men and women don't have bodies that are *that* different from one another. It's silly to think that women should be that much tinier than men. Remember, everybody's body is fine the way it is, and except at the doctor's office, the number on the scale doesn't matter."

2. THE GENDER STEREOTYPES

As modern Disney Princesses, Elsa and Anna defy several stereo-types regarding feminine behavior. They are active, not passive. Although Elsa is often anxious, she is authoritative and speaks plainly to Anna during moments of conflict. Elsa also has real power and decision-making authority once she becomes queen, as indicated by the Duke of Weselton's eagerness to discuss matters of trade with her.

On the other hand, in the first part of the film, men are portrayed as the ones who wield power and have voices worthy of attention.

For example, the king of Arendelle and the troll king together decide the course of Elsa and Anna's futures. Meanwhile, the queen of Arendelle hardly speaks: the king has twelve lines of dialogue, the troll has seven, and the queen speaks only two brief lines: "Anna!" and "She's ice cold."

Subsequently, the course of action the king elects is decisive but clearly ineffective. It is not in their best interest to be isolated from others and from one another; in fact, as the film plays out, this decision proves to be psychologically damaging.

With children ages four and five, if you wish to address these gendered representations of authority and power while co-viewing, be as specific as possible. Here are some examples:

- "In the opening scene, the ice harvesters sing that ice's magic is stronger than a hundred men. That makes it sound like only men are strong. But I know women are strong, too!"
- "The king and the troll are doing all the talking in this scene. I wish the girls' mommy, the queen, talked more in this part of the movie. I bet she would have had some good ideas about how to help Elsa with her ice powers! Shutting the girls away didn't help them at all."
- "It's so brave of Anna to go find her sister. I like the way she takes charge and lets other people know that she will handle things with Elsa. Did you know that as the youngest of the two sisters, she is second in line to the throne? That means she has real power and authority in the kingdom, and if anything happened to Elsa, she would become queen herself. It's great to see her take charge and be such a good leader."

With children ages six to eight, you can raise these points while co-viewing, but you could also connect some dots in a later conversation. For example:

- "In the beginning of *Frozen*, I noticed that men like the king and the troll king have all the power. But what's interesting is that later in the movie, Elsa becomes queen and doesn't just have snow and ice power. She has real political power to make decisions for other people, too. For example the Duke of Weselton mentions that Weselton is Arendelle's trading partner. Do you know what that means? It means that Weselton and Arendelle do business together. They sell each other the things that they make and the queen has an important role to play in that process. This is just one of the ways in which being queen of a country is a big job. Once she is queen, Elsa has real work to do to as the leader of Arendelle."

Make it real: In the middle part of the song "Do You Want to Build a Snowman," Anna speaks to a painting of an armored Joan of Arc riding into battle ("Hang in there, Joan!"). Joan of Arc is an interesting, complex, and brave historic role model for girls. You could point out the painting in *Frozen* to your child and then tell her more about Joan—referencing either online sources or an illustrated book such as Diane Stanley's *Joan of Arc*. Also noteworthy for parents seeking to broaden their daughters' princess toy collections: the Papo toy line sells a small Joan of Arc action figure (wearing a suit of armor as in the Arendelle portrait gallery) and horse.

3. THE ROMANCE NARRATIVE

All of Walt Disney Studios's previous princess-themed films were romance stories first and foremost, in which young women are in search of a romantic "Happily Ever After"—sometimes after falling in love at first sight. In contrast, *Frozen* is the first Walt Disney Studios film to argue *against* love at first sight.

With children ages four to five, offer concrete points of agreement and criticism so that they know where you stand. For example:

- When characters such as Elsa and Kristoff warn Anna against marrying someone she just met, you can state your agreement and support by saying, "That's right! You shouldn't marry someone you just met. It's important to really get to know another person first."
- When Anna sings about how she dreams she will find romance, you might comment, "It's too bad she's focused on finding romance right away! She is so lonely and it would be healthier if she focused on finding new friends."
- At the end of the film when Kristoff asks Anna if it's okay for him to kiss her, you could say, "Wow, it's really good that Kristoff asks Anna if it's okay to kiss. He is showing his respect for her. They are still getting to know one another, and that was a healthy question for him to ask."

With children ages six to eight, or perhaps younger depending on the child, feel free to make these same observations while co-viewing, but *plan a conversation about healthy relationships of various types later on*, when you're not in front of the screen. Some talking points:

- "At the beginning of *Frozen*, little Anna begs Elsa to do the magic, because she thinks her big sister is amazing. I think a lot of girls think their sisters (or brothers) are amazing even though they don't have magic powers! It's nice to see a movie that focuses on sisters learning to get along. Too many movies make it seem like a girl's main goal should be finding a boyfriend, or a prince, but other relationships are also really important—just like Merida's relationship with her mother in *Brave*."

- "I think it's really interesting that in *Frozen*, Elsa's mantra, 'Conceal, don't feel,' actually makes matters worse. When her father taught her that he meant well, but it was really bad advice. It's actually important for us all to be in touch with our feelings and pay attention to how we react to the problems we face in life. If you are ever in a situation or a relationship with someone who is making you upset or uncomfortable or sad, please don't ignore it or try to hold it in. We can talk about it together. I want you to know that you can always tell me about your feelings."

4. THE RACE REPRESENTATION

The setting of *Frozen* is a fictitious Scandinavian kingdom in the pre-industrial era. The human characters depicted in *Frozen* all appear to be white, though the film does offer some ethnic diversity that might be lost on U.S. audience members—specifically Kristoff and the other ice harvesters are supposed to be members of the Saami people, the northernmost indigenous people in Europe. Their Saami culture is indicated in the film by markers such as their manner of dress and their use of reindeer for transportation.

You can also mention that the Saami people are from a range of racial backgrounds and that many people have objected to the fact that all of the characters in *Frozen* are white. For example, you can look together at images online that have reimagined Elsa as a person of color at www.dailydot.com/fandom/tumblr-disney-frozen-princess/.

5. TEACHING CHILDREN ABOUT MEDIA CREATION

As our children's pop culture coaches, we can help them become media literate by always reminding them that media are created by other people—people who are making choices about who and what to depict on-screen.

In the case of *Frozen*, there are a lot of wonderful websites and videos to browse about the making of the film, ranging from the way the ice and snow was rendered on-screen to the decisions about costume design, textiles, and scenery. You can emphasize for your child that many people contributed to this project.

You can also carry over the conversation about race representation into your conversation about media creation. For example you might note that the woman who voices the troll who sings the lead vocals in "Fixer-Upper," is Maia Wilson, a successful African American actress and singer. Her credits include several Broadway shows, and if you do a YouTube or Google Video search for her, you can witness her singing. It's unfortunate that Disney characters played by people of color are so often not human characters and therefore do not help diversify on-screen representations of people of color. However, we can point out Wilson's involvement in the film to our children, for in a soundtrack full of gifted professional singers like Idina Menzel and Josh Gad, her soaring vocals are an impressive contribution to the movie.

FOR FURTHER READING

Books

The Body Image Survival Guide for Parents: Helping Toddlers, Tweens, and Teens Thrive by Marci Warhaft-Nadler.

Born to Buy: The Commercialized Child and the New Consumer Culture by Juliet B. Schor.

Cinderella Ate My Daughter: Dispatches from the Front Lines of the New Girlie-Girl Culture by Peggy Orenstein.

Consuming Kids: Protecting Our Children from the Onslaught of Marketing & Advertising by Susan Linn.

Dads and Daughters: How to Inspire, Understand, and Support Your Daughter When She's Growing Up So Fast by Joe Kelly.

Good Girls Don't Get Fat: How Weight Obsession Is Messing Up Our Girls and How We Can Help Them Thrive Despite It by Robyn Silverman.

Growing Up with Girl Power: Girlhood On Screen and in Everyday Life by Rebecca Hains.

Her Next Chapter: How Mother-Daughter Book Clubs Can Help Girls Navigate Malicious Media, Risky Relationships, Girl Gossip, and So Much More by Lori Day.

How to Say It to Girls: Communicating with Your Growing Daughter by Nancy Gruver.

Killing Monsters: Why Children Need Fantasy, Super Heroes, and Make-Believe Violence by Gerard Jones and Lynn Ponton.

The Lolita Effect: The Media Sexualization of Young Girls and Five Keys to Fixing It by M. Gigi Durham.

Nurture Shock: New Thinking about Children by Po Bronson and Ashley Merryman.

Packaging Girlhood: Rescuing Our Daughters from Marketers' Schemes by Sharon Lamb and Lyn Mikel Brown.

Pink and Blue: Telling the Boys from the Girls in America by Jo B. Paoletti.

Pink Brain, Blue Brain: How Small Differences Grow into Troublesome Gaps— And What We Can Do about It by Lise Eliot.

Princess Recovery: A How-to Guide to Raising Strong, Empowered Girls Who Can Create Their Own Happily Ever Afters by Jennifer Hartstein.

Redefining Girly: How Parents Can Fight the Stereotyping and Sexualization of Girlhood, from Birth to Tween by Melissa Atkins Wardy.

So Sexy So Soon: The New Sexualized Childhood and What Parents Can Do to Protect Their Kids by Diane Levin and Jean Kilbourne.

Blogs

Beauty Redefined. www.beautyredefined.net/blog

Brenda Chapman's blog. brenda-chapman.com/blog

Campaign for a Commercial-Free Chilhood. www.commercialfreechildhood.org/blog

Dr. Jennifer Shewmaker's Operation Transformation. Jennifershewmaker.com

Dr. Robyn Silverman's blog. www.drrobynsilverman.com

Gamine Expedition. gamineexpedition.blogspot.com

Girl w/ Pen. thesocietypages.org/girlwpen

Peggy Orenstein's blog. Peggyorenstein.com/blog.html

Pigtail Pals and Ballcap Buddies. pigtailpalsblog.com

Princess Free Zone. princessfreezone.com

Rachel Simmons's blog. www.rachelsimmons.com/blogs/rachels-blog

Rebecca Hains's blog. RebeccaHains.com

Reel Girl: Imagining Gender Equality in the Fantasy World. Reelgirl.com

Renee Hobbs at the Media Education Lab. mediaedlab.com

Shaping Youth. shapingyouth.org

Sociological Images. thesocietypages.org/socimages

SPARK Movement. www.sparksummit.com

ACKNOWLEDGMENTS

*T*he *Princess Problem* had its earliest beginnings during my research for my previous book, *Growing Up With Girl Power: Girlhood On Screen and in Everyday Life*. The little girls in my study loved girl power cartoons, but during our conversations, I learned how much they loved princesses, too. Many thanks to them for inspiring me to take this path of inquiry.

Conducting the research for *The Princess Problem* spanned more than three years, during which three graduate assistants worked with me on this project: Timothy Magill, who assisted with the early stages of this project; Krista Andberg, who offered substantial recruiting, interviewing, and transcription help; and Karen Loughlin, who worked tirelessly on transcription and data analysis. I am grateful to the three of them for their contributions and to Salem State University's School of Graduate Studies for assigning me such terrific students and providing additional grant funding. Gratitude also to my friend Florrie Marks, who was always willing to fill in with additional transcribing as needed.

I would also like to thank the Communications Department for supporting this study, particularly department chairs Judi Cook and Peter Oehlkers. With their blessing, four communications undergraduates—Jenna Burpee, Morgan Grogan, Caitlin Mannix, and Nadine Solimine—each spent a summer session immersed in princess research. Many thanks to the university's Provost, Dr. Kristin Esterberg, as well. She encouraged me to write a trade (rather than academic) book about the study, making a complicated decision easier.

To the parents and other pseudonymous people whom I interviewed for this book: Because of our confidentiality agreement, I can't thank you by name—but please know that I am incredibly grateful to each of you for spending time talking with me about your children, princess culture, the media, and parenting in general. I am also appreciative of all the experts and professionals in the field who allowed me to interview them "on the record" for this book. Your perspective is invaluable. I'm likewise indebted to my Facebook community and Melissa Wardy's Facebook community at Pigtail Pals and Ballcap Buddies for answering research-related questions on occasion, and to all the friends, family members, and acquaintances who eagerly suggested potential interviewees. There's been such enthusiasm surrounding this project that it's sometimes been overwhelming (in a good way!).

Several friends and colleagues generously read drafts of the book proposal and/or manuscript chapters. I owe debts of gratitude to my fellow writers' group members Christa Terry and Lori Day; my sister Sarah Jackson, herself an incredible writer; Dr. Miriam Forman-Brunell of the University of Missouri–Kansas City, who is coediting the scholarly anthology *Princess Cultures: Mediating Girls' Identities and Imaginations* with me and is contagiously enthusiastic about princess scholarship; Dr. Cyndy Scheibe of Ithica College; Dr. Dafna Lemish at Southern Illinois University Carbondale, editor of the *Journal of Children and Media*; and Froswa' Booker-Drew of Soulstice

Consultancy. Also, my colleagues Dr. Robert Brown and Beverly Gerson of Salem State University, Dr. Jody Madeira of Indiana University, Dr. Sharon Mazzarella of James Madison University, Dr. Renee Hobbs of the University of Rhode Island, Dr. Gigi Durham of the University of Iowa, and Dr. Sharon Lamb at University of Massachusetts Boston were helpful sounding boards at critical points in the project.

My colleagues at the Brave Girls Alliance were always willing to answer questions and share resources. Inês Almeida, Lyn Mikel Brown, Lori Day, Nancy Gruver, Peggy Orenstein, Jean Kilbourne, Lexie Kite, Lindsay Kite, Elline Lipkin, Margot Magowan, Jennifer Shewmaker, Robyn Silverman, Melissa Wardy, and Marci Warhaft-Nadler: Thank you for being true allies. Much gratitude also goes to my agent Jill Marsal of Marsal Lyon Literary Agency and my editor Shana Drehs at Sourcebooks for their excellent advice and guidance along the way.

Finally, I would like to thank my children, Theodore and Alexander, for being constant sources of inspiration and joy, whose love and laughter brighten my days. And last but not least, all my love and gratitude to my husband Tyler. His loving support makes everything possible.

NOTES

Introduction

xv *Disney Princess is the number-one brand for licensed entertainment merchandise in the United States and Canada*: Mayer, 2013.

Chapter 1

1 *In consequence, boys grow up in an active, rough-and-tumble, building-oriented world, while girls grow up in a passive, frilly, image- and appearance-oriented world*: Paoletti, 2012.

4 *He noted that* Fallen Princesses *"comment critically on the Disney world and raise many questions about the lives women are expected to lead…"*: Zipes, no date.

5 *When Disney Junior announced the impending release of its new television cartoon* Sofia the First…: Barnes, 2011.

6 *Orenstein was incredulous. She accused Disney of trying to have it both ways*: Orenstein, Dec. 14, 2011.

8 *As author Colette Dowling has argued*: Dowling, 2000.

8 *Ultimately, girls are dropping out of sports at two times the rate…*: Sabo and Veliz, 2008.

8 *Studies show that this is in part because girls feel worried about how they look while exercising…*: Robbins, Pender, and Kazanis, 2003; Dwyer, Allison, Goldenberg, Fein, Yoshida, and Boutilier, 2006.

10 *As early as 1975, scholar Kay Stone…*: Stone, 1975.

10 *"not only passive and pretty, but also unusually patient, obedient, industrious, and quiet"*: Stone, 1975, p. 45.

10 *Since then, many other studies have agreed…*: Baker-Sperry and Grauerholz, 2003; Beres, 1999; Dundes, 2000; Giroux, 1998; Pewewardy, 1996/97; Trites, 1991.

14 *And as the Disney Princess brand evolved into a megabrand worth $4 billion…*: Setoodeh, 2007.

14 *Orenstein's* New York Times Magazine *article "What's Wrong with Cinderella?" proved a cultural touchstone*: Orenstein, 2006.

14 *Orenstein later expanded her argument into a bestselling book,* Cinderella Ate My Daughter: Orenstein, 2011.

15 *…the* Christian Science Monitor *covered the issue in an article called "Little Girls or Little Women? The Disney Princess Effect"*: Hanes, 2011.

15 *And when powerful stars add their voices to the mix—as Meryl Streep did in an awards ceremony speech in 2014, calling Walt Disney himself a "gender bigot" who had "racist proclivities"…*: Schulman, 2014.

16 *As author Gerard Jones explains in the book* Killing Monsters: Why Children Need Fantasy, Super Heroes, and Make-Believe Violence: Jones, 2002, p. 96.

16 *…for all the reasons Stone outlined back in 1975*: Stone, 1975.

Chapter 2

24 *When you parent proactively, you anticipate*: Padilla-Walker, 2006.

25 *The American Academy of Pediatrics (AAP) recommends*: American Academy of Pediatrics, no date.

26 *One study found that children in home-based day cares watch an average of 2.4 hours of television at day care, versus 0.4 hour a day in a child-care center*: Christakis and Garrison, 2009.

27 *Organizations that advocate for this*: RobbGrieco and Hobbs, 2013, p. 7.

28 *After all, people learn how to behave by observing and imitating others:* Bandura, 1977.

28 *When children see characters rewarded or punished for their actions and attitudes, they learn about cultural norms and rules that might apply to them:* Gerbner and Gross, 1976.

29 *When researchers conducted an experiment on how* Mighty Morphin Power Rangers *influenced children's behavior:* Boyatzis and Matillo, 1995.

29 *Although there are disagreements on this point:* Freedman, 2002; Baker and Petley, 2001.

29 *...a 2010 report in the journal* Pediatrics *argued:* Strasburger et al., 2010, p. 759.

29 *For example, researchers studying the effect of fast-paced shows on preschool children conducted an experiment with* SpongeBob SquarePants: Lillard and Peterson, 2011.

31 *Studies show that children acquire television-viewing patterns in early childhood:* Singer and Singer, 1981; Huston et al., 1990.

34 *...the decades of research on* Sesame Street: Fisch and Truglio, 2000.

40 *Their attention to what's on-screen may be due to a basic human reflex known as the orienting response:* Anderson and Pempek, 2005.

40 *When an unfamiliar sight or sound occurs, the orienting response makes babies focus on it, in case it is a threat:* Pavlov, 1927.

40 *As Rich has argued:* Rich, 2013.

42 *Research suggests that with young children especially, when parents use a warm approach, the children's desire to identify with their parents increases:* Grusec and Goodnow, 1994.

42 *Studies indicate that 96 percent of teenagers lie to their parents:* Bronson and Merryman, 2009.

42 *Studies show that authoritative parenting is most effective:* Grusec and Goodnow, 1994.

45   *...children can take parents' silence regarding negative material as a form of
      endorsement*: Nathanson, 1999.

45   *"...parents should be aware that the popular advice to 'watch television with
      your children'..."*: Nathanson, 2001, p. 217.

45   *...the simple advice to watch television together may actually be counterproduc-
      tive*: Austin et al., 1990, p. 190.

52   *Academic studies show that even prosocial children's media, like the kind
      found on PBS that are meant to teach lessons about good behavior, spend way
      too much time modeling bad behavior*: Ostrov, Gentile, and Crick, 2006;
      Scheibe and Figueroa, 2007.

56   *As you're viewing, you might ask yourself: "Who is harmed, who benefits, and
      who is left out?"*: RobbGrieco and Hobbs, 2013, p. 14.

56   *...whether different movies pass the Bechdel test*: For more information,
      visit BechdelTest.com.

62   *Learning how to make their own books, videos, and storyboards will help chil-
      dren develop creative skills and problem-solving skills, as well*: RobbGrieco
      and Hobbs, 2013, p. 8.

Chapter 3

68   *While Disney Princess films have earned more than $2.6 billion at the box
      office worldwide, the Disney Princess brand boasts more than $4 billion in
      global retail sales. In the United States, Disney Princess is actually the number-
      one licensed toy brand among all girls, and it's also the number-one toy brand
      for dolls and role play among two- to five-year-old girls*: Disney Consumer
      Products, 2011.

79   *When synergy happens, one plus one no longer equals two. It can equal three,
      four, five, or more*: Wayne, no date.

80   *It's only at about the age of seven that children understand that sex is both
      biological and stable over time*: Slaby and Frey, 1975.

80 *Roughly two-thirds of girls ages three to four, and roughly half of boys ages five to six, develop what researchers call "appearance rigidity"*: Halim et al., in press.

80 *This is so common, in fact, that researchers use the acronym "PFD" to describe this syndrome*: Ruble, Lurye, and Zosuls, 2007.

81 *During this developmental stage, boys and girls will typically play only with children of their own sex and reject anything associated with the opposite sex*: Paoletti, 2012, p. 13.

81 *As a general rule, boys really like being boys, and girls really like being girls*: Martin and Ruble, 2009.

81 *So when young kids treat gender stereotypes as religion...*: Halim et al., in press.

81 *Girls and boys announce their genders in very different ways, though*: Chiu et al., 2006.

83 *Meanwhile, new research has found that in elementary school, children don't necessarily avoid playing with the opposite sex...*: Neal, Neal, and Capella, 2013; Michigan State University, 2014.

85 *...a study that Harvard put out that says that one out of every ten kids is gender nonconforming*: Roberts, Rosario, Corliss, Koenen, and Austin, 2012.

Chapter 4

113 *In a study of children's animated films, including many of Disney's princess films such as* Cinderella, The Little Mermaid, *and* Beauty and the Beast: Herbozo, Tantleff-Dunn, Gokee-Larose, and Thompson, 2004.

114 *Because of these problems, experts such as Diane Levin and Jean Kilbourne argue in their book* So Sexy So Soon: Levin and Kilbourne, 2009.

114 *Media studies expert Gigi Durham echoes these concerns...*: Durham, 2008.

114 *...psychologist Jennifer Hartstein believes girls' princess obsessions can lead them to fixate on appearance*: Hartstein, 2012.

115 *Indeed, as Levin and Kilbourne explain in* So Sexy So Soon: p. 48.

117 *We assume—without thinking critically about it—that outward appearance tells us truths about a person's life*: Dion, Berscheid, and Walster, 1972.

117 *…the cosmetics and diet industries earn profits of tens of billions of dollars a year—and the cosmetic surgery industry isn't too far behind*: Wolf, 1992, p. 17.

117 *In fact, research shows that people who are deemed unattractive are approximately as happy and satisfied…*: Diener, Wolsic, and Fujita, 1995.

118 *Psychologists claim that two things strongly influence our beliefs about the lives of attractive people*: Eagly, Ashmore, Makhijani, and Longo, 1991.

118 *"the wicked witch and giant are ugly, and the heroic prince and virtuous princess are attractive"*: Eagly et al., 1991, p. 112.

118 *in a classic study, professors Margaret Clifford and Elaine Walster…*: Clifford and Walster, 1973.

118 *Previous studies had shown that when a teacher is told a random child is an early bloomer…*: Rosenthal and Jacobson, 1968.

120 *In our culture, women are constantly objectified. Our physical appearances are constantly evaluated*: Frederickson and Roberts, 1997.

120 *Most women are physically unable to meet these cultural beauty ideals*: Botta, 1999; Fallon, 1990.

120 *The media are dominated by images of young women who are tall and exceptionally thin*: Fouts and Burggraf 1999, 2000; Malkin et al., 1999.

120 *…and the media almost never offer diverse ideas about what constitutes beauty*: Aapola, Gonick and Harris, 2005, p. 134.

121 *We compare our own bodies with the images around us, internalizing the ideal as a personal goal*: Keery et al., 2004a, 2004b.

121 *The ideal is nearly impossible to achieve*: Katzmaryzk and Davis, 2001; Wiseman et al., 1992.

121 *This dissatisfaction leads to a host of psychological consequences…*: Engeln-Maddox, 2006.

121   *...often falling well below what doctors would consider a healthy weight for women*: Engeln–Maddox, 2006.

121   *...women who have internalized the ideal of extreme thinness are at risk...*: Thompson and Stice, 2001.

122   *as one study of five-year-old girls and their mothers found*: Abramovitz and Birch, 2000.

122   *...if mothers feel critical about their daughters' bodies, even if they have kept those critical feelings to themselves...*: Hahn-Smith and Smith, 2001.

122   *When it comes to girls' body images, moms are their daughters' role models and influencers*: Davison et al., 2000; Lowes and Tiggemann, 2003; Ricciardelli et al., 2003.

122   *According to one striking study, when nine- to eleven-year-old girls simply attended the same school as older girls, they had higher rates of body-image issues*: Wardle and Watters, 2004.

123   *according to the U.S Census Bureau, 49.9 percent of children younger than five are categorized as minorities*: U.S. Census Bureau, 2013.

123   *Thanks to media, parents, and peers, most girls feel that policing their own and other girls' appearances is "normal"*: Pomerantz, 2008, p. 69.

123   *According to one experiment, three- to five-year-old girls were already using negative adjectives to describe fat body types and positive adjectives to describe thin body types*: Harriger, Calogero, Witherington, and Smith, 2010.

124   *When asked why, their replies included statements like, "I don't want to be her. She is fat and ugly," and "I hate her because she has a fat stomach"*: Harriger, Calogero, Witherington, and Smith, 2010, p. 616.

125   *Unfortunately, one in ten children between the ages of four and six is bullied, and in consequence, bullying experts suggest that children need to begin learning about bullying at the age of three*: O'Connell, 2007.

125   *Girls who are bullied about their appearances deal with many consequences*: Puhl and Luedicke, 2012.

125 *One study of teen girls who have been bullied about their weight found...*: Puhl and Luedicke, 2012.

125 *Children who have been bullied have a reduced quality of life—as do children who have a negative body image*: Haraldstad et al., 2011.

125 *At about five or six years of age—not in adolescence, as previously thought— girls begin expressing dissatisfaction with their own bodies*: Ambrosi-Randic, 2000; Davison et al., 2000; Davison et al., 2003; Dohnt and Tiggeman 2004, 2005; Hendy et al., 2001; Williamson and Delin, 2001.

125 *In recent years, some girls in this age group have even begun showing signs of eating disorders*: Tanofsky-Kraff et al., 2004.

125 *In the long term, girls who are concerned about their weight at this age are significantly more likely to diet or have problem eating behaviors by the age of nine*: Davison et al., 2003.

125 *Sadly, girls' self-worth tends to decrease when others make negative assessments of their appearances*: Davison and McCabe, 2006.

126 *Studies suggest that for a girl to be considered "popular"...*: Duncan and Owens, 2011.

126 *And when a girl is teased on the basis of her appearance, studies show the effects are more marked...*: Agliata, Tantleff-Dunn, and Renk, 2007.

127 *...some experts claim that popular culture is the most powerful influence in the areas of beauty and the hyper-thin ideal*: Tiggemann, 2003.

127 *...in one study, researchers gave six- to ten-year-old girls dolls of varying sizes to play with*: Anschutz and Engels, 2010.

127 *The authors were certain this was cause and effect: "The dolls directly affected actual food intake in these young girls," they wrote*: Anschutz and Engels, 2010.

127 *When girls internalize the ideal of extreme thinness prior to adolescence, they are especially at risk later for chronic dissatisfaction with their bodies and eating disorders*: Sinton and Birch, 2006.

127 *...when girls reach puberty, their bodies typically change in ways that take*

them even further from the hyper-thin ideal female body: Levine and Smolak, 2002.

127 *This is markedly different from boys' experiences, for in puberty, their bodies move closer to the muscular ideal male body*: Ata et al., 2007; Tiggemann, 2005.

128 *During adolescence, girls' dissatisfaction with their bodies increases, and girls are more likely to experience lowered self-esteem and depression:* Ata et al., 2007; Jones, 2004; Tiggemann, 2005.

128 *No wonder girls who develop eating disorders usually do so in adolescence*: Stice, 2002; Touyz and Beaumont, 1985.

128 *…studies show that girls will only identify with female characters if they consider them attractive…*: Hoffner, 1996; Reeves and Greenberg, 1977; Reeves and Lometti, 1979.

128 *…research suggests that early exposure to unrealistically thin dolls can be detrimental to girls' body image, putting them at greater risk of eating disorders*: Dittmar, Halliwell, and Ive, 2006.

129 *When a child plays with a toy weapon, he or she is generally aware that it's fantasy*: Jones, 2002.

153 *Studies show that when mothers instruct their daughters on media content, their daughters are less likely to sexualize themselves; and, conversely, they are more likely to have better critical-viewing skills, better body esteem, and better self-esteem*: Starr and Ferguson, 2012.

Chapter 5

160 *Experts argue that rough-and-tumble play shouldn't just be for boys. It actually enables girls to feel "stronger as individuals and therefore less at the mercy of peer approval and matters of appearance and dress"*: Jones, 2002.

161 *The resulting mind-set is called the Cinderella complex, and it is psychologically unhealthy and limiting. In fact, in the long term, it can be economically detrimental to women*: Dowling, 1981.

163 *Cosmopolitan's list of the best and worst colleges for meeting men*: Panariello, 2013.

172 *In a different Disney film, Elsa could easily have been cast as a villain for this. In fact, this was Disney's original plan for the character*: Associated Press, 2013.

174 *According to the* Los Angeles Times, *Lee helped break* Frozen *out of the one-leading-girl-only rut found in the rest of the Disney Princess films. After joining the team…*: Keegan, 2013.

174 *Media critic Akash Nicholas, writing for the* Atlantic…: Nicholas, 2013.

175 *Writing for* Slate, *Amanda Marcotte complained…*: Marcotte, 2013.

175 Boston Globe *columnist Joanna Weiss lamented…*: Weiss, 2013.

184 *…according to outlets such as the* Los Angeles Times: Sperling, 2011.

192 *One day, in the mid-1970s, his wife asked him…*: Munsch, 2013.

200 *you might say: "Let's pretend we're pioneers going to live on the moon. You're the captain of the spaceship"*: Gruver, 2004, p. 342.

201 *you might say: "I don't like it when the girl needs to be rescued all the time. What do you think?" or "It seems like all the girls in this movie act pretty ridiculous. How do you feel about it?"*: Gruver, 2004, p. 319.

Chapter 6

208 *For decades, critics have lamented that fashion dolls meant to represent African Americans and other races are too often simply "dye-dipped"*: DuCille, 1994.

208 *"…it goes back to slave times, when it was a status symbol to be able to look like you're mixed, like you're part of the master's family"*: see also Patton, 2006, p. 27.

214 *a series of doll studies conducted since the 1940s has repeatedly shown the damage this does to young children*: Clark and Clark, 1947; Dweck, 2009.

217 *Studies show that prejudice is a learned behavior, not an instinctive one, and*

that what we see in the world around us—from parents and society at large, including media—determines whether or not we become prejudiced people: Bergen, 2001.

217 *Family, society, and media have their strongest influence on children's development of prejudices when kids are ages eight and under*: Bergen, 2001.

218 *...children's attitudes toward African American people quickly improve*: Vittrup and Holden, 2011.

221 Mulan *invented a form of female oppression (matchmaking) that did not historically exist in China*: Sun, Picker, and Media Education Foundation, 2001.

221 Pocahontas *also included an original song about "savages" that is racist and offensive...inexplicably, the film concludes with the English explorers leaving the natives in peace*: Pewewardy, 1996/97; Sun, Picker, and Media Education Foundation, 2001.

227 *...some viewers expressed concern that the sinister voodoo magic of Doctor Facilier (or "the Shadow Man") implies that "African people are spooky and scary and have magical powers"*: Stewart, 2009.

227 *...critics complained that Tiana spends too much of the film as a frog*: Wiltz, 2009.

229 *Megan Condis—a PhD candidate at the University of Illinois—conducted a scholarly analysis of how Disney films portray girls' labor*: Condis, forthcoming.

231 *The other dolls are inevitably off to the sides in Barbie advertisements and books, or they're excluded entirely*: Rand, 1998.

231 *Rhea and Madison, two nine-year-old African American girls who participated in a study I conducted in 2005*: Hains, 2012.

236 *When they see their parents act in certain ways around people of other races or ethnicities, they pick up on it. They internalize their parents' nonverbalized attitudes*: Castelli et al., 2008.

236 *And when they see television shows segregate people of different races and*

ethnicities, they believe this is the natural order of things: Vittrup and Holden, 2011; Bigler and Brown, 2002.

236 *...until the age of seven or eight, children strongly identify with their parents and want to be like them*: Bergen, 2001.

236 *Therefore, we can be explicit about the messages we want our children to internalize, model the kinds of behaviors we want them to practice, and expose them to diversity*: Vittrup and Holden, 2011; Bergen, 2001.

237 *According to a 2007 study at Vanderbilt University*: Brown et al., 2007.

237 *They fear that even a positive statement like "It's wonderful that a black person can be president" could teach children to see divisions in society, rather than unity*: Bronson and Merryman, 2009.

237 *African American families in mixed neighborhoods frequently talk about race relations to prepare their children for discrimination. Pre-arming their children is a survival strategy*: Padilla-Walker, 2006.

237 *But when white parents don't discuss race with their kids, peer and media influences fill in the gaps—often with terrible consequences*: Hughes et al., 2006; Katz, 2003.

237 *Children start noticing race at as young as six months of age*: Katz, 2003.

237 *Phyllis Katz, PhD, from the University of Maryland advises parents to talk with children about race from an early age*: Katz, 2003.

239 *Children's attitudes toward race are strongly influenced by what they perceive their parents' attitudes to be*: Vittrup and Holden, 2011.

239 *...studies conducted by researchers at Sesame Street...*: Truglio et al., 2001.

239 *When parents don't tell their children that they like racially diverse people, kids' assumptions about how their parents feel are way off the mark*: Vittrup and Holden, 2011.

239 *If moms are "color-blind" or "color-mute" during the storytelling, the children fail to understand that their mothers agree with the book's message*: Pahlke, Bigler, and Suizzo, 2012.

239 *It's not good enough to offer platitudes like "Everybody's equal," "God made all of us," and "Under the skin, we're all the same"*: Bronson and Merryman, 2009.

240 *Vittrup and Holden suggest that parents of children ages five to seven discuss race using clear statements and questions:* quoted in Bronson and Merryman, 2009.

240 *For maximum effect, though, these conversations should be meaningful—not just a brief mention, but a real dialogue that is age-appropriate*: Bergen, 2001.

240 *According to the research, children of color who have a strong racial or ethnic identity…have better self-esteem than those who do not*: Phinney, 2003.

241 *Lacking the vocabulary to discuss race, instead they use phrases such as "skin like ours" to describe their racial group*: Bronson and Merryman, 2009.

245 *Studies show that when children of color both respect other groups and have a strong racial or ethnic identity, they are more resilient when they encounter discrimination*: Phinney, 2003.

245 *They are also better able to overcome the stereotyping that can damage their academic performance and self-esteem*: Branscombe, Schmitt, and Harvey, 1999; Buckley and Carter, 2005; Ethier and Deaux, 1990; Davis, Aronson, and Salinas, 2006.

246 *…in one study conducted by researchers from the City University of New York and Columbia University*: Buckley and Carter, 2005.

246 *…they were "likely to use other black people as a reference group for their thoughts, feelings, and behaviors"*: Buckley and Carter, 2005, p. 657.

249 *Latina girls who have high racial self-esteem nevertheless have low body esteem…*: Poran, 2002.

249 *…Latino children feel less positive about themselves and the color of their skin than children who are white, African American, and Chinese American*: Truglio et al., 2001.

250 *While many Latina girls are socialized into* marianismo—*an ideal form of womanhood that values self-sacrifice and submissiveness*: Gil and Vazquez, 1996.

250 ...*many African American girls are raised to value their own independence*: Ridolfo, 2007; Ridolfo, Chepp, and Milkie, 2013.

250 *When their mothers encourage them to "think, act, and make decisions independently," African American girls develop a strong sense of self-worth*: Ridolfo, 2007, p. 54.

251 *Vittrup and Holden's study of how parents influence their children's racial attitudes offered strong support for this point, at least among Caucasian families*: Vittrup and Holden, 2011, p. 92.

251 ...*knowledge of parents' friendships is an even better way of reducing racial biases in children than attending diverse preschools*: Pahlke, Bigler, and Suizzo, 2012.

251 *Although studies have shown that interracial friendships and cooperative learning can help reduce children's biases*: Aboud, 2009; Paluck and Green, 2009.

251 ...*doctoral research at the University of Texas at Austin found that children's mothers' friendships were the much more influential factor*: Pahlke, Bigler, and Suizzo, 2012.

252 *Even though Caucasians don't typically realize it*: Poran, 2002.

252 *girls of Asian descent who strongly embrace Western beauty ideals are more prone to eating disorders*: Jennings, Forbes, McDermott, Juniper, S., and Hulse, 2005.

252 ...*and may develop a more subservient attitude toward men*: Lee and Vaught, 2013.

252 ...*while the Latina girls who watch the most television have especially low self-esteem*: Rivadeneyra, Ward, and Gordon, 2007; see also Albarran and Umphrey, 1993, and Greenberg, Heeter, Burgoon, Burgoon, and Korzenny, 1983.

253 *And if you rank the self-esteem levels of African American, Caucasian, and Latina girls...no one-size-fits-all approach will work*: Iglesias and Cormier, 2002.

253 *When African American girls reject mainstream beauty standards and focus instead on broader standards, they are happier with their physical appearances*: Duke, 2002; Buckley and Carter, 2005.

253 *When African American girls reject the Western beauty ideal, their self-esteem is substantially better than their Caucasian peers'*: Patton, 2006; Milkie, 1999; Lakoff and Scherr, 1984; Parker et al., 1995; Wardle and Marsland, 1990.

253 *One study suggests that young Latina women who embrace Latina beauty standards may not benefit to the same extent*: Goodman, 2002.

253 *...when Latina girls watch black-oriented television, their body image is better than that of Latina girls who watch mainstream television*: Schooler, 2008.

253 *...Tracey Owens Patton, PhD, who argues that women must "create their own standards of beauty" to escape the escape the negative consequences of the Western beauty ideal*: Patton, 2006, p. 46.

255 *Researchers have noted that children under the age of eight...the potential to improve their racial attitudes*: Wright et al., 1997; Katz and Zalk, 1978; Wham, Barnhart, and Cook, 1996; Cameron et al., 2007; Cameron et al., 2006.

255 *Just remember...we have to be clear*: Johnson and Aboud, 2012; Pahlke, Bigler, and Suizzo, 2012.

264 *Elizabeth Iglesias, PhD, and Sherry Cormier, PhD, of West Virginia University argue, "The most important thing adults can do for teenage girls is to validate them"*: Iglesias and Cormier, 2002, p. 267.

WORKS CITED

Introduction

Mayer, I. (2013, Oct. 21). Disney Princess, Stars Wars, Hello Kitty topped $1B each in licensed merchandise sales in 2012: 34 properties sell $100M or more in U.S./Canada; Disney accounts for 51% of total. EPM Communications, Inc. Retrieved February 6, 2014 from www.epmcom.com/public/Disney_Princess_Stars_Wars_Hello_Kitty_Topped_1B_Each_In_Licensed_Merchandise_Sales_in_2012_34_Properties_Sell_100M_or_More_in_USCanada_Disney_Accounts_for_51_Of_Total.cfm.

Chapter 1

Baker-Sperry, L. and Grauerholz, L. (2003). The pervasiveness and persistence of the feminine beauty ideal in children's fairy tales. *Gender and Society*, 17(5):711–726.

Barnes, B. (2011, Dec. 11). For Disney, a younger princess. *New York Times*. mediadecoder.blogs.nytimes.com/2011/12/11/for-disney-a-younger-princess/.

Beres, L. (1999). Beauty and the beast: The romanticization of abuse in popular culture. *European Journal of Cultural Studies*, 2(2):191–207.

Dowling, C. (2000). *The Frailty Myth: Redefining the Physical Potential of Women and Girls*. New York: Random House.

Dundes, L. and Dundes, A. (2000). The trident and the fork: Disney's *The Little Mermaid* as a male construction of an Electral fantasy. *Psychoanalytic Studies*, 2(2):117–129.

Dwyer, J. J., Allison, K. R., Goldenberg, E. R., Fein, A. J., Yoshida, K. K., and Boutilier, M. A. (2006). Adolescent girls' perceived barriers to participation in physical activity. *Adolescence*, 41(161): 75–89.

Giroux, H. (1998). Are Disney movies good for your kids? In S. R. Steinberg and J. L. Kincheloe (Eds.) *Kinderculture: The corporate construction of childhood*. Boulder: Westview Press.

Hanes, S. (2011, Sept. 24). Little girls or little women? The Disney Princess effect. *Christian Science Monitor: Modern Parenthood* [blog].

Jones, G. (2002). *Killing Monsters: Why Children Need Fantasy, Super Heroes, and Make-Believe Violence*. New York: Basic Books.

Orenstein, P. (2006). What's wrong with Cinderella? *New York Times Magazine*. www.nytimes.com/2006/12/24/magazine/24princess.t.html?_r=0.

Orenstein, P. (2011). *Cinderella ate my daughter: Dispatches from the front lines of the new girlie-girl culture*. New York: HarperCollins.

Orenstein, P. (2011, Dec. 14). Disney agrees: Princesses are unhealthy for girls! *Peggy Orenstein's Blog*. peggyorenstein.com/blog/sofia-the-cynical.

Paoletti, J. (2012). *Pink and Blue: Telling the Boys from the Girls in America*. Bloomington, IN: University of Indiana Press.

Pewewardy, C. (1996/97). The Pocahontas paradox: A cautionary tale for educators. *Journal of Navajo Education*. www.hanksville.org/storytellers /pewe/writing/Pocahontas.html.

Robbins, L. B., Pender, N. J., and Kazanis, A. S. (2003). Barriers to physical activity perceived by adolescent girls. *Journal of Midwifery and Women's Health*, 48(3): 206–12.

Sabo, D. and Veliz, P. (2008). *Go out and play: Youth sports in America*. East Meadow, NY: Women's Sports Foundation.

Schulman, M. (2014, Jan. 9). Meryl Streep pokes back at male Hollywood. *The New Yorker*. www.newyorker.com/online/blogs/culture/2014/01/meryl-streeps-feminist-tribute-to-emma-thompson.html?mobify=0.

Setoodeh, R. (2007, Nov. 17). Disney's $4B "Princess" brand. *Newsweek*. www.newsweek.com/disneys-4b-princess-brand-96993.

Stone, K. (1975). Things Walt Disney never told us. *Journal of American Folklore*, 88(347):42–50.

Sun, C. F., Picker, M., and Media Education Foundation. (2002). *Mickey Mouse Monopoly*. Northampton, MA: Media Education Foundation.

Trites, R. (1991). Disney's sub/version of Andersen's *The Little Mermaid*. *Journal of Popular Film & Television*, 18(4):145–152.

Zipes, J. (no date). Subverting the myth of happiness: Dina Goldstein's "Fallen Princesses." www.dinagoldstein.com/essays.

Chapter 2

American Academy of Pediatrics (no date). Media and children. www.aap.org/en-us/advocacy-and-policy/aap-health-initiatives/pages/media-and-children.aspx.

Anderson, D. and Pempek, T. (2005) Television and very young children. *American Behavioral Scientist*, 48(5):505–522.

Austin, E. W., Fujioka Y., Bolls P., and Engelbertson J. (1999). How and why parents take on the tube. *Journal of Broadcasting and Electronic Media*, 43:175–192.

Baker, M. and Petley, J. (2001). *Ill Effects: The Media Violence Debate*. New York: Routledge.

Bandura, A. (1986). *Social Foundations of Thought and Action*. Englewood Cliffs, NJ: Prentice Hall.

Boyatiz, C. J. and Matillo, G. M. (1995): Effects of *The Mighty Morphin Power Rangers* on children's aggression with peers. *Child Study Journal*, 25(1):45–55.

Bronson, P. and Merryman, A. (2009). *Nurture Shock: New Thinking about Children*. New York: Twelve.

Christakis, D. A. and Garrison, M. H. (2009). Preschool-aged children's television viewing in child care settings. *Pediatrics*, 124(6):1627 32.

Fisch, S. M. and Truglio, R. T., eds. (2001). *G is for Growing: Thirty Years of Research on Children and Sesame Street*. Mahwah, NJ: Lawrence Erlbaum.

Freedman, J. L. (2002). *Media Violence and Its Effect on Aggression: Assessing the Scientific Evidence*. Toronto, Canada: University of Toronto Press.

Gerbner, G. and Gross, L. (1976). Living with television: The violence profile. *Journal of Communication*, 26: 172–199.

Grusec, J. E. and Goodnow, J. J. (1994). Impact of parental discipline methods on the child's internalization of values: A reconceptualization of current points of view. *Developmental Psychology*, 30(1):4–19.

Huston, A. C., Wright, J. C., Rice, M. L., Kerkman, D., and St. Peters, M. (1990). Development of television viewing patterns in early childhood: A longitudinal investigation. *Developmental Psychology*, 26(3):409–420.

Lillard, A. S. and Peterson, J. (2011). The immediate impact of different types of television on young children's executive function. *Pediatrics*, 128(4):644–649.

Nathanson, A. I. (1999). Identifying and explaining the relationship between parental mediation and children's aggression. *Communication Research*, 26:124–164.

Nathanson, A. I. (2001). Parent and child perspectives on the presence and meaning of parental television mediation. *Journal of Broadcasting and Electronic Media*, 45:201–220.

Ostrov, J. M., Gentile, D. A., and Crick, N. R. (2006). Media exposure, aggression, and prosocial behavior during early childhood: A longitudinal study. *Social Development*, 15(4):612–627.

Padilla-Walker, L. M. (2006). Peers I can monitor, it's media that really worries me! *Journal of Adolescent Research*, 21(1):56–82.

Pavlov, I. P. (1927). *Conditioned Reflexes: An Investigation of the Physiological Activity of the Cerebral Cortex*. Oxford, England: Oxford University Press.

Rich, M. (2013). Presentation at the Consuming Kids Summit, the meeting of the Campaign for a Commercial-Free Childhood. Brookline, MA.

RobbGrieco, M. and Hobbs, R. (2013). *A field guide to media literacy education in the United States*. [Working paper, available online.] Media Education Lab, Harrington School of Communication and Media, University of Rhode Island, Kingston, RI.

Scheibe, C. and Figueroa, G. (2007). Sticks and stones: Teasing, put-downs, and derogatory language on TV shows for children and adolescents. Poster presented at the biennial meeting of the Society for Research in Child Development, Boston, MA.

Singer, J. L. and Singer, D. G. (1981). *Television, Imagination, and Aggression: A Study of Preschoolers*. Hillsdale, NJ: Erlbaum.

Strasburger, V. C., Jordan, A. B., and Donnerstein, E. (2010). Health effects of media on children and adolescents. *Pediatrics*, 125(4):756–767.

Chapter 3

Chiu, S. W., Gervan, S., Fairbrother, C., Johnson, L. L., Owen-Anderson, A. F. H., Bradley, S. J., and Zucker, K. J. (2006). Sex-dimorphic color preference in children with gender identity disorder: A comparison to clinical and community controls. *Sex Roles*, 55:385–395.

Disney Consumer Products (2011). Disney Princess. Retrieved from web .archive.org/web/20120224082342/https://www.disneyconsumer products.com/Home/display.jsp?contentId=dcp_home_ourfranchises _disney_princess_us&forPrint=false&language=en&preview=false &imageShow=0&pressRoom=US&translationOf=null&region=0.

Halim, M. L., Ruble, D. N., Tamis-Lemonda, C. S., Zosuls, K. M., Lurye, L. E., and Greulich, F. (In press.) Pink frilly dresses and the avoidance of all things "girly": Children's appearance rigidity and cognitive theories of gender development. *Developmental Psychology*.

Martin, C. L. and Ruble, D. N. (2009). Patterns of gender development. *Annual Review of Psychology*, 61:353–81.

Michigan State University (2014, January 9). Kids have skewed view of gender segregation. *ScienceDaily*. Retrieved January 12, 2014, from www.sciencedaily.com/releases/2014/01/140109103701.htm.

Neal, J. W., Neal, Z. P., and Cappella, E. (2013) I know who my friends are, but do you? Predictors of self-reported and peer-inferred relationships. *Child Development*. Online version. Retrieved February 6, 2014 from onlinelibrary.wiley.com/doi/10.1111/cdev.12194/abstract ?deniedAccessCustomisedMessage=&userIsAuthenticated=false.

Paoletti, J. (2012). *Pink and Blue: Telling the Boys from the Girls in America*. Bloomington, IN: Indiana University Press

Roberts, A. L., Rosario, M., Corliss, H. L., Koenan, K. C., and Austin, S. B. (2012). Childhood gender nonconformity: A risk indicator for childhood abuse and posttraumatic stress in youth. *Pediatrics*. Retrieved Feb. 6, 2014 from pediatrics.aappublications.org/content/early/2012 /02/15/peds.2011-1804.

Ruble, D. N., Lurye, L. E., Zosuls, K. M. (2007). Pink Frilly Dresses (PFD) and early gender identity. *Princeton Report on Knowledge*, 2(2). Retrieved February 6, 2014 from www.princeton.edu/prok/issues/2-2/pink _frilly.xml.

Slaby, R. G. and Frey, K. S. (1975). Development of gender constancy and selective attention to same-sex models. *Child Development* 46(4):849–856.

Wayne, J. (No date.) Definition of synergy in marketing. *Houston Chronicle*:

Small Business. Retrieved February 6, 2014 from smallbusiness.chron
.com/definition-synergy-marketing-21786.html.

Chapter 4

Aapola, S., Gonick, M., and Harris, A. (2005). *Young Femininity: Girlhood, Power and Social Change*. New York: Palgrave Macmillan.

Abramovitz, B. A. and Birch, L. L. (2000). Five-year-old girls' ideas about dieting are predicted by their mothers' dieting. *Journal of the American Dietetic Association*, 100:1157–1163.

Agliata, A. K., Tantleff-Dunn, S., and Renk, K. (2007). Interpretation of teasing during early adolescence. *Journal of Clinical Psychology*, 61(1):23–30.

Ambrosi-Randic, N. (2000). Perception of current and ideal body size in preschool age children. *Perception and Motor Skills*, 90: 885–889.

Anschutz, D. J. and Engels, R. C. M. E. (2010). The effects of playing with thin dolls on body image and food intake in young girls. *Sex Roles*, 63(9–10):621–630.

Ata, R. N., Ludden, A. B., and Lally, M. M. (2007). The effects of gender and family, friend, and media influences on eating behaviors and body image during adolescence. *Journal of Youth and Adolescence*, 36:1024–1037.

Botta, R. (1999). Television images and adolescent girls' body image disturbance. *Journal of Communication*, 49:22–41.

Clifford, M. M. and Walster, E. (1973). Research note: The effects of physical attractiveness on teacher expectations. *Sociology of Education*, 46:248–258.

Davison, K. K., Markey, C. N., and Birch, L. L. (2000). Etiology of body dissatisfaction and weight concerns among 5-year-old girls. *Appetite*, 35:143–151.

Davison, K. K., Markey, C. N., and Birch, L. L. (2003). A longitudinal examination of patterns in girls' weight concerns and body dissatisfaction from ages 5 to 9 years. *International Journal of Eating Disorders*, 33:320–332.

Davison, T. E. and McCabe, M. P. (2006). Adolescent body image and psychosocial functioning. *Journal of Social Psychology*, 146(1):15–30.

Diener, E., Wolsic, B., and Fujita, F. (1995). Physical attractiveness and subjective well-being. *Journal of Personality and Social Psychology*, 69(1):120–129.

Dion, K., Berscheid, E., and Walster, E. (1972). What is beautiful is good. *Journal of Personality and Social Psychology*, 24:285–290.

Dittmar, H., Halliwell, E., and Ive, S. (2006). Does Barbie make girls want to be thin? The effect of experimental exposure to images of dolls on the body image of 5- to 8-year-old girls. *Developmental Psychology*, 42(2):283–92.

Dohnt, H. K. and Tiggemann, M. (2004). The development of perceived body size and dieting awareness in young girls. *Perceptual and Motor Skills*, 99:790–792.

Dohnt, H. K. and Tiggemann, M. (2005). Peer influences on body image and dieting awareness in young girls. *British Journal of Developmental Psychology*, 23:103–116.

Duncan, N. and Owens, L. (2011). Bullying, social power, and heteronormativity: Girls' constructions of popularity. *Children & Society*, 25: 306–316.

Durham, M. G. (2008). *The Lolita Effect: The Media Sexualization of Young Girls and What We Can Do About It*. New York: Overlook Press.

Eagly, A. H., Ashmore, R. D., Makhijani, M. G., and Longo, L. C. (1991). What is beautiful is good, but…A meta-analytic review of research on the physical attractiveness stereotype. *Psychological Bulletin*, 110 (1):109–128.

Engeln-Maddox, R. (2006). Buying a beauty standard or dreaming of a new life? Expectations associated with media ideals. *Psychology of Women Quarterly*, 30:258–266.

Fallon, A. (1990). Culture in the mirror: Sociocultural determinant of body image. In T. F. Cash and T. Pruzinsky (Eds.) *Body Images: Development, Deviance, and Chance* (pp. 80–109). New York: Guilford.

Fouts, G. and Burggraf, K. (1999). Television situation comedies: Female body images and verbal reinforcements. *Sex Roles*, 40:473–481.

Fouts, G. and Burggraf, K. (2000). Television situation comedies: Female weight, male negative comments, and audience reactions. *Sex Roles*, 42:925–932.

Frederickson, B. L. and Roberts, T. (1997). Development of body image in preschool girls. *Homeostasis in Health and Disease*, 40:161–169.

Hahn-Smith, A. and Smith, J. E. (2001). The positive influence of maternal identification on body image, eating attitude, and self-esteem of Hispanic and Anglo girls. *International Journal of Eating Disorders*, 29:429–440.

Haraldstad, K., Christopersen, K. A., Eide, H., Natvig, G. K., and Helseth, S. (2011). Predictors of health-related quality of life in a sample of children and adolescents: a school survey. *Journal of Clinical Nursing*, 20:3048–3056.

Harriger, J. A., Calogero, R. M., Witherington, D. C., and Smith, J. E. (2010). Body size stereotyping and internalization of the thin ideal in preschool girls. *Sex Roles*, 63:609–620.

Hartstein, J. L. (2012) *Princess Recovery: A How-To Guide to Raising Strong, Empowered Girls Who Can Create Their Own Happily Ever Afters*. Avon, Mass: Adams Media.

Hendy, H. M., Gustitus, C., and Leitzel-Schwalm, J. (2001). Social cognitive predictors of body image in preschool children. *Sex Roles* 44:557–597.

Herbozo, S., Tantleff-Dunn, S., Gokee-Larose, J., and Thompson, J. K. (2004). Beauty and thinness messages in children's media: A content analysis. *Eating Disorders*, 12:21–34.

Hoffner, C. (1996). Children's wishful identification and parasocial interaction with favorite television characters. *Journal of Broadcasting & Electronic Media*, 40:389–402.

Jones, D. C. (2004). Body image among adolescent girls and boys: A longitudinal study. *Developmental Psychology*, 40:823–835.

Jones, G. (2002). *Killing Monsters: Why Children Need Fantasy, Super Heroes, and Make-Believe Violence*. New York: Basic Books.

Katzmarzyk, P. T. and Davis, C. (2001). Thinness and body shape of Playboy centerfolds from 1978 to 1998. *International Journal of Obesity*, 25:590–592.

Keery, H., Shroff, H., Thompson, J. K., Wertheim, E., and Smolak, L. (2004a). The Sociocultural Internalization of Appearance Questionnaire—Adolescents (SIAQ-A): psychometric analysis and normative data for three countries. *Eating and Weight Disorders*, 9:56–61.

Keery, H., van den Berg, P., and Thompson, J. K. (2004b). An evaluation of the tripartite influence model of body dissatisfaction and eating disturbance with adolescent girls. *Body Image*, 1:237–251.

Levin, D. E. and Kilbourne, J. (2009). *So Sexy So Soon: The New Sexualized Childhood and What Parents Can Do To Protect Their Kids*. New York: Ballantine Books.

Levine, M. P. and Smolak, L. (2002). Body image development in adolescence. In T. F. Cash and T. Pruzinsky (Eds.), *Body Image: A Handbook of Theory, Research and Clinical Practice* (pp. 74–82). New York: Guilford.

Lowes, J. and Tiggemann, M. (2003). Body dissatisfaction, dieting awareness and the impact of parental influence in young children. *British Journal of Health Psychology*, 8:135–147.

Malkin, A. R., Wornian, K., and Chrisler, J. C. (1999). Women and weight: Gendered messages on magazine covers. *Sex Roles*, 40:647–655.

O'Connell, D. (2007, Sept.). Tiny tormentors. *Scholastic*, 19.

Pomerantz, S. (2008). Style and girl culture. In C. Mitchell and J. Reid-Walsh (Eds.) *Girl Culture: An Encyclopedia*, Vol. 1 (pp. 64–72). Westport, CT: Greenwood Press.

Puhl, R. M. and Luedicke, J. (2012). Weight-based victimization among adolescents in the school setting: Emotional reactions and coping behaviors. *Journal of Youth and Adolescence*, 41:27–40.

Reeves, B. and Greenberg, B. S. (1977). Children's perceptions of television characters. *Human Communication Research*, 3:113–127.

Reeves, B. and Lometti, G. (1979). The dimensional structure of children's perceptions of television characters: A replication. *Human Communication Research*, 5:247–256.

Ricciardelli, L. A., McCabe, M, P., Holt, K., and Finemore, J. (2003). A biopsychosocial model for understanding body image and body change strategies among children. *Journal of Applied Developmental Psychology*, 24:475–495.

Rosenthal, R. and Jacobson, L. (1968). *Pygmalion in the Classroom*. New York: Holt, Rinehart and Winston.

Sinton, M. and Birch, L. (2006). Individual and sociocultural influences on pre-adolescent girls' appearance schemas and body dissatisfaction. *Journal of Youth and Adolescence*, 35(2), 165–175.

Starr, C. R. and Ferguson, G. M. (2012). Sexy dolls, sexy grade-schoolers? Media and maternal influences on young girls' self-sexualization. *Sex Roles*, 67:463–476.

Stice, E. (2002). Risk and maintenance factors for eating pathology: A meta-analytic review. *Psychological Bulletin*, 128:825–848.

Tanofsky-Kraff, M., Yanovski, S. Z., Wilfley, D. E., Marmarosh, C.,

Morgan, C. M., and Yanovski, J. A. (2004). Eating-disordered behaviours, body fat, and psychopathology in overweight and normal weight children. *Journal of Consulting and Clinical Psychology*, 72(1):53–61.

Thompson, J. K. and Stice, E. (2001). Thin-ideal internalization: Mounting evidence for a new risk factor for body image disturbance and eating pathology. *Current Directions in Psychological Research*, 10:181–183.

Tiggemann, M. (2003). Media exposure, body dissatisfaction, and disordered eating: Television and magazines are not the same! *European Eating Disorders Review*, 11:418–430.

Tiggemann, M. (2005). Television and adolescent body image: The role of program content and viewing motivation. *Journal of Social and Clinical Psychology*, 24:193–213.

Touyz, S. W. and Beaumont, P. J. V. (1985). *Eating Disorders: Prevalence and Treatment*. Sydney, Australia: William and Wilkins/Adis.

U.S. Census Bureau (2013, June 13). Asians fastest-growing race or ethnic group in 2012, Census Bureau Reports. Retrieved February 6, 2014 from www.census.gov/newsroom/releases/archives/population/cb13-112.html.

Wardle, J. and Watters, R. (2004). Sociocultural influences on attitudes to weight and eating: Results of a natural experiment. *International Journal of Eating Disorders*, 34(4):589–596.

Williamson, S. and Delin, C. (2001). Young children's figural selections: Accuracy of reporting and body size dissatisfaction. *International Journal of Eating Disorders* 29:80–84.

Wiseman, C. V., Gray, J. J., Mosimann, J. E., and Ahrens, A. H. (1992). Cultural expectations of thinness in women: An update. *International Journal of Eating Disorders*, 11:85–89.

Wolf, N. (1992). *The Beauty Myth: How Images of Beauty Are Used against Women*. New York: Anchor Books.

Chapter 5

Associated Press (2013, Dec. 9). Disney's *Frozen* cools *Catching Fire* at box office. *Yahoo! News*. Retrieved February 6, 2014 from news.yahoo .com/disney-39-39-frozen-39-cools-39-catching-210529237.html.

Dowling, C. (1981) *The Cinderella Complex: Women's Hidden Fear of Independence*. New York: Summit.

Jones, G. (2002). *Killing Monsters: Why Children Need Fantasy, Super Heroes, and Make-Believe Violence*. New York: Basic Books.

Gruver, N. (2004). *How to Say It to Girls: Communicating with your Growing Daughter*. New York: Prentice Hall.

Keegan, R. (2013, November 22). *Frozen, Get a Horse!* female directors mark firsts for Disney. *Los Angeles Times*. Retrieved February 6, 2014 from articles.latimes.com/2013/nov/22/entertainment/la-et-mn -frozen-get-a-horse-female-director-20131124.

Marcotte, A. (2013, Dec. 18). New Disney heroine's eyes are bigger than her wrists. *Slate*. Retrieved February 6, 2014 from www.slate.com /blogs/xx_factor/2013/12/18/anna_in_frozen_her_eyes_are_bigger _than_her_wrists.html.

Munsch, R. (2013). *The Official Robert Munsch Site*. robertmunsch.com /book/the-paper-bag-princess.

Nicholas, A. (2013, Jan. 8). Does Prince Charming really need to be invented? *Atlantic*. Retrieved February 6, 2014 from www.theatlantic .com/entertainment/archive/2014/01/does-prince-charming-really -need-to-be-reinvented/282908/.

Panariello, L. (Oct. 2013). The best and worst colleges for meeting men. *Cosmopolitan*. Retrieved February 6, 2014 from www.cosmopolitan .com/sex-love/dating-advice/best-worst-colleges-to-meet-men.

Sperling, N. (2011, May 25). When the glass ceiling crashed on Brenda Chapman. *Los Angeles Times*. Retrieved February 6, 2014 from articles

.latimes.com/2011/may/25/entertainment/la-et-women-animation-sidebar-20110525.

Weiss, J. (2013, Dec. 8). The problem with princesses. *Boston Globe*. Retrieved February 6, 2014 from www.bostonglobe.com/opinion/2013/12/08/disney-frozen-when-pretty-boring/w2HG4hUPI4FFM17R3YDjZM/story.html.

Chapter 6

Aboud F.E. (2009). Modifying children's racial attitudes. In Banks J. (Ed.), *The Routledge International Companion to Multicultural Education* (pp. 199–209). New York, NY: Routledge.

Albarran, A. B., and Umphrey, D. (1993). Profile: An examination of television motivations and program preferences by Hispanics, blacks, and whites. *Journal of Broadcasting and Electronic Media*, 37(1): 95–103.

Bergen, T. J. (2001). The development of prejudice in children. *Education* 122:154–163.

Bigler, R. and Brown, C. (2002). Can separate be equal? The role of segregation in the formation of children's intergroup attitudes. Paper presented at the annual meeting of the Southwestern Society for Research on Human Development, Austin, TX.

Branscombe, N. R., Schmitt, M. T., and Harvey, R. D. (1999). Perceiving pervasive discrimination among African Americans: Implications for group identification and well-being. *Journal of Personality and Social Psychology*, 77:135–149.

Bronson, P. and Merryman, A. (2009). *NurtureShock: New Thinking about Children*. New York: Twelve.

Brown, T. N., Tanner-Smith, E. E., Lesane-Brown, C. L., and Ezell, M. E. (2007). Child, parent, and situational correlates of familial ethnic/race socialization. *Journal of Marriage and Family*, 69(1): 14–25.

Buckley, T. R. and Carter, R. T. (2005). Black adolescent girls: Do gender role and racial identity impact their self-esteem? *Sex Roles*, 53(9–10):647–661.

Cameron, L., Rutland, A., and Brown, R. (2007). Promoting children's positive intergroup attitudes towards stigmatized groups: Extended contact and multiple classification skills training. *International Journal of Behavioral Development*, 31:454–466.

Cameron, L., Rutland, A., Brown, R., and Douch, R. (2006). Changing children's intergroup attitudes toward refugees: Testing different models of extended contact. *Developmental Psychology*, 77:1208–1219.

Castelli, L., De Dea, C., and Nesdale, D. (2008). Learning social attitudes: Children's sensitivity to the nonverbal behaviors of adult models during interracial interactions. *Personality & Social Psychology Bulletin*, 34:1504–1513.

Clark, K. B. and Clark, M. P. (1947). Racial identification and preference among Negro children. In E. L. Hartley (Ed.) *Readings in Social Psychology*. New York: Holt, Reinhart, and Winston.

Condis, M. (forthcoming). Applying for the position of princess: Race, labor, and the privileging of whiteness in the Disney Princess line. In M. Forman-Brunell and R. C. Hains (Eds.) *Princess Cultures: Mediating Girls' Imaginations and Identities*. New York: Peter Lang.

Davis, C., Aronson, J., and Salinas, M. (2006). Shades of threat: Racial identity as a moderator of stereotype threat. *Journal of Black Psychology*, 32:399–417.

DuCille, A. (1994). Dyes and dolls: Multicultural Barbie and the merchandizing of difference. *Differences: A Journal of Feminist Cultural Studies*, 6(1):47–68.

Duke, L. (2002). Get real!: Cultural relevance and resistance to the mediated feminine ideal. *Psychology and Marketing*, 19:211–233.

Dweck, C. S. (2009). *Prejudice: How It Develops and How It Can Be Undone.* Switzerland: Karger. doi:10.1159/000242351.

Ethier, K. A. and Deaux, K. (1990). Hispanics in ivy: Assessing identity and perceived threat. *Sex Roles*, 22:427–440.

Gil, R. M. and Vazquez, C. I. (1996). *The Maria Paradox: How Latinas Can Merge Old World Traditions with New World Self-Esteem.* Premier Digital Publishing.

Goodman, J. R. (2002). Flabless is fabulous: How Latina and Anglo women read and incorporate the excessively thin body ideal into everyday experience. *Journalism and Mass Communication Quarterly*, 79:712–727.

Greenberg, B. S., Heeter, C., Burgoon, M., Burgoon, J., and Korzenny, F. (1983). Mass media use, preferences, and attitudes among young people. In B. Greenberg, M. Burgoon, J. Burgoon, and F. Korzenny (Eds.) *Mexican Americans and the Mass Media* (pp. 202–223). Norwood, NJ: Ablex.

Hains, R. C. (2012). *Growing Up with Girl Power: Girlhood On Screen and in Everyday Life.* New York: Peter Lang.

Hughes, D., Rodriguez, J., Smith, E., Johnson, D., Stevenson, H., and Spicer, P. (2006). Parents' ethnic-racial socialization practices: A review of research and directions for future study. *Developmental Psychology*, 42:747–770.

Iglesias, E. and Cormier, S. (2002). The transformation of girls to women: Finding a voice and developing strategies for liberation. *Journal of Multicultural Counseling and Development*, 30:259–271.

Jennings, P. S., Forbes, D., McDermott, B., Juniper, S., and Hulse, G. (2005) Acculturation and eating disorders in Asian and Caucasian Australian adolescent girls. *Psychiatry and Clinical Neurosciences*, 59(1): 56–61.

Johnson, P. J. and Aboud, F. E. (2012). Modifying ethnic attitudes in young children: The impact of communicator race and message strength. *International Journal of Behavioral Development*, 37(3):182–191.

Katz, P. (2003). Racist or tolerant multiculturalists? How do they begin? *American Psychologist*, 58:897–909.

Katz, P. A. and Zalk, S. R. (1978). Modification of children's racial attitudes. *Developmental Psychology*, 14:447–461.

Lakoff, R. T. and Scherr, R. L. (1984) *Face Value: The politics of Beauty*. Boston: Routledge.

Lee, S. J. and Vaught, S. (2013). "You can never be too rich or too thin": Popular and consumer culture and the Americanization of Asian American girls and young women. *Journal of Negro Education*, 72(4):457–466.

Milkie, M. A. (1999). Social comparisons, reflected appraisals, and mass media: The impact of pervasive beauty images on black and white girls' self-concepts. *Social Psychology Quarterly*, 62(2):190–210.

Padilla-Walker, L. M. (2006). Peers I can monitor, it's media that really worries me! *Journal of Adolescent Research*, 21(1):56–82.

Pahlke, E., Bigler, R. S., and Suizzo, M. (2012). Relations between color-blind socialization and children's racial bias: Evidence from European American mothers and their preschool children. *Child Development*, 83(4):1164–1179.

Paluck, E. L., and Green, D. P. (2009). Prejudice reduction: What works? A review and assessment of research and practice. *Annual Review of Psychology*, 60: 339–367.

Parker, S., Nichter, M., Nichter, M., Vockovic, N., Sims, C., and Ritenbaugh, C. (1995). Body image and weight concerns among African American and white adolescent females: Differences that make a difference. *Human Organization* 54:103–114.

Patton, T. O. (2006). Hey girl, am I more than my hair? African American women and their struggles with beauty, body image, and hair. *NWSA Journal*, 18(2):24–51.

Pewewardy, C. (1996/97). The Pocahontas paradox: A cautionary tale for educators. *Journal of Navajo Education*. www.hanksville.org/storytellers /pewe/writing/Pocahontas.html.

Phinney, J. S. (2003). Ethnic identity and acculturation. In K. M. Chun, P. S. Organista, and G. Marin (Eds.) *Acculturation: Advances in Theory, Measurement, and Applied Research* (pp. 63–82). Washington, DC: American Psychological Association.

Poran, M. A. (2002). Denying diversity: Perceptions of beauty and social comparison processes among Latina, black, and white women. *Sex Roles*, 47(1/2):65–81.

Rand, E. (1998). Older heads on younger bodies. In H. Jenkins (Ed.) *The Children's Culture Reader* (pp. 382–93). New York: New York University Press.

Ridolfo, H. E. (2007). Race and self-image: How mothers' socialization matters. Master's thesis, Department of Sociology, University of Maryland. www.drum.lib.umd.edu/bitstream/1903/6708/1/umi-umd-4181 .pdf.

Ridolfo, H., Chepp, V., and Milkie, M. A. (2013). Race and girls' self-evaluations: How mothering matters. *Sex Roles*, 68:496–509.

Rivadeneyra, R., Ward, L. M., and Gordon, M. (2007). Distorted reflections: Media exposure and Latino adolescents' conceptions of self. *Media Psychology*, 9:261–290.

Schooler, D. (2008). Real women have curves: A longitudinal investigation of TV and the body image development of Latina adolescents. *Journal of Adolescent Research*, 23(2):132–153.

Stewart, D. (2009, Sept. 10). 5 possible problems with *The Princess and the Frog*. *Jezebel*. Retrieved February 13, 2014 from jezebel.com/5356476/5 -possible-problems-with-the-princess-and-the-frog.

Sun, C. F., Picker, M., and Media Education Foundation. (2002). *Mickey Mouse Monopoly*. Northampton, MA: Media Education Foundation.

Truglio, R. T., Lovelace, V. O., Segui, I., and Scheiner, S. (2001). The varied role of formative research: Case studies from 30 years. In S. M. Fisch and R. T. Truglio (Eds.) *"G" is for Growing: Thirty Years of Research on Children and Sesame Street* (pp. 61–79). Mahwah, NJ: Lawrence Erlbaum.

U.S. Census Bureau (2013, June 13). Asians fastest-growing race or ethnic group in 2012, Census Bureau Reports. Retrieved February 6, 2014 from www.census.gov/newsroom/releases/archives/population/cb13-112.html.

Vittrup, B. and Holden, G. W. (2011). Exploring the impact of educational television and parent–child discussions on children's racial attitudes. *Analyses of Social Issues and Public Policy*, 11(1):82–104.

Wardle J. and Marsland, L. (1990). Adolescent concerns about weight and eating: A social-development perspective. *Journal of Psychosomatic Research*, 34:377–91.

Wham, M., Barnhart, J., and Cook, G. (1996). Enhancing multicultural awareness through the storybook reading experience. *Journal of Research and Development in Education*, 30(1):1–7.

Wiltz, T. (2009, Dec. 11). The froggiest of them all: Is Disney hedging its bets, afraid of letting too much blackness play front and center on the big screen? *The Root*. Retrieved November 15, 2013 from www.theroot.com/articles/culture/2009/12/the_princess_and_the_frog_disneys_first_black_princess_is_mostly_a_frog.html.

Wright, S. C., Aron, A., McLaughlin-Volpe, T., and Ropp, S. A. (1997). The extended contact effect: Knowledge of cross-group friendships and prejudice. *Journal of Personality and Social Psychology*, 73:73–90.

ABOUT THE AUTHOR

Dr. Rebecca C. Hains is a children's media culture expert. As a media studies professor at Salem State University in Salem, Massachusetts, Hains has published her research about girls and media in various academic journals and anthologies, as well as her academic book *Growing Up With Girl Power: Girlhood On Screen and in Everyday Life* (Peter Lang Press, 2012). Her musings on children's popular culture frequently appear on the *Christian Science Monitor*'s popular *Modern Parenthood* blog.

PHOTO BY KELLY LINDSEY

She has appeared in media including NPR, Fox News, the *Boston Globe*, the *Christian Science Monitor*, *Cosmopolitan*, the *Atlanta Journal-Constitution*, the *National Journal*, the *Harvard Political Review*, and the *Huffington Post*, which have featured her expert perspective on media culture, as well as her work advocating for better media for girls and women. She holds a PhD in Mass Media and Communication from Temple University and lives north of Boston with her husband and two children.